Redefining European Economic Governance

The global financial crisis and sovereign debt crisis exposed the inadequacy of European economic governance. Despite the multitude of new mechanisms and institutions that have arisen over the last few years, many contend that economic governance remains inadequate and the EU must integrate even further to calm still volatile markets. A tension exists between creating effective instruments that will not overstep the authority delegated to an EU that has integrated economically but not politically. Can the EU's economic governance system satisfy the demands of markets and politics? Relevant issues include the ability of supranational institutions to dictate policy to national governments, the harmonisation of economic policies and institutions across Europe, and a substantial increase in the transfer of funds across borders. Can monetary union continue without political union? How will the new institutions alter the distribution of power between EU institutions as well as between member states?

This edited volume analyses the major policy challenges and institutional mechanisms at the EU and international levels to combat the global financial crisis and the EU's sovereign debt crisis such as financial integration, fiscal cooperation, and the rising power of the ECB.

This book was previously published as a special issue of the *Journal of European Integration*.

Michele Chang (College of Europe), **Georg Menz** (Goldsmiths University of London) and **Mitchell P. Smith** (University of Oklahoma) are former co-chairs of the European Union Studies Association's Political Economy Interest Section.

Journal of European Integration Special Issues

Series editors:
Thomas Christiansen, Maastricht University, Netherlands
Simon Duke, European Institute of Public Administration, Netherlands

The *Journal of European Integration* book series is designed to make our Special Issues accessible to a wider audience. All of the themes covered by our Special Issues and the series are carefully selected with regard to the topicality of the questions addressed in the individual volumes, as well as to the quality of the contributions. The result is a series of books that are sufficiently short to appeal to the curious reader, but that also offer ample depth of analysis to appeal to the more specialist reader, with contributions from leading academics.

Representation and Democracy in the EU
Does one come at the expense of the other?
Edited by Richard Bellamy and Sandra Kröger

Coping with Crisis: Europe's Challenges and Strategies
Edited by Jale Tosun, Anne Wetzel and Galina Zapyanova

Globalization and EU Competition Policy
Edited by Umut Aydin and Kenneth Thomas

Redefining European Economic Governance
Edited by Michele Chang, Georg Menz and Mitchell P. Smith

PREVIOUSLY PUBLISHED BOOKS FROM THE JOURNAL

The Maastricht Treaty: Second Thoughts after 20 Years
Edited by Thomas Christiansen and Simon Duke

Europe after Enlargement
Edited by Yannis Stivachtis and Mark Webber

Euroscepticism within the EU Institutions
Diverging Views of Europe
Edited by Nathalie Brack and Olivier Costa

The Performance of the EU in International Institutions
Edited by Thomas Oberthür, Knud Erik Jørgensen and Jamal Shahin

Functional and Territorial Interest Representation in the EU
Edited by Michèle Knodt, Christine Quittkat and Justin Greenwood

European Neighbourhood through Civil Society Networks?
Policies, Practices and Perceptions
Edited by James Wesley Scott and Ilkka Likanen

European Parliament Elections after Eastern Enlargement
Edited by Hermann Schmidt

The Common Agricultural Policy
Policy Dynamics in a Changing Context
Edited by Grace Skogstad and Amy Verdun

The External Dimension of Justice and Home Affairs
A Different Security Agenda for the European Union?
Edited by Sarah Wolff, Nicole Wichmann and Gregory Mounier

Policy Coherence and EU Development Policy
Edited by Maurizio Carbonne

The Future of European Foreign Policy
Edited by Erik Jones and Saskia van Genugten

The EU as a Global Player
The Politics of Interregionalism
Edited by Fredrick Soderbaum and Luk Van Langenhove

Redefining European Economic Governance

Edited by
Michele Chang, Georg Menz and
Mitchell P. Smith

LONDON AND NEW YORK

First published 2015
by Routledge
2 Park Square, Milton Park, Abingdon, Oxon, OX14 4RN, UK

and by Routledge
711 Third Avenue, New York, NY 10017, USA

Routledge is an imprint of the Taylor & Francis Group, an informa business

© 2015 Taylor & Francis

All rights reserved. No part of this book may be reprinted or reproduced or utilised in any form or by any electronic, mechanical, or other means, now known or hereafter invented, including photocopying and recording, or in any information storage or retrieval system, without permission in writing from the publishers.

Trademark notice: Product or corporate names may be trademarks or registered trademarks, and are used only for identification and explanation without intent to infringe.

British Library Cataloguing in Publication Data
A catalogue record for this book is available from the British Library

ISBN 13: 978-1-138-79406-1

Typeset in Sabon
by RefineCatch Limited, Bungay, Suffolk

Publisher's Note
The publisher accepts responsibility for any inconsistencies that may have arisen during the conversion of this book from journal articles to book chapters, namely the possible inclusion of journal terminology.

Disclaimer
Every effort has been made to contact copyright holders for their permission to reprint material in this book. The publishers would be grateful to hear from any copyright holder who is not here acknowledged and will undertake to rectify any errors or omissions in future editions of this book.

Contents

Citation Information ix

1. Introduction: Kicking the Can Down the Road to More Europe? Salvaging the Euro and the Future of European Economic Governance 1
   Georg Menz & Mitchell P. Smith

2. Sworn to Grim Necessity? Imperfections of European Economic Governance, Normative Political Theory, and Supreme Emergency 13
   Kenneth Dyson

3. 'Tough Love': How the ECB's Monetary Financing Prohibition Pushes Deeper Euro Area Integration 29
   Jonathan Yiangou, Mícheál O'Keeffe & Gabriel Glöckler

4. Time Will Tell: The EFSF, the ESM, and the Euro Crisis 45
   Ledina Gocaj & Sophie Meunier

5. Fiscal Policy Coordination and the Future of the Community Method 61
   Michele Chang

6. The Politics of Risk-sharing: Fiscal Federalism and the Greek Debt Crisis 77
   Nikolaos Zahariadis

7. The EMU's Legitimacy and the ECB as a Strategic Political Player in the Crisis Context 93
   Francisco Torres

8. The Little Engine that Wouldn't: Supranational Entrepreneurship and the Barroso Commission 107
   Dermot Hodson

9. Merged Into One: Keystones of European Economic Governance, 1962–2012 121
   David Andrews

10. Banking on Stability: The Political Economy of New Capital Requirements in the European Union 139
    David Howarth & Lucia Quaglia

CONTENTS

11. Keeping the Agents Leashed: The EU's External Economic Governance in the G20   153
Charlotte Rommerskirchen

12. Eurozone Crisis and European Integration: Functional Spillover, Political Spillback?   167
Ramūnas Vilpišauskas

Index   181

Citation Information

The chapters in this book were originally published in the *Journal of European Integration,* volume 35, issue 3 (April 2013). When citing this material, please use the original page numbering for each article, as follows:

Chapter 1
Kicking the Can Down the Road to More Europe? Salvaging the Euro and the Future of European Economic Governance
Georg Menz & Mitchell P. Smith
Journal of European Integration, volume 35, issue 3 (April 2013) pp. 195–206

Chapter 2
Sworn to Grim Necessity? Imperfections of European Economic Governance, Normative Political Theory, and Supreme Emergency
Kenneth Dyson
Journal of European Integration, volume 35, issue 3 (April 2013) pp. 207–222

Chapter 3
'Tough Love': How the ECB's Monetary Financing Prohibition Pushes Deeper Euro Area Integration
Jonathan Yiangou, Mícheál O'Keeffe & Gabriel Glöckler
Journal of European Integration, volume 35, issue 3 (April 2013) pp. 223–238

Chapter 4
Time Will Tell: The EFSF, the ESM, and the Euro Crisis
Ledina Gocaj & Sophie Meunier
Journal of European Integration, volume 35, issue 3 (April 2013) pp. 239–254

Chapter 5
Fiscal Policy Coordination and the Future of the Community Method
Michele Chang
Journal of European Integration, volume 35, issue 3 (April 2013) pp. 255–270

Chapter 6
The Politics of Risk-sharing: Fiscal Federalism and the Greek Debt Crisis
Nikolaos Zahariadis
Journal of European Integration, volume 35, issue 3 (April 2013) pp. 271–286

CITATION INFORMATION

Chapter 7
The EMU's Legitimacy and the ECB as a Strategic Political Player in the Crisis Context
Francisco Torres
Journal of European Integration, volume 35, issue 3 (April 2013) pp. 287–300

Chapter 8
The Little Engine that Wouldn't: Supranational Entrepreneurship and the Barroso Commission
Dermot Hodson
Journal of European Integration, volume 35, issue 3 (April 2013) pp. 301–314

Chapter 9
Merged Into One: Keystones of European Economic Governance, 1962–2012
David Andrews
Journal of European Integration, volume 35, issue 3 (April 2013) pp. 315–332

Chapter 10
Banking on Stability: The Political Economy of New Capital Requirements in the European Union
David Howarth & Lucia Quaglia
Journal of European Integration, volume 35, issue 3 (April 2013) pp. 333–346

Chapter 11
Keeping the Agents Leashed: The EU's External Economic Governance in the G20
Charlotte Rommerskirchen
Journal of European Integration, volume 35, issue 3 (April 2013) pp. 347–360

Chapter 12
Eurozone Crisis and European Integration: Functional Spillover, Political Spillback?
Ramūnas Vilpišauskas
Journal of European Integration, volume 35, issue 3 (April 2013) pp. 361–373

Please direct any queries you may have about the citations to
clsuk.permissions@cengage.com

INTRODUCTION

Kicking the Can Down the Road to More Europe? Salvaging the Euro and the Future of European Economic Governance

GEORG MENZ & MITCHELL P. SMITH

Department of European Political and Administrative Studies, College of Europe, Belgium

Recent assessments of the nature of the eurozone's problems, their origins, and of policy choices and likely outcomes inform our understanding of the crisis and explain its persistence. These accounts detail weaknesses in design of economic and monetary union (EMU) and its implementation (Meyer 2010; Dadush and Stancil 2010; Cooley and Marimon 2011); the manner in which political constraints have limited or distorted policy choices (Scharpf 2011); and the failings of political leadership at both European and national levels (Featherstone 2011). But more or less lost in the welter of commentary is any account of how we identify and account for the trajectory of European economic governance in response to the eurozone's troubles.

Few observers of the single currency correctly predicted the extraordinary economic problems the euro has created for Europe: mass unemployment, depression, social unrest, and rule by technocratic government in southern Europe and billions of public funds diverted to sustain the speculative transactions of French and German banks with concomitant years of debt service for future generations in the North. If the economic instability caused by the euro were not serious enough, the political ramifications have been equally severe: an exchange of xenophobic stereotypes in the German and Greek press cast serious doubt on just how much pan-European sentiment the integration process has produced, while imposed austerity in southern Europe appears to nourish the emergence of far-right movements as in Greece, also strengthening separatism as in Spain.

As students of European integration we are intrigued by a currency upheld as a symbol of European integration that is purportedly worth saving at any cost and by the political implications of the recast architecture of European economic governance. While the prevailing narrative inscribes the euro crisis as one of irresponsible budgetary policy in southern Europe (Scharpf 2011), the official response strategy is one of making the Maastricht criteria stick, whilst marginalizing treaty provisions to allow the creation of well-funded vehicles that convey northern public funds to purchase largely worthless southern government bonds originally acquired by northern banks.

Economic governance — the set of institutions and mechanisms for ensuring the orderly pursuit of shared economic policy objectives — has in fact evolved at multiple levels, including policy processes, policy outcomes, and institutional dynamics. Collectively, these shifts amount to a redefinition of European economic governance consisting of an unlikely amalgam of diminished reliance on the 'Community method' characterized by European Commission agenda setting, along with a series of institutional innovations that strengthen common fiscal surveillance and oversight of macroeconomic imbalances and thereby advance integration. Institutionally, select nodes within the Council of Ministers — the permanent Council presidency and the Economics and Finance Council — have taken a firmer hand in agenda-setting; the actions of the European Central Bank have drawn national economic domains more directly into the European governance mix; and the European Parliament has sought to become a more active interlocutor of all of these actors as the voice of European citizens. Ironically, amidst the eurozone's severe strains, we are witnessing the emergence of a more 'European' European economic governance through unexpected means.

This trajectory provokes critical questions. How can we explain the form taken by institutional innovations? What role do existing EU institutional structures and policy inheritance play in determining the contours of these arrangements? How have institutional roles in the establishment of those mechanisms varied over time, and why? And what is the significance of the national economic divergence highlighted in much of the recent analysis of the eurozone crisis — not simply as outcome of the flaws in the design of EMU, as emphasized in the recent commentary — but as *cause* of policy patterns and decision processes?

In this issue, we assemble contributors who explore the dynamics of European economic governance in response to the ongoing troubles of the single currency, which are intertwined, of course, with the major global recession sparked by the collapse of trade in overvalued US home loans and the subsequent closer attention paid by international banks to the macroeconomic data of southern and northwestern European governments whose securities they had readily purchased in the early 2000s. Our common theme is an *institutional* focus that analyzes both *policy output* produced by European institutions in the wake of the crisis and the *dynamic interactions of these institutions* themselves. Consequently, several contributors employ historical institutionalist arguments about path dependency as a central element shaping policy choices, while others deploy the prism of a principal-agent framework to explain the evolution of European economic governance.

Through these approaches, the volume brightly illuminates the choice of institutional innovations. Elements of the EU treaties and existing institutional arrangements, choices and constraints appear to have been vital in shaping the overall response to the mounting eurozone banking and sovereign debt crisis. The response itself has hardly been either linear or inevitable. As observers have explained relentlessly, the Maastricht Treaty did not create sufficiently powerful corrective mechanisms (especially in the fiscal realm), yet also closed off policy options by placing restraints on actions (the prohibition on monetary financing of national governments, for example) and actors (ECB). Crisis resolution has as a consequence proven elusive. But our analysis cannot end there. These treaty components not only account for the casting about for politically acceptable and economically effective solutions throughout the crisis; these omissions and constraints also help us understand the course that *has* been taken by eurozone member state governments.

Of course, the very existence of prohibitions that produced policy paralysis pushes to the fore the question of incorporating into European economic governance an ultimate element of supranational executive discretion authorizing measures to salvage the eurozone in dire circumstances, creating once and for all a credible commitment to irreversibility of economic and monetary union. Kenneth Dyson carefully maps this terrain of 'supreme emergency' in his article, motivated by the insight that rules relying on the behaviour of markets and states are unlikely to operate as expected in crisis conditions. He establishes that any authority to invoke such a prerogative would have to be vested in an independent agent. Nonetheless, as Dyson informs us, this is inherently a normative question that, inevitably raised by the tensions inherent in European economic governance, inevitably will remain unresolved.

It is a widely accepted insight that European integration has often thrived on difficulty and proceeded because of and in spite of extremely adverse circumstances. A number of — very cautionary — regulatory attempts have been made to somewhat limit the awesome powers of financial markets, while EU actors have created rescue vehicles, crucially the European Stability Mechanism (ESM) and the European Financial Stabilisation Facility (EFSF). Critically, in the process of attempting to salvage the single currency new power dynamics have unfolded, with a decisive shift away from the 'community method' and a much more intergovernmentally inspired response pattern. Initially, of course, eurozone crisis response efforts adhered to the community method. This was true of the 'six-pack' of economic reforms proposed by the European Commission in fall 2010, which addressed tighter fiscal surveillance, oversight of macroeconomic imbalances, and strengthening of the Stability and Growth pact and followed traditions of Commission agenda-setting. But a change in the dynamics of policy making quickly ensued, as national governments actively sought to reduce agency slack accruing to supranational institutions, shifting agenda setting authority to the Council President and members of the Economics and Finance Council (Ecofin) and in essence established a hierarchy that subordinated the role of the Commission to these actors.

Such a shift towards what Angela Merkel describes as the 'Union method' is perhaps unsurprising given the substantial long-term financial commitments entered into by northern governments. However, the robust role that key national governments, especially the German, but also the French, have played in the process of elaborating a response, must not distract us from the noteworthy policy entrepreneurship of an institution that has quietly emerged from relative obscurity to being a major *eminence gris*. The European Central Bank (ECB) has been a crucial actor in helping usher in the institutional and practical foundations for fresh cash injections into the strapped governments of the South. The ECB is also playing a role in the enforcement of austerity programmes largely resembling Washington Consensus-style structural adjustment programmes in Greece. In the ongoing tug-of-war between the Commission and the member states, the response thus far seems ultimately more shaped by member state influence, the latter understandably keeping the rescue vehicles on a tight leash. However, broadly speaking, European-level influence in devising a response is hardly absent, notably in the form of both the enlarged ECB role and a very activist European Parliament (EP).

Rather than confining ourselves to one preferred approach or school, our contributors employ a variety of mid-level theoretical approaches, while all broadly subscribing to an institutional focus. All concur that the response seems to be geared towards affirming both the single currency and the Maastricht criteria with tougher enforcement mechanisms and imposed austerity and structural adjustment programmes meant to redress the mounting and persistent economic imbalances highlighted during the past few years. Whether such strategy is viable, as senior economists openly question, whether the euro has been salvaged once and for all given the obvious economic mismatch in terms of its membership basis and the severe dislocations this will continue to produce, and whether the response strategy has thus merely 'kicked the can down the road' are valid questions worth contemplating.

In their contribution to the volume, Jonathan Yiangou, Mícheál O'Keeffe and Gabriel Glöckler demonstrate how the monetary financing prohibition, by closing off one channel to the resolution of the eurozone crisis, pushed the process onto an alternative path. Consistent with the European Central Bank's independence and mandate to pursue price stability, the prohibition on financing of governments' debts was intended to protect monetary policy from the intrusion of a fiscal imperative generated by the budget positions of national governments. Both this group of authors and Nikos Zahariadis in his essay on the Greek debt crisis point out that the dynamics of fiscal federalism, according to which markets and voters were to hold individual governments accountable — through risk premia and electoral choice — did not function effectively. Costs of fiscal choices spilled across national borders. As contagion spread, the potential costs of eurozone disintegration rose sharply.

At this point, institutional constraints become critical to the course of EU economic governance. The ECB resisted any dramatic deviation from its mandate and limits. As Yiangou, O'Keeffe and Glöckler indicate, this impasse accounts for the shape of the first concrete efforts toward alleviating the crisis: restructured mechanisms to address macroeconomic imbalances; measures to assure sound national reporting of economic data; closer monitoring of peer fiscal policies, since financial assistance was to come in the form of fiscal transfers from other governments rather than monetary financing from the ECB; plans for centralized bank supervision and a framework for bank capitalization.

Initial economic governance choices made in the face of deteriorating conditions and diverse and uncertain preferences also have had lasting consequences for the subsequent course of European economic governance. Ledina Gocaj and Sophie Meunier establish that the creation of the European Financial Stability Facility (EFSF) in spring 2010 decisively shaped the permanent European Stability Mechanism (ESM) devised less than a delete second part of sentence 8 October 2012. The EFSF, to be available to governments cut off from capital markets, itself was hardly pre-determined; the institution was crafted in the context of near panic in financial markets, grave worries about domestic political constraints, and a wide range of conflicting views on how to respond effectively. In this environment, the EFSF emerged as a wholly inadequate instrument, as market and political forces quickly demonstrated. The response was a push from several quarters — from the ECB to national finance ministers — to expand the resources available to the EFSF. The apparent inadequacies of the EFSF structure and its intended temporary nature notwithstanding, time compression and the political dynamics of approval of any new bailout mechanism generated an ESM that was a modified version of the EFSF.

The decision of the Economics and Finance Council to create the EFSF represented an alternative to a European Commission proposal for an EU stabilization fund that would borrow on the strength of guarantees from member state governments. In this sense, as Meunier and Gocaj underscore, the form of the EFSF put economic governance decision making on a firmly intergovernmental path. Picking up on this very dynamic, Dermot Hodson explores the role of the Barroso Commissions, finding them a cautious player carefully safeguarding the institution's political capital and strategically supporting minimalist re-regulatory activity with substantial political support in the member states. The center-right political leaning of Commission President Barroso further contributes to an ultimately limited Commission-led response, effectively affirming the monetarist-inspired Maastricht criteria and avoiding substantial taming of the financial markets.

Michele Chang similarly investigates the weight of member states relative to the Commission, arguing that through the skilful appointment of constrained agents the member states maintain a key role in controlling the re-financing of southern government debt. Resonating with Chang's argument, while turning toward the external representation of the EU in institutions of global economic governance, Charlotte Rommerskirchen explores the incomplete Europeanization of representation of member states in international economic institutions, where despite some cautious delegation at the G-20, principals remain very restrained in employing agents and jealously safeguard their hold on interest representation in global fora.

Ironically, while Commission entrepreneurship appears to have waned in the crisis, at least in part due to divergence of national economic positions, national economic divergence and insufficient economic policy coordination have produced a very different institutional dynamic involving the European Central Bank. The operation of the ECB is based on delegation by the national governments to a completely independent agent, an act required to achieve credibility in the pursuit of price stability. Coupled with national economic divergence and the incomplete contracting characteristic of economic and monetary union, the process was likely from the start to require additional policy coordination. As indicated by Francisco Torres, soft policy mechanisms (such as the Lisbon Strategy) proved wholly inadequate to this purpose. The result has been the creation of a succession of new institutional mechanisms to advance the goal of stability amidst national economic divergence.

More precisely, the ECB has been driven by crisis into national policy domains in pursuit of its mission to provide stability 'in a highly fragmented political system' — and, critically, to protect its independence. Put differently, national economic policies become a matter of common concern as the ECB pursues its role as guardian of the objectives of economic and monetary union. This disjuncture between ECB independence and the production of new economic policy coordination mechanisms inevitably produces serious challenges for procedural legitimacy in the monetary policy realm.

What does this institutional constellation suggest about the likely sources of institutional innovation in European economic governance? As David Andrews explains in his comparison of the European Commission's 2008 assessment of successes and challenges confronting economic and monetary union after its first decade with its 1962 'Action Programme for the Second Stage' of the development of the Common Market, the Commission was quite insightful in its identification of the eurozone's problems at a relatively early stage, focusing on macroeconomic imbalances between countries and divergent developments in unit labour costs and competitiveness. Resonating with the 1962 action programme, the Commission also adhered to a general approach of long-standing: moving towards 'ever closer union' and a more European approach through embracing the principle of *engrenage*. All the more perplexing, then, is why the Commission was quite reserved as an entrepreneur initially in taking steps to rectify the obvious problems that emerged with the single currency during the second half of the 2000s in particular or why it hesitated to challenge the two heavyweights of the eurozone, France and Germany, in 2003 when both countries' macroeconomic data already diverged from the Maastricht criteria. As Dermot Hodson might suggest, entrepreneurial activity by the Commission seems to be heavily conditioned by strategic considerations — picking battles wisely — and the ideological orientation of the Barroso Commissions, as opposed to earlier Commission leadership which historically assumed a more technocratic stance.

Coinciding with Hodson's observation, Andrews finds that while a sort of 'bicycle theory' of the need for incessant forward movement of integration persists, the Commission has in contrast with its earlier incarnation abandoned an insistence that steps toward the breaking down of barriers between national markets — negative integration — must be accompanied by parallel developments in positive integration. Furthermore, the constancy of the Commission's conceptualization of the dynamic of the integration process suggests it is not likely to be a source of fresh thinking or innovative institutional reform.

National economic divergence provides one clue to the prominence of national governments in defining the emerging contours of EU economic governance. At the same time, such divergence may well be an impediment to efficient decision-making and effective outcomes. We see evidence for this, for example, in the manner in which the EU has translated financial rules negotiated in multilateral fora — such as the banking regulation agreed in the context of the Basel Committee on Banking Supervision in 2010 — into EU law. As David Howarth and Lucia Quaglia demonstrate, member state preferences shaped by structural features of national political economies, including the capital position and leverage ratios of banks and the nature of their financing arrangements, both reinforced the intergovernmental nature of the bargaining process and altered the application of the multilateral agreement in the EU context in ways likely to render it less effective.

National divergence also features prominently in Nikolaos Zahariadis's account of fiscal federalism, which draws on work by Hallerberg (2011) focused on three key disciplining factors to reign in spendthrift governments: market signals, a no bailout policy, and corrective action as well as an active populace punishing profligate governments in democratic elections. Hallerberg's argument suggests these conditions were met until mid-2009, but that bailouts developed in spring 2010 broke the link between national government finances and assessments of the sustainability of those finances by markets (Hallerberg 2011, 128). Zahariadis develops the argument for the Greek case, demonstrating that problems emerge when costs of fiscal choices are not confined to national borders, creating perverse incentives for individual governments to depart from the behaviour expected by market and political signals — and for collective deviation from adherence to the principles of fiscal federalism as well. At the systemic level — for the eurozone as a whole — problems are exacerbated where agreed fiscal limits cannot be met by most members, undermining the credibility of those limits. The spread of contagion across the eurozone rendered the cost of bailout potentially less than the cost of adhering to rules of fiscal federalism. Additionally, as Zahariadis points out, lack of adherence to principles of fiscal federalism has locked in structural inequalities by failing to impose adjustment on surplus and deficit countries alike, while efforts to rescue fiscal federalism have not made the threat of default any more credible.

Zahariadis' argument finds its counterpart in the analysis provided by Ramūnas Vilpišauskas, who underscores the formative role of popular sentiment in the member states in moulding the response to the crisis. In contrast with the analysis advanced by Howarth and Quaglia, Vilpišauskas places less emphasis on structural elements of national polities and more on preferences derived from domestic politics — illustrated, for example, in the divergent positions on a financial transactions tax backed by 11 countries and supported by the European Parliament. Vilpišauskas underscores the more intensive politicization of redistributive policies relative to regulatory policies, which in turn intensifies national divergence as a constraint on efforts to address the problems of the eurozone.

The response to the crisis of the euro has been uneven across both mechanisms and institutions. At the *EU level*, cautious and modest re-regulation has been passed, as detailed in Hodson's and Zahariadis' articles, though in no way does this limited tinkering with financial markets amount to the radical recast of the financial service industry seemingly demanded by the crisis since 2009. From a Commission previously known for its commitment to the neoliberal growth course articulated in the Lisbon Agenda, this was perhaps unrealistic to expect for both ideological reasons (Smith 2012) and political considerations.

An intriguing institutional re-arrangement points to three key findings of our analysis. *First*, rather than permitting facile generalizations about the response to economic turmoil in the eurozone being coloured by a supranational or an intergovernmental shade, the empirical and analytical reality is significantly more complex. As we document, the actions of member state governments and EU institutions have not simply followed the 'Community method'. The 'Union method' seems to be shaped significantly more by member states than might have been anticipated given the political constellations prior to the crisis. In truth, member state governments have been faced by an indecisive and uninspiring Commission, but they also hesitated to accept top-down Europeanization and a significant power shift to European-level institutions. In fact, one of the more interesting empirical phenomena is the ongoing power struggle between the German government, the Bundesbank and its representatives in the ECB and the rest of the central bank's apparatus. The struggle seems as much informed by disagreements over policy content as over the desirability of full fiscal union, with the 'German' argument reasonably highlighting the ignored dangers implicit in higher inflation, unsustainable and undesirable debt burdens, and massive wealth redistribution to a limited number of financial institutions. Thus, the somewhat muddled response is yet again a case of containing both strongly intergovernmental elements — the rescue vehicles in particular — and intergovernmental touches, notably in the form of the six-pack and the European semester. Ultimately, however, given the strong interest of the German government in securing and re-affirming the Maastricht criteria even this ostensibly supranational element is strongly coloured by one government's preferences.

Second, our analysis points to the emergence of two key actors, only one of which, the European Parliament, appears to have been the object of significant attention in the scholarly literature. The post-Lisbon ordinary legislative procedure enabled the EP to avoid Commission attempts to water down financial market re-regulation, asserting itself as a self-confident actor willing — and more importantly, able — to flex its muscles. A second pivotal actor, which deserves more scholarly scrutiny, is the ECB, which has engaged in extensive policy entrepreneurship. We detect a divided policy agenda here, with bank officials dedicated to not only salvaging the euro at any cost, but also pushing for fiscal union in the absence of unlimited lending or Eurobonds, effectively curtailed by the German Constitutional Court ruling of 12 September 2012. This agenda is not shared by all representatives in the governing council because of its obvious financial and political fall-out. The ECB can be said to have acted as a decisive, at times even shrewd actor in pursuing its favoured strategy. In fact, much of the empirical story reads like one of quiet, yet powerful, mission creep.

Third, our work points to the importance of delegation, its limits, its potential, and its implications for policy output and its legitimacy. The recently reawakened scholarly interest in applying the principal-agent framework to European studies bears testimony to the increasing significance of delegation as a governance tool at the EU level. A number of our contributors deploy this framework, exploring the often very tight room for manoeuvre afforded to the appointed agents. In politically sensitive and extremely costly affairs, principals are understandably conservative in allotting influence to the executing agents.

At the *national* level, the developments charted and analyzed here point to the familiar picture of the Franco–German alliance acting as an engine (or not) in European integration, with the October 2010 Deauville meeting between Angela Merkel and Nicolas Sarkozy, and their tentative bilateral deal imposing some of the costs of bailouts on private bond holders, a case in point. The proactive role of the Germans, not quite mirrored by developments in Paris, where a weak and confused leadership struggled to identify a coherent policy response and was ultimately replaced in national elections, is unsurprisingly linked to the financial responsibility implied by the current response strategy. Rapid and decisive action in 2010 was eschewed in favour of a piecemeal response to what were then portrayed as largely self-inflicted severe economic difficulties in one marginal southern member state. Events since have both highlighted the enormous financial cost of the initial dithering and hesitation, including that by German Chancellor Angela Merkel, at another singular historical moment.

Events at the national level also point to significant potential for political upheaval. It is worth highlighting the potential for government default on debts in Greece, as well as escalating political violence in the repression of anti-austerity demonstrations and the anti-immigrant tensions actively promoted by the Golden Dawn movement. Serious and sustained financial difficulties by both the Spanish governments and some of the autonomous regions, coupled with a vocal separatist movement not only in Catalonia and the Basque Country, along with mass youth employment provide all ingredients necessary for sustained political and economic turmoil. Meanwhile, in Italy as elsewhere in Mediterranean Europe, the consequences of a pronounced competitiveness gap with Germany, the inability to meaningfully compete in product markets with cheaper producers in East Asia, and the dire political consequences of extended austerity, at least for a government still wedded to liberal democracy and regular elections, are such that it has not been possible to entirely rule out a voluntary eurozone exit by any of the southern countries throughout the course of the crisis.

As if there was not enough uncertainty and potential for serious political conflict and civil unrest in the south, central European countries both within and outside the eurozone, such as Slovenia, Slovakia, and Hungary, are experiencing severe budgetary problems; Hungary is in addition witnessing the re-emergence of colourful populists with little more than a nominal commitment to the values of liberal democracy. Not only is it necessary to raise the question whether the can has been merely kicked down the road, it is also worth pondering why and in whose interest the kicking continues, given the hefty political and economic price tag for the ideological commitment to the desirability of a single currency.

Future academic work might chart the emergence of a consensus on the desirability of salvaging the euro and 'toughening up' of the Maastricht criteria amongst European elites as an ideational prerequisite for the course of action (cf. Heipertz & Verdun 2004). In an important update to her seminal monograph, McNamara wrote in 2006 (813–4):

> ... a second key issue now that EMU is out in the open is whether we should look to the central bankers' consensus to provide an adequate foundation, or is consensus needed (but unlikely to be secured) across a broader range of political elites as well as their publics? ... If the ECB is staffed by professionals largely educated and socialized along similar lines, consensus is relatively likely in the ECB as national policy traditions become less dominant over the past decades of monetary co-operation. Here the findings of a systematic sociological study of the ECB professional staff would be helpful to determine whether consensus is being reinforced by the new bureaucratization of the monetary policy realm and the creation of a professional socialization within the ranks.

We largely concur with these sentiments, but would add that for various and often pragmatic reasons, elite consensus stretches well beyond the narrow confines of the Eurotower in Frankfurt. In fact, despite the steep price associated with saving the euro, those policy makers expressing dissent in the principal contributor country — Germany — have been written off as political mavericks (Sarrazin 2012). Given political contestation and the implications of austerity for southern Europe and a massive debt burden for the North, it remains to be seen whether such consensus will prevail over time.

In sum, Europe's economic governance mechanisms have been reconfigured and the interplay between European and national institutions has generated a response strategy that ultimately consists of more communautarisation. The revised Stability and Growth Pact entails penalties for member state governments failing to implement required economic reforms and surveillance of macroeconomic imbalances of surplus and deficit countries alike. Europeanised banking regulation and supervisions appear to be in the cards. The conditionalities attached to financial support to the Greek, and less dramatically so the Spanish and Italian governments, will lead to a significant restructuring of the economies, the role and size of the public sector and the scope for redistribution, social, health and education policy. With a muddled response, yet ultimately one headed towards more Europe and the distinct prospect of fiscal union appearing more likely, there remains significant potential for political conflict and indeed economic instability.

In the long term, the refusal of certain member states to partake in the single currency will create stronger tensions for European governance than is the case already. A managed exit for weaker member states, for which no adequate institutional or legal parameters exist at present, would of course lead to substantial political upheaval. Curiously, the attraction of membership in the eurozone seems fairly undiminished amongst elites in central European countries. A more pernicious, yet distinctly possible outcome is persistent stagnation in southern Europe, necessitating the stark choice between either an end to the eurozone project in its current incarnation or a full-fledged transfer union with a more substantial contribution from northern European member states. At present, the political support amongst the European populace for the second option seems weaker than that for the first. Past choices in European integration have thus conditioned the present array of options available for policymakers, though crisis has a way of lending energy to creative ways of exploring uncharted territory.

References

Cooley, T.F., and R. Marimon. 2011. A credible commitment for the Eurozone. VOX, 20 July, http://www.voxeu.org/article/constitutional-solutions-eurozone-s-design-flaw (accessed 19 March 2013).

Dadush, U., and B. Sancil. 2010. Paradigm lost: the euro in crisis. *Carnegie Endowment for International Peace*, June 2, http://carnegieendowment.org/2010/06/02/europe-s-debt-crisis-more-than-fiscal-problem/bl8k (accessed 19 March 2013).

Featherstone, K. 2011. The Greek sovereign debt crisis and EMU: a filing state in a skewed regime. *Journal of Common Market Studies* 49, no. 2: 193–217.

Fioretos, O. 2001. The domestic sources of multilateral preferences: varieties of capitalism in the European Community. In *Varieties of capitalism*, ed. P. Hall and D. Soskice, 231–44. Oxford: Oxford University Press.

Hallerberg, M. 2011. Fiscal federalism reforms in the European Union and the Greek crisis. *European Union Politics* 12, no. 1: 127–42.

Heipertz, M., and A. Verdun. 2004. The dog that would never bite? What we can learn from the origins of the stability and growth pact. *Journal of European Public Policy* 11, no. 5: 765–80.

McNamara, K. 2006. Economic governance, ideas and EMU: what currency does policy consensus have today? *Journal of Common Market Studies* 44, no. 4: 803–21.

Meyer, H. 2010. The eurozone's critical design flaws. *The Guardian*, 17 February.

Sarrazin, T. 2012. *Europa braucht den Euro nicht: Wie uns politisches Wunschdenken in die Krise geführt hat.* Munich: Deutsche Verlagsanstalt.

Scharpf, F. 2011. Monetary union, fiscal crisis and the preemption of democracy. *Zeitschrift für Staats- und Europawissenschaften* 9, no. 2: 163–98.

Smith, M. 2012. *Europe and national economic transformation: the EU after the Lisbon decade*. New York: Palgrave Macmillan.

Sworn to Grim Necessity? Imperfections of European Economic Governance, Normative Political Theory, and Supreme Emergency

KENNETH DYSON

School of European Studies, Cardiff University, Cardiff, UK

ABSTRACT   This contribution examines the Euro Area crisis and European economic governance reforms through a less technocratic lens. It argues for the need to reframe debate around foundation issues in normative legal and political theory. The defining issue is supreme emergency. The credibility of its capacity to act in supreme emergency is of existential significance for the Euro Area. At the same time this capacity poses is bound up with basic legitimacy issues. In particular, it involves ultimately contentious requirements for supranational executive discretion, including credible contingent commitments to take exceptional measures. Meeting these requirements exposed a power vacuum within the Euro Area, consequent on domestic political constraints. This vacuum was filled—if reluctantly—by the European Central Bank. However, difficult legitimacy issues remain. They leave open the credibility of the ECB contingent commitment to act in supreme emergency.

To think our former state a happy dream;
From which awaked, the truth of what we are
Shows us but this: I am sworn, brother sweet,
To grim Necessity, and he and I
Will keep a league till death...
(William Shakespeare, *Richard II*, Act V, Scene 1)

The lesson from Shakespeare's magisterial tragedy is that, once a ruler is shaken out of complacency, and recognizes the need for decisive action, firm resolution is vital. King Richard II is found wanting. He prevaricates and perishes, a case of too little, too late. His tragedy can be read as a commentary on the first decade of the euro—a happy dream inducing procrastination and complacency. It can also be seen as reflected in the limitations of a strategy of 'buying time' that came to characterize Euro Area crisis management from 2007 onwards. King Richard II's words pose the—still open—question of whether, faced by supreme emergency, the Euro Area can, and should, firmly commit to do whatever 'grim necessity' requires for its survival. The answer is bound up with the will and the capacity of the Euro Area to endow supranational institutions with the executive discretion to act in this way.

This contribution analyses central challenges to the Maastricht paradigm of economic governance, posed by supreme emergency, and the unanswered questions to which they give rise. These questions relate to the incomplete nature of Economic and Monetary Union (EMU), despite major reforms from 2008; the tension between requirements of democratic legitimacy and justificatory principles for supranational executive discretion to take exceptional measures; and the modest expectations that can be held of rules in the face of the imperfections of states and markets and of the inducements to complacency.

Above all, the contribution highlights the central tension between conceptual analysis of the nature of the crisis prevention and management capacities of the Euro Area and its historically and institutionally specific character. Two sources of this distinctiveness are the treaty prohibitions on the monetary financing of member state governments (Article 123, Treaty on the Functioning of the European Union, TFEU) and on Community or member state liability for the debts of other governmental bodies (Article 125). The former forbids European Central Bank (ECB) purchases of sovereign bonds, at least in the primary market; the latter serves to support a 'no-bail-out' interpretation of the Treaty.

The contribution goes on to examine the competing principles for justifying exceptional measures in supreme emergency in the EU context; the difficulties in minimizing risk of moral hazard by credible contingent commitments to exceptional measures; and the complex issues of institutional design. Finally, the contribution outlines the problems in developing a political strategy for supreme emergency, notably in building creditor state support and in justifying enhanced supra-national executive discretion at a time of deepening political concerns about the EU 'democratic deficit'. However much one tries to dress up debate about exceptional measures in technocratic terms, the supra-national will and capacity to act in supreme emergency remains normative, politically contestable, deeply unwelcome in key official and political circles, and – in the absence of a 'pivotal event'—off the public political agenda.

Challenges to the Maastricht Governance Paradigm: Unanswered Questions

Lawyers and statesmen place enormous weight on honouring Treaty commitments, for very good reasons of history, legitimacy, and consent. With respect to the Maastricht constitution of EMU, this commitment means strict compliance with the fundamental principle of stability-oriented policies and its four pillars: strict central bank independence, no co-responsibility for each other's public debts, no monetary financing of member state governments, and the strict separation of fiscal and monetary policies. Corrosion of these pillars risks mounting mistrust and resentment, hostility within creditor states, threat of legal redress, and the loss of market as well as political credibility. This historical and institutional specificity of the Euro Area has fundamental implications in narrowing debate about economic governance reforms and for building its will and capacity to act in supreme emergency in the form of supra-national institutions with the appropriate executive discretion.

The Maastricht governance paradigm faces three fundamental challenges. They beg the question whether the Euro Area can rely *only* on stability-oriented crisis prevention and management mechanisms and a rules-based approach. Firstly, the Euro Area operates in the context of a growing mismatch. On the one hand, it is mired in the mounting complexity, dense opacity, and accelerating speed, of financial markets. On the other, it confronts the limited capacity for comprehensive and rapid collective action by its member states (and by the larger international political economy of global governance). EU political logic is grounded in multiple interacting domestic electoral calendars and in the temporal scheduling of Council meetings. It is imperfectly synchronized with faster-moving financial markets that focus on very short-term returns (Dyson 2009). The unanswered question is: how is the Euro Area to escape from being characteristically 'behind the curve' of market-created events?

Secondly, the Euro Area—and the wider EU—places great faith in one—or both—of two approaches to crisis prevention and management: the capacity of reinforced rules and surveillance and monitoring procedures, quasi-automatic in character, to secure compliance by Member States; and the capacity of financial markets to discipline member states in a manner consistent with their long-term economic and political stability and with sustainable economic growth.

Both approaches rest on the Enlightenment faith in the triumph of rationality. However, reliance on them exposes the Euro Area to the imperfections of states and markets. The Euro Area and wider EU have internal problems of state capacity to comply with commitments. States contain powerful incentives to avert compliance, associated with elections and party and coalition management. They face the obstacles of entrenched domestic veto points. Governments are induced to indulge citizens and special interests, including tolerating asset-price booms. State capacity is further compromised when states exhibit rent-seeking activity, their resources being used for partisan and personal gains. Many states are bound up in clientelist political practices and deeply factionalized and personalized politics. Efficacy of EU and Euro Area economic governance mechanisms is further compromised by 'sinners (actual and potential) voting on sinners'. From the perspective of long-term stability-oriented policies, financial markets contain perverse incentives. They are driven by alternating fear and greed, exhibit short-term predatory activity, especially in purely financial transactions, and are notoriously creative in evading and subverting supervision and regulation (Dyson forthcoming). Crisis situations reveal the modest capacity of formalized rule-based approaches to deal with these imperfections of states and markets. Rule-based approaches fit uncomfortably with short-term, opportunistic, and herd-like financial market activity and with deficiencies of collective action in taming financial markets. The unanswered question is: how is the Euro Area to manage this logic of imperfect states and imperfect markets?

Thirdly, the creation of the Euro Area, in conjunction with the single market programme, means that much more is at stake in crisis management than in earlier crises of the 1970s–1990s. The context and character of the oil crises and of Exchange Rate Mechanism (ERM) crises of 1983, 1987, and 1992–1993 were very different. By spurring banking and financial market integration, the Euro Area intensified cross-national supervisory and regulatory problems on a scale, and at a speed, that outstripped its institutional capacity. Financial market integration reinforced the potential for interlinked and contagious Euro Area sovereign debt and banking crises. Major financial market supervisory and regulatory reforms, in the wake of the Lamfalussy report and Basle III, were unable to keep pace with this growing complexity and interdependence. In addition, unlike in the 1970s–1990s, the Euro Area (and the wider EU) was bound together in a complex web of euro-denominated contracts, compounding the costs of exit for member states. The unanswered question is: how is the Euro Area to act once the limits of its capacity to act as a banking and financial union are breached?

The Central Tension

The three challenges to the Maastricht governance paradigm—and the unanswered questions to which they give rise—underline the central tension between the conceptual analysis of crisis prevention and management capacities and the historically and institutionally specific character of the Euro Area. The difficulties in resolving this tension illustrate that conceptual analysis of supreme emergency provision gets one only so far. After the disaster of the Nazi seizure of power in 1933, German lawyers retained a particularly deep, and comprehensible, aversion to endowing public authorities with emergency powers. Eventual incorporation of emergency powers in the German Basic Law in 1968–1969 took place against the background of widespread political protest. It required a framework of Grand Coalition government. The idea of emergency powers was contaminated by association with the foremost German legal theorist of the 'power state', Carl Schmitt (1963), whose work had been used to legitimize the Nazi revolution. In reaction, attachment to the

Rechtsstaat (state ruled by law) assumed fundamental doctrinal importance in post-war Germany.

Like Germany itself, the EU is seen as, above all, a polity based on law. German thinking on what the EU and its institutions can, and should be enabled to do in crisis management is profoundly constrained by respect for primary Treaty rules and formal legal arguments, grounded in painful historical experience. Such formalistic thinking is less prevalent in Anglo-American jurisprudence, which places more emphasis on the 'open texture' and uncertainties of primary rules and the margin of discretion left to officials and courts (notably Hart 1961, 121–32).

This underlying tension at the heart of the Euro Area invites comparison with, and possible learning from, debates in normative political theory about 'just war', specifically the liberal democratic state and the so-called 'supreme emergency exemption'. As the liberal theorist John Rawls (1999, 98–9) argued, all polities face the basic existential question of whether, in supreme emergency, there are limits on what they can do, and how. This question of the limits of normal moral reasoning arises when polities are faced by clear and imminent danger to their integrity and survival and to the understandings that were at the heart of their constitution-making process.

In the case of the EU and EMU, such understandings might relate to treaty provisions on irreversibility and solidarity. On this basis, it can be argued that the Euro Area is a matter of existential national interest for its member states. They are politically committed to 'making the euro work' and to ensuring its survival as 'irrevocable', as a 'community of destiny'. Making credible this commitment means 'doing what has to be done' so that intertwined banking collapses and disorderly sovereign defaults do not trigger the collapse of the Euro Area and place the survival of the wider EU, including the single market, at risk. Politically, this kind of argument involves a commitment to 'consequentialism': namely, that the costs of not acting in this way would be too awful to contemplate. In legal theory, it finds expression in the notion of establishing legal validity by reference to sources of authoritative criteria outside specific constitutional or treaty provisions. The so-called 'rule of recognition' is established in use as officials, government leaders, and courts balance different parts of treaty text, give priority to one part over another, and look for principles of justification to general declarations and to customary practice (Hart 1961, 92–104).

Justificatory Principles: The Problem of Legitimizing Supreme Emergency Action in the Euro Area

Exceptional measures by supranational institutions with executive discretion to deal with supreme emergency require justification. Differing kinds of justificatory arguments can be derived from legal and political theory, notably Thomas Hobbes, Jeremy Bentham, G.W.F. Hegel, and H.L.A. Hart. Their critical analysis raises the question of whether the Euro Area can be understood as a single 'order of worth', based on stability culture as the principle of evaluation and on arguments grounded strictly in avoidance of moral hazard. This position is advocated by those—notably

Germans—who argue for a return to the original Maastricht Treaty construction. However, an examination of normative legal and political theory opens up the prospect of reframing the Euro Area as an arena of multiple, mutually incompatible, orders. Each offers its own distinctive justification for exceptional measures, and each is available for mobilization in crises (cf. Boltanski and Thévenot 2006). Seen in these terms, the practical challenge is to construct compromises, however fragile and specific to individual situations, amongst these competing principles of justification by reference to the notion of a European common good. The practical constraint on this process of compromise and reframing is the underlying structures of power that support particular principles of evaluation and kinds of argument. Within the Euro Area, they privilege the stability culture principle and serve to keep supreme emergency away from the public political agenda of European economic governance reforms. In particular, they constrain the political room for manoeuvre of German and other creditor state leaders in addressing Euro Area crises (on which Dyson 2013).

However, other principles—sovereignty, community, utility, and legal reasoning—can be evoked to justify exceptional measures in supreme emergency. Following Hobbes, justification can be found in the need for a European sovereign power with the discretionary authority to take such measures to avert economic, social, and political breakdown within the EU. A second justificatory principle rests on Benthamite utilitarian calculus. Social welfare is, on balance, best secured by exceptional measures in supreme emergency. An alternative and very different principle is Hegelian appeal to the superior moral claims of community over economic calculus. In these terms, the EU and the Euro Area are fundamentally a humanistic project to overcome fragmentation and particularity through a 'community of destiny'. A fourth principle is rooted in a form of legal reasoning that justifies exceptional measures by the 'rule of recognition'. Their legal validity is derived from general characteristics of the composite set of treaty and legislative texts on which the EU and Euro Area are based and from accompanying general declarations that are invoked as authoritative.

There are obvious problems in trying to construct a claim for the EU or the Euro Area to be given the supra-national discretionary authority to act in supreme emergency on Hobbesian or Hegelian foundations. Assertion of a right based on sovereignty lacks credibility in the absence of a fully-fledged European federal state with independent democratic legitimacy. In its absence, supra-national assumption of mutual and shared liabilities on behalf of taxpayers faces severe legitimacy problems. The Lisbon Treaty does not provide the EU with exclusive or shared formal competence to act in supreme emergency. Similarly, assertion of the moral claims of community is fraught with difficulties in the absence of a European *demos*. The Euro Area lacks a shared public sphere for debating how macro-economic problems should be resolved. Not least, the European Parliament does not have a high profile within the architecture of European economic governance. Co-decision is a minor element, limited mainly to single market issues. In contrast, Benthamite utilitarian calculus fits well with existing claims that the EU depends on its 'output' legitimacy, its policy performance in meeting the aspirations and expectations of member state citizens. However, economic calculus is a 'thin', contestable, and fragile basis for claiming a right to take exceptional measures. In a supreme emergency it may prove more difficult to make such claims on a purely utilitarian basis.

These serious difficulties in constructing a normative argument for supra-national executive discretion suggest an examination of the implications of H.L.A Hart's 'rule of recognition' and his emphasis on the open texture of rules. Hart argues that attempts to establish legal validity generate conflicts over the ranking of different authoritative criteria and over the priority between different parts of treaty text. Thus one might invoke treaty and extra-treaty texts on irrevocability of monetary union; and one might place different stress on how to rank Articles 125 and 136 (TFEU), dealing respectively with no co-responsibility for public debts and with collective financial assistance. However, in thinking about how a rule of recognition might work in practice, one needs to be more alert than Hart to underlying power relations. Above all, the ECB and German negotiators have power in framing the terms of such debates. In this of power relations justifying exceptional measures on the basis of this type of legal reasoning could prove very difficult. Nevertheless, in 2012, with the Outright Monetary Transactions (OMT) Programme, and the commitment to buying sovereign bonds in the secondary market, the ECB showed itself willing to move ahead of key German public opinion formers, notably the Bundesbank, in embracing the role of supra-national authority of 'last resort'.

However normatively justified, and whatever the difficulties that follow from the historical and institutional specificities of the EMU, the argument remains the same. Given the imperfections of states and markets, and pervasive inducements to procrastination and complacency, the Euro Area requires the ultimate capacity to exercise supra-national executive discretion when the danger to it is 'close and serious' and its very existence is threatened. 'Just war' theory offers an intriguing, if imperfect parallel. Advocacy of the supreme emergency exemption from stability-oriented principles of the Maastricht governance paradigm rests on emphasis on the existentially significant costs in rigid formal compliance with principle-based treaty law that deals with normality. According to Michael Walzer (1992, 254), supreme emergency places a polity under 'the rule of necessity (and necessity knows no rules).'

Credible Contingent Commitment and Supreme Emergency: The Challenge of Minimizing Moral Hazard

Acceptance of the case for exceptional measures in supreme emergency poses serious intellectual and design challenges. The foremost problem is whether existential threats are 'real': that is, firmly grounded in evidence and clearly justified by indicators that enjoy broad support. Supreme emergency is readily amenable to 'creative' construction by self-interested domestic political actors, who wish to evade responsibility for pursuing unpopular stability-oriented policies. It is also amenable to abuse by supra-national officials, who seek opportunities for task expansion and bureaucratic empire-building. In short, supreme emergency risks fostering a discursive process in which politicians and officials construct and dramatize threats as justifying exceptional supra-national discretionary action. Similar processes have been identified in 'securitization' theory (Waever 1995, 55). The supreme emergency 'exemption' offers an incentive to construct the Euro Area as in a state of semi-permanent emergency. In these circumstances, exceptional measures become the new normality; moral hazard become endemic; supra-national institutions take on excessive credit risks; and the Euro Area founders on the question 'who then rescues the rescuer?'

The danger is that building supranational capacity for executive discretion in supreme emergency creates new perverse incentives, generating unanticipated and unwanted consequences, not least deterioration in the risk profile of supranational credit institutions. Minimizing these incentives depends on contingent commitments to exceptional measures when certain preconditions are met or thresholds are crossed. Contingent commitments have several virtues. They give politicians, citizens, and markets clarity about how policy will evolve, so that the principle that 'stability begins at home' retains its central importance. Contingent commitments also help to reduce political uncertainty. They offer an umbrella under which the most dangerous social and political manifestations of harsh economic austerity can be averted. Not least, by recognizing the high volatility and extreme uncertainty that characterize macro-economic performance, contingent commitments to exceptional measures help provide confidence and protect credibility.

However, translating contingent commitments into institutional design in a way that minimizes moral hazard is enormously difficult and potentially highly contentious. It rests on two requirements, which are difficult to reconcile. Firstly, the threshold of harm that justifies overriding the fundamental principle of stability-oriented policies in crisis management must be set very high. Specification of the threshold of harm might be set in different ways, generating controversy. One set of indicators would focus on the severe and protracted welfare costs from the failure to act, measured by scale of recession risks and threats to jobs and incomes. Indicators would focus on the real economy of GDP and unemployment. Alternatively, resort to supra-national emergency action might depend on thresholds for sovereign bond yield spreads, including so-called 'conversion' risk when pricing in premium for euro exit disrupts the monetary transmission mechanism. Another set of indicators would deal with institutional risks to the EU from loss of public confidence and trust. These more qualitative indicators would examine the growth of different forms of social unrest, mobilization of populist protest, and the rise of Euro-sceptic political parties and political sentiment. The question is whether the threshold of harm could be set in purely technical, numeric terms or would require subjective judgment.

Secondly, there would need to be strong incentives for early exit from exceptional measures. Management of the supreme emergency exemption—from activation to exit—would need to be entrusted to an independent supra-national professional institution. It must be founded on a basis that ensures that the responsible institution has an inbuilt self-interest in limiting use of the supreme emergency exemption and in ensuring early exit from temporally delimited exceptional measures. This requirement suggests distancing the supreme emergency exemption from the European Council, ECOFIN, the Eurogroup, and other inter-governmental bodies like the European Stability Mechanism (ESM). It points to a pivotal role for the ECB.

These two requirements pose dilemmas in institutional and procedural design that are not easily managed. Some key aspects of threshold specification might be deemed technical, reducible to numeric indicators. At the same time, there remains an irreducible political judgment that falls more appropriately to the European Council than to the ECB. Most problematically, building supra-national capacity to act in supreme emergency has the effect of binding the ECB into a political process. German Ordo-liberalism, and the Bundesbank as its guardian, remains deeply averse to this development. The dilemma might be managed on the (suitably modified) model of exchange-rate policy provisions in the Maastricht Treaty. A Council decision would have to be based on the recommendation of an unimpeachably independent professional institution (the ECB), and on that institution's ongoing consent.

Design Issues in Supreme Emergency: Instruments, Agencies, and Procedures

Empirically, the issue of supranational executive capacity in supreme emergency is defined by certain policy tools or instruments and by how practice evolves in their use. One element is the 'lender of last resort' function, a well-established central bank role in providing liquidity to the banking system, conducted by non-standard monetary policy operations. In putting this set of tools in place, the ECB emerged as the supra-national discretionary authority of last resort, conducting this supreme emergency function independently of the Council. Its key elements are the three-year unlimited liquidity provision to Euro Area banks, with relaxed collateral requirements, introduced in December 2011; and the TARGET2 payment system balances within the Eurosystem of ECB and national central banks, which by January 2012 left the Bundesbank with liabilities of €498 billion.

By February–March 2012 these unconventional ECB measures provoked German fears that the lender-of-last-resort function was serving as an indirect route to circumvent the 'no monetary financing of governments' provision. Banks could make sizeable profits by obtaining very cheap money from the ECB and using it to invest in sovereign bonds that offered high yields, notably in Italy and Spain. Moreover, cheap unlimited long-tem liquidity provision risked sustaining insolvent and imprudent banks rather than inducing overdue change in bank business models The ECB stressed its decisive action to avert imminent macro-economic risk of recession, consequent on a credit crunch. In contrast, the Bundesbank, leading German economists and the financial press highlighted the long-term risks from the accumulation of weak collateral, asset-price bubbles, and heightened inflation expectations. The difference of views came to a head with the leak of a letter from the Bundesbank president to the president of the ECB (Frankfurter Allgemeine Zeitung 2012).

The institutional constraints on developing policy instruments for supra-national executive discretion in supreme emergency are even more severe in the fiscal sphere. In the last resort, the Euro Area has to assume collective responsibility for sovereign debt and for bank recapitalization and resolution. It implies banking union as well as fiscal union, with their attendant transfers.

A number of problems arise. Firstly, neither Article 122.2 (TFEU) nor Article 136 (as amended) provides a satisfactory treaty basis for acting in supreme emergency, at least viewed narrowly in their own terms. The European Financial Stabilization Facility (EFSF) and the ESM fall well short of possessing supra-national executive discretion. They also lack the scale of fiscal 'firepower' to use in supreme emergency. The ESM did not provide a credible contingent commitment at the systemic level. When created, the ESM was resourced only to deal with smaller periphery Member States, not Italy and Spain, let alone France. Although the ESM Treaty makes a gesture in its provisions for emergencies, the discretion of the ESM remains bounded and anchored in unanimity. The ESM is an intergovernmental body and sub-optimal in terms of capacity to take exceptional measures. It fits the so-called 'Union method', evolved and endorsed by the French and German governments during the post-2007 crisis, rather than the traditional Community method that would empower the European Commission and the European Parliament. Germany possesses a *de facto* veto power within the ESM. Hence its credibility is contingent on German domestic constraints.

Secondly, a key lesson of the post-2007 crisis was the close interdependence of sovereign debt and bank debt. Debt problems spill from one to the other in chain reaction, meaning that fiscal union required parallel banking union. However, the coordinated use of fiscal and monetary policy tools risks subverting key pillars of the Maastricht economic governance paradigm and inducing rejection by the German Bundesbank. In its absence, the institutional capacity of the Euro Area to take exceptional action in supreme emergency looks inferior to US and UK practices.

Ultimately, however, developing a supranational fiscal capacity for exceptional measures, including bank recapitalization and resolution, encounters the problem of how to resource such a capacity in the absence of justificatory principle for extracting taxation. The EU/Euro Area is not a federal state with an independent basis of political legitimacy. The design of the ESM follows this logic in the resources made available to it by its member states, in its limited discretion, and its intergovernmental character.

If one accepts the logic of a supra-national executive capacity to act in supreme emergency, serious and difficult institutional design questions remain in the context of the historical and institutional specificities of the Euro Area, above all the lack of a federal state. Within the bounds of this context, there is room for argument about better design with respect to collective responsibility for sovereign debt and bank recapitalization and resolution. What kind of institutional arrangement minimizes risk of moral hazard? How is political, fiscal, monetary, and banking and financial market authority to be organized and coordinated? How high should be the threshold for triggering action? How can incentives for exit be maximized?

The risk in avoiding addressing these difficult and unwelcome questions is that grim necessity may force them to be answered in imprudent, unsustainable ways. In the face of the historical and institutional specificities of the Euro Area, the consequences could prove fatal. In the final analysis, given the imperfections of state capacity and implementation, and the consequent modest role that rules can play, the capacity to act in supreme emergency is essential to deter short-term, speculative financial trading. It involves the threat of imposing losses on those who put at risk the long-term collective good of European integration founded on economic stability.

The treaty provision that prohibits monetary financing of member state governments precludes a major direct role for the ECB in sovereign bond markets, at least in primary markets. The ECB Securities Markets Programme (SMP) of May 2010, which conducted interventions in secondary bond markets, was justified by reference to the ECB obligation to ensure depth and liquidity in dysfunctional market segments and restore the smooth functioning of the monetary transmission mechanism. However, it lacked a clear direct link to conditionality requirements. For this reason, and for reasons of principle, the SMP encountered deep reservations from the Bundesbank. It was connected to the early departure of its president, Axel Weber, as well as of the German Chief Economist of the ECB, Jürgen Stark (2011). The ineffectiveness of the SMP in gaining credible commitments to fiscal and structural reforms by the Italian government in late 2011 led to erosion of support within the ECB itself. The SMP was wound down by the new ECB president Mario Draghi. It was replaced with the longer-term bank liquidity provision programme and by the OMT Programme. The OMT was a contingent commitment to buy sovereign bonds in secondary markets subject to an agreed fiscal consolidation and structural reform programme with the EFSF/ESM and its timely implementation.

Minimizing hazard in the incentive structure suggests a strong case for entrusting a central role to the ECB in any procedure to activate and terminate exceptional measure in supreme emergency. The ECB would have a strong corporate self-interest in protecting stability-oriented principles both by setting a very high threshold for activation and by early exit from exceptional measures. Institutional self-interests might lead to a more relaxed approach by a special-purpose vehicle like the ESM or some future European Monetary Fund (EMF). Less damage would be done to moral hazard.

In addition, central banks have carefully honed skills in 'constructive ambiguity', keeping markets guessing. The ECB had the internal capacity to develop a set of indicators that would signal readiness for exceptional measures once warning lights began to flash. At the same time it would act as a reassurance that the threshold might be fixed at a suitably high level. Hence the process of activation would have to give the ECB a clear veto role.

As the banking and sovereign debt crises mounted, the ECB encountered conflicting incentives in developing its role as a supranational authority with discretion to act in supreme emergency. One incentive for it to abandon its principled opposition to crossing the Rubicon of fiscal policy stemmed from the greater risks in allowing this function to fall into the hands of a politicized body or a intergovernmental bureaucratic structure with self-interest in expansion. Another incentive was provided by the ECB's own bureaucratic self-interest in protecting the currency that it manages. Its own survival was at issue. The ECB had evolved a corporate self-interest and identity as a supranational institution that distanced it from the Bundesbank. It recognized that markets abhorred a vacuum and that the European Council was driven by domestic political incentives that generated complacency and procrastination. Only the ECB had the instruments to act to avert extreme emergency. At the same time, this shift to a more innovatory and politically visible and contested institution co-existed with more conservative instincts within the Eurosystem. There was discomfort with the subversion of the formal principle of central bank independence, notably the separation of fiscal and monetary policies and the provision for no privileged access for governments to central bank finance.

Whatever the constraints posed by historical and institutional specificities, and the inherent caution and conservatism of central bankers, the will and capacity to take supra-national discretionary action in supreme emergency remains the ultimate insurance device. It provides a credible commitment to irreversibility in EMU and a device that would further legitimate exceptional closer surveillance and intervention in domestic policies, as Draghi stressed with respect to the OMT programme. In addition, a supranational capacity to act in supreme emergency offers a shield for protecting state sovereignty and for enabling longer-term, growth-focused policies that help restore debt sustainability. However, its attractions diminish if the threshold of harm is lowered, increasing moral hazard. Lowering the threshold and giving too much authority to the European Council would simply pose the existential question in a new, equally unwelcome form—'who rescues the rescuer?' (Wulff 2011). Supranational executive discretion to act in supreme emergency becomes self-defeating once the institution involved suffers deterioration in its risk profile and loses creditworthiness and credibility. Hence commitments have to be contingent.

Political Strategy for Building Supra-national Executive Discretion to Act in Supreme Emergency

The political problems of legitimacy and consent in building capacity for supra-national discretionary authority in supreme emergency within the Euro Area are formidable. They stem in part from debtor states, where political elites and public opinion resent the attached conditionality as excessive interference in their sovereignty and as destructive of the core of national cultural identity. Legitimacy and consent problems are if anything even greater in creditor states, above all Germany. These states are fewer in number than debtor states and fear out-voting. Above all, the creditor states are the source of the credible guarantees that underpin the capacity for supranational executive discretion in supreme emergency and are anxious to limit their liabilities.

The Maastricht Treaty provisions on EMU represented an accommodation of these different sets of debtor and creditor state interests. The abridgement of the central principles of the Maastricht 'monetary constitution' in the interests of capacity building to act in supreme emergency was therefore bound to be highly contentious. It required major concessions by German Ordo-liberals and was welcomed neither by the Bundesbank nor by the German Federal Chancellor. Angela Merkel's Christian Democratic Union/ Christian Social Union (CDU/CSU) parliamentary party, her coalition government with the Free Democratic Party (FDP), and German public opinion remained deeply wedded to safeguarding 'stability culture'. They were committed to a long-term approach to Euro Area crisis management. This approach rested on strengthening the incentives for states to take individual responsibility for their own liquidity and solvency problems and on minimizing risks to the creditor state guarantors. It was based on two principles: European solidarity is based on effort, not transfers; and greater mutual liability must be matched by stronger supranational controls. The German government sought to put in place legal constructs, like the 'fiscal compact' treaty and the ESM treaty, to reinforce these principles. Above all, the German government feared that it might assume commitments and liabilities that it could not honour. In consequence, it would sacrifice its own creditworthiness and reputation and lose its claim to a special responsibility as economic motor and stability anchor within EMU (Merkel 2012).

Building a German-centred coalition of support for supra-national executive discretion to act in supreme emergency is an exceedingly difficult challenge. Most problematic of all, the Bundesbank has to be persuaded that acceptance of the Eurosystem having a 'bridging' function of 'buying time' for domestic management of fiscal consolidation and structural reforms was necessary but not enough (Weidmann 2012). As the OMT Programme showed, a political strategy of continuing to rely on 'binding-in' the Bundesbank threatened to meet its limits. The federal government had to assert the primacy of fundamental German security interests in European integration. This position had been adopted by Chancellor Helmut Kohl in the final Maastricht negotiations in 1991 and later in the transition to stage three of EMU (Dyson and Featherstone 1999). In order to 'bind-in' the Bundesbank, the Federal Chancellor would have to craft a discourse that focused on legal and political commitment to 'irreversibility'. This commitment was a key resource employed by Kohl. The shift of discourse would also need to emphasize the asymmetric gains to Germany from European monetary union. Correspondingly, disorderly defaults and the unraveling of the Euro Area would have prohibitively high political and macro-economic costs to Germany. Finally, the return of the SPD and/or Greens to the German federal government after the 2013 elections would lead to demotion of 'stability culture' discourse (as in 1998–2009 under SPD federal finance ministers). The SPD and Greens proved willing to commit to the principle of greater collective responsibility in crisis management (Bofinger et al. 2011). However, they were ultimately constrained by the electoral risks of being less in tune with German public opinion than Chancellor Merkel.

Shift in the centre of gravity of German debate mattered in two respects. Firstly, internal advocates of a more interventionist ECB policy depended on the political skills of its president in gaining the support of the German Chancellor. By 2012 Draghi was explaining the OMT programme to a special committee of the German Bundestag and directly engaging in helping shape the terms of German political debate. Secondly, the market and political credibility of ECB contingent commitment under the OMT programme was dependent on German political support. ECB willingness and capacity to act seemed contingent not just on debtor state compliance with EFSF/ESM fiscal consolidation and restructuring programmes but also on what German public and elite opinion would tolerate. Consequently, the logic of the supranational discretion to act in supreme emergency remained imperfectly reflected in the Euro Area.

Conclusions

Faith might be placed in the Euro Area eventually acting under the 'rule of a necessity that knows no rules'. Resort to exceptional measures in the face of grim necessity would involve a deeply unwelcome admission of the modest capacity of stability-oriented rules to tame both volatile, herd-like financial markets and states with variable, often weak compliance capacity. More problematically, it would expose a deep dilemma at the heart of the Euro Area. On the one hand, the need for supra-national executive discretion to deal with supreme emergency reflected the gaps of the Maastricht economic governance paradigm both in preventing and in managing crises. On the other hand, these design flaws exposed the weakness of justificatory principles for enhancing supranational executive discretion to take exceptional measures. In the specific historical and institutional context of the Euro Area, equipping its institutions to take exceptional measures in supreme emergency is fraught with enormous legitimacy and consent difficulties. The issue of supranational executive discretion to act in supreme emergency inevitably provokes intensified debate about the 'democratic deficit' and the technocratic character of the EU. It risks the alienation of public opinion in creditor states, notably Germany, and continuing resort to judicial review. Hence debate about supreme emergency is unlikely to be welcomed by policy-makers and likely to be kept off the public political agenda.

Reframing the core problem of European economic governance in terms of supranational executive discretion to act in supreme emergency helps to embed the debate about its reform in broader normative political arguments. These arguments were neglected in official EU thinking about the justificatory principles for reforms of crisis prevention and management arrangements. They suggest that the stability-oriented principles of the Maastricht economic constitution are fundamental to legitimacy but remain insufficient. Debate needs to move beyond the narrowly technocratic and procedural to normative justification.

The fundamental question remains: 'what ultimate claim to legitimacy can the Euro Area make in the absence of a supra-national executive capacity to act in supreme emergency?' Making this claim in the absence of a federal state structure, founded on independent democratic legitimacy for a 'transfer union', is inherently problematic. The political and institutional design problems that supreme emergency throw up for European economic governance may seem insuperable. Conversely, failure to adequately address this fundamental question exposes the Euro Area to the grim necessities that follow from the imperfect character of states and of financial markets. It is time for those who reform European economic governance to turn to Rawls and Walzer and to Hobbes, Bentham, Hegel, and Hart for inspiration on how to put flesh on the normative basis for acting in supreme emergency.

Ultimately, there are costs both in endorsing and in rejecting the need for supra-national discretionary authority to act in supreme emergency. Equally, minimizing these costs by credible contingent commitments is fraught with difficulties. On the one hand, capacity to take exceptional measures in supreme emergency assumes existential significance for the Euro Area, given the sheer complexities of euro-denominated debt contracts, the interconnected and contagious nature of banking and state debt, and the threat that they pose to EU integrity and survival. Endorsing it can be judged essential in order to protect European integration as the core historical project of the post-1945 period and to secure the irreversibility of EMU. Supra-national executive discretion to act in supreme emergency provides insurance against the inherent imperfections of states and markets, the modest role that can be attributed to rules of economic governance, and enduring political inducements to procrastination and complacency, especially in good times.

On the other hand, endorsement of the principle of supra-national executive discretion risks abandonment of ground-floor principles of the Maastricht Treaty and the ECB being drawn into filling a political vacuum. Its endorsement may be judged too costly in subverting the Treaty, encouraging moral hazard, and putting at risk the credibility and creditworthiness of the ECB and thus the larger European integration project. In the absence of convincing justificatory principle, building this capacity for supra-national executive discretion threatened to erode the fragile basis of consent to the EU, notably in creditor states. Weighing these risks goes beyond technical arguments in economics. It enters the contested realm of normative political argument and strategic calculations of party political, coalition, and electoral interests.

References

Bofinger, P., S. Gabriel, F.W. Steinmeier, C. Özdemir, C. Roth, R. Künast, and J. Trittin. 2011. Der Euroraum darf nicht an der Engstirnigkeit der deutschen Regierung scheitern. *Süddeutsche*.de, 8 December.

Boltanski, L., and L. Thévenot. 2006. *On justification: the economies of worth*. Princeton: Princeton University Press.

Dyson, K. 2009. The evolving timescapes of European economic governance: contesting and using time. *Journal of European Public Policy* 16, no. 2: 286–306.

Dyson, K. 2013. Maastricht plus: managing the logic of inherent imperfections. *Journal of European Integration* 35, no. 2, pp. 791-808.

Dyson, K. Forthcoming. *States, debt, and power: saints and sinners in European history and integration*. Oxford: Oxford University Press.

Dyson, K., and K. Featherstone. 1999. *The road to Maastricht: negotiating economic and monetary union*. Oxford: Oxford University Press.

Ruhkamp, S. (2012). 'Die Bundesbank fordert von der EZB bessere Sicherheiten', *Frankfurter Allgemeine Zeitung*, 1 March.

Hart, H.L.A. 1961. *The concept of law*. Oxford: Clarendon Press.

Merkel, A. 2012. Regierungserklärung vor dem Deutschen Bundestag zum Europäischen Rat am 28/29 Juni 2012, Berlin, 27 June.

Rawls, J. 1999. *The law of peoples*. Cambridge, MA: Harvard University Press.

Schmitt, C. 1963. *Der Begriff des Politischen*. Berlin: Duncker and Humblot.

Stark, J. 2011. Ich konnte mich nicht mehr durchsetzen. *Börsen-Zeitung*, 31 December.

Waever, O. 1995. Securitization and desecuritization. In On security, ed. R. Lipschutz, New York: Columbia University Press, pp. 46–86.

Walzer, M. 1992. *Just and unjust wars*. New York: Basic Books.

Weidmann, J. 2012. Wir müssen klare Kante zeigen. *Der Tagesspiegel*, 2 January.

Wulff, C. 2011. Wer rettet die Retter? *ZDF heute journal*, 24 August.

'Tough Love': How the ECB's Monetary Financing Prohibition Pushes Deeper Euro Area Integration

JONATHAN YIANGOU, MÍCHEÁL O'KEEFFE & GABRIEL GLÖCKLER

International and European Relations, European Central Bank, Frankfurt am Main, Germany

ABSTRACT This paper analyses the underlying dynamics of institutional change in economic governance in EMU. We show that the crisis revealed significant gaps between the intentions of the designers of EMU and the observed outcome. Building on the path dependence literature we use the framework of historical institutionalism to understand how policy-makers were constrained in their options for the containment and resolution of the sovereign debt crisis. We argue that the principle which prohibits the central bank from financing governments as enshrined in the Maastricht Treaty was a causal factor in fostering reform and deeper integration.

Introduction

The sovereign debt crisis that has befallen Europe since early 2010 has led to a fundamental overhaul of economic governance in EMU. Member states have strengthened rules and procedures for fiscal governance, erected a framework to monitor macroeconomic imbalances, and established a large and flexible mechanism for cross-border financial assistance. These are significant developments in the evolution of the European Union and its institutions which go beyond the predictions of most observers as recently as four years ago. Indeed, when marking the tenth anniversary of

EMU in 2008, the EU essentially celebrated the stability of the 'Maastricht' *status quo* (European Commission 2008).

Ex post, much of the observed institutional evolution may appear as a logical sequence of steps, with each incremental decision clearly building upon, and deriving from, the previous ones, and setting the stage for the subsequent one. *Ex ante*, however, there was nothing inevitable or logical about why the EU's institutional evolution in response to the crisis should turn out the way it did. This begs the question what precisely happened, why it happened and what this development might imply for the future. Specifically, this contribution aims to address the following questions: first, why did these specific institutional developments occur? Second, and more generally, why did the sovereign debt crisis lead to deeper EMU integration rather than disintegration, as a significant number of observers had predicted (Roubini 2011; Münchau 2011)?

These questions are especially pertinent given that deeper integration and reinforced economic governance imposes costs on the member states involved. For instance, stronger fiscal rules backed up by an effective sanctioning regime are evidently more challenging for countries with high existing deficit and debt levels and weaker fiscal institutions. Similarly, the burden of cross-border financial assistance falls disproportionately on a small number of creditworthy member states, where financially supporting less creditworthy countries may not be popular with domestic taxpayers. *Prima facie*, it therefore cannot be assumed that governments would have pursued the path of strengthening governance had other options been available to them.

In seeking to understand the principal dynamics which made these fundamental institutional changes possible, this contribution argues that governments were compelled to respond to the crisis in this way by the prohibition on monetary financing (Art. 123 TFEU)—the Treaty rule that forbids the central bank to finance government spending by through money creation. We contend that the ECB's strict interpretation of this provision forced member states to choose between two options: to accept a deeply destabilising break-up of the euro area; or to strengthen economic governance and provide the required financing to countries in difficulty. The undesirability of the former option forced member states into the latter: to take responsibility for stabilising the sovereign debt crisis through coordinated policy measures. Very much in contrast to the earlier reluctance to move towards deeper economic integration, the crisis confronted euro area policy-makers with a situation in which they realised, like Sherlock Holmes, that 'once you eliminate the impossible, whatever remains, no matter how improbable, must be the truth' (Sir Arthur Conan Doyle).

In making this argument, we employ the framework of historical institutionalism (HI) to explain systemic level changes. Specifically, we contend, with reference to Pierson's (1996) account of European integration, that there were significant 'gaps' between the intended functioning of EMU's institutional framework and the effects of those institutions in practice. When the sovereign debt crisis struck, these 'gaps'—which have, for example, been conceptualised as a variety of 'trilemmas' or inconsistencies (Pisani-Ferry 2012; Schoenmaker 2011)—became visible and contributed to the emergence of a vicious circle which threatened EMU with a series of sovereign defaults. In line with HI, we argue that path dependent processes created by the initial choices in the Treaty of Maastricht constrained policy-makers' options for crisis containment and resolution (Thelen 1999; Pierson 2000). We maintain that the monetary financing prohibition acts as a form of 'tough love' which led to a closer economic union in the euro area than would have been the case otherwise.

The paper is structured as follows. Building on the path dependence literature, the second section sets out the approach of historical institutionalism. The third section analyses the original framework of economic governance in EMU, and outlines the central role accorded to financial markets to ensure discipline. The fourth section explains why there were 'gaps' between the intended design of the governance framework and its actual operation, and how this created instability. The fifth section presents the subsequent options available—(i) accepting a break-up, (ii) large-scale, potentially unlimited, purchases of government debt by the ECB or (iii) national reforms and stronger governance—and demonstrates how path dependent processes impacted policy choice. The sixth section outlines the reforms in economic governance that are taking place, and the seventh section concludes.

Theory and Framework of Analysis

In analysing institutional stability and change, this paper draws on the dynamic framework of historical institutionalism (HI). HI explains the effects of institutions over time (Pierson 2000; Pierson 2004), with institutions here defined as the 'rules of the game' (North 1990). Central to HI is the theory of path dependence which characterises institutional development as a path and suggest that previous institutional choices will constrain future options for institutional change. Increasing returns and positive feedback processes trigger self-reinforcing dynamics which can enhance stability (Pierson 2000; Streeck and Thelen 2005; Mahoney and Thelen 2010). However, 'gaps' can emerge between the intentions of the institutional designers and the effects of those institutions. We employ the framework put forward by Pierson (1996, 131) where European integration is driven by those 'gaps' which can occur because of:

- the large potential for unintended consequences;
- short time horizons of decision-makers;
- changing preferences of member state governments; or
- the autonomous actions of European institutional actors.

Pierson (1996) argues these 'gaps' create room for some actors to influence European integration.[1] However, the options available to these actors may be constrained because of:

- sunk costs and the rising price of exit;

- the resistance of supranational actors; or
- institutional barriers to reform ('sticky institutions').

We argue that to understand the institutional changes that have taken place during the crisis—notably the reform of EMU governance—we must first understand the 'gaps'. We aim to explain how the efforts of policy-makers to fill these 'gaps' were constrained by previous institutional choices. We use counterfactual analysis to analyse the empirical plausibility of our argument (Fearon 1991).

Designing EMU: What was the Intention?

The economic basis for EMU was provided for by three key factors. First, EMU was believed to be a logical step in the context of economic spillover from the Single European Act, as a single market with the continued existence of national currencies was considered suboptimal. This conviction was neatly encapsulated in the title of the Delors Report, 'One Market, One Money' (Delors 1989). Second, a neoliberal 'sound money and public finances' policy consensus emerged with price stability at the centre (McNamara 1998). This was reinforced by the growth of capital mobility whereby financial markets could be used as a disciplinary device on national budgets and increase allocational efficiency (Dyson and Featherstone 1999, 754). Third, the macroeconomic expansion of the 1980s meant negotiators believed they could converge upon certain criteria like low inflation and deficits easily (see Dyson and Featherstone 1999).

Accordingly, the institutional design of EMU—laid down in the Maastricht Treaty sought to reflect these factors. In order to enshrine the principle of 'sound money and public finances', Article 101[2] forbade the ECB from directly financing government deficits—the so-called monetary financing prohibition—reflecting the principle of the 'law as the guardian of economic wisdom' (Herdegen 1998). The legal force of this provision was designed to remove expectations that deficits would ever be 'monetised' by the central bank. This would ensure 'monetary dominance' and exclude the possibility of 'fiscal dominance': a situation where fiscal policy would manoeuvre governments into such an untenable position that monetary policy-makers would be forced into deficit financing (Sargent and Wallace 1981; ECB 2008). Art. 102 TEU[3] also prohibited privileged access to credit for any government.

In line with the consensus on low inflation and deficits, Article 104c and 109j and a protocol annexed in the Treaty outlined what became known as the 'Maastricht criteria'. Member states would have to maintain a deficit-to-GDP ratio of 3 per cent, a debt-to-GDP ratio of 60 per cent, a stable inflation and interest rate and no devaluation of the currency in the ERM for the previous two years before the final stage of EMU. The Stability and Growth Pact (SGP), which contained a European Council resolution (OJ C 236, 2.8.1997) and two Regulations (EC No 1466/97 and EC No 1467/97) were subsequently designed to complement the fiscal targets. It consisted of a 'preventive arm' which required member states to submit stability and convergence programmes and pursue 'close to balance or in surplus' medium term budgetary positions, and a 'corrective arm' to

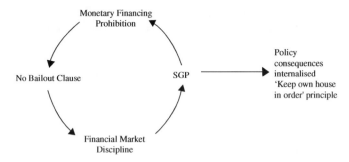

Figure 1. A schematic of positive feedback mechanisms in EMU's design

ensure the implementation of the excessive deficit procedure—whereby member states had to ensure their general government deficit and debt was below 3 per cent and 60 per cent respectively. Sanctions were to be imposed against those who exceeded the threshold.

Against the background of a general acceptance of the efficient market hypothesis (Beechey *et al.* 2000), the Maastricht construction was intended to encourage market discipline and differentiation between euro area borrowers. The effectiveness of this discipline would rest, in theory, upon certain institutional and informational conditions being fulfilled: governments would not have privileged access to capital markets, a country would bear the consequences of any default risk, and timely and accurate information would be available for financial markets to assess financial sustainability (ECB 2006, 73–4). The monetary financing prohibition, the prohibition on privileged access, and reporting under the SGP sought to create this framework. In addition, the so-called 'no bail-out clause' embodied in Art. 103 (1)[4] forbade member states from assuming each other's liabilities, thereby concentrating default risk in the member state responsible.

Taken together, these elements were designed to reinforce each other and create positive feedback mechanisms which would ensure a stable economic and monetary system (Figure 1). Overall, this would ensure that policy failures would be internalised, which would encourage member states to keep their 'own houses in order'. The effect of this framework was to create an incentive structure where financial markets, in theory, had a clear rationale to enforce discipline. As creditors were exposed to potential losses, they would respond to a deteriorating outlook for public finances by demanding higher risk premia, which in turn would ensure that governments did not pursue profligate fiscal policies. However, the incentives for member states were less clear: if policy failures would be internalised, why should they enforce the SGP and exercise peer pressure? The incentive system built into the original design of EMU, therefore, relied fundamentally on 'governance through financial market discipline'.

EMU in Practice: Where Were the 'Gaps'?

The effects of this institutional framework deviated significantly in practice from the intentions of its designers. The emergence of these 'gaps' reflects a number of the causal factors identified by Pierson (1996). First, the central role afforded to 'governance through market discipline' did not have the consequences expected by EMU's designers. Markets in fact showed little willingness to punish deficit or debt levels above the Maastricht thresholds. This was because, despite the threat of default implicit in the 'no bail-out' clause and monetary financing prohibition, euro area government bonds were not seen by markets as containing credit risk. Positive returns were expected in all states of the world, rather than a full probability distribution of returns, leading to an under-pricing of risk (Turner 2011). As a result, euro area member states received inappropriate signals about their future solvency, leading to deficit and debt levels not supported by underlying economic fundamentals (ECB 2006). However, when some bad news emerged—for example, the announcement by the new Greek government in October 2009 that the annual deficit would be more than 12 per cent of GDP, double the level previously communicated—markets suddenly had to price in the 'neglected risks', leading to rapid and volatile adjustments, as visible in Figure 2 (Gennaioli et al. 2010).

Second, euro area fiscal governance proved to be not as effective as intended. As noted above, the Maastricht framework did not contain strong incentives for member states to exercise peer pressure and to effectively enforce the SGP. In practice, peer pressure was rarely employed for fear of reprisal, creating what Lorenzo Bini Smaghi has termed a 'mutual non-aggression pact' (Bini Smaghi 2011). Moreover, the SGP was insufficiently robust to restrain the shifting preferences of member states over time. The Commission's decisions to initiate formal procedural steps under the SGP required the support of the College of Commissioners, leaving it susceptible to 'watering down' of proposals as individual Commissioners came under pressure from their respective 'home countries'. Member states were also able to block procedural steps being taken through collusion in

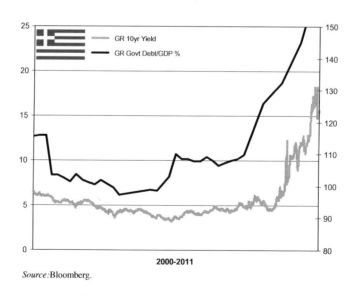

Figure 2. Greek government debt levels and sovereign bond yields

the ECOFIN (Schuknecht *et al.* 2011). A clear example of this was the Council decision in 2001 not to adopt a proposal for a Recommendation for Ireland under Article 99(4), despite the Commission presenting evidence of increasingly unbalanced economic and budgetary developments. When in 2004-05 the SGP *did* threaten to restrain policy discretion, it was amended to include differentiated medium term objectives. This was ostensibly to provide the SGP with sufficient flexibility to deal with asymmetric shocks that have a cyclical component (de Grauwe 2006). However, the reforms introduced greater discretion, political control by member states and complexity—which made it more difficult for the markets to monitor member states (Schuknecht *et al.* 2011).

Third, the 'own-house-in-order' principle proved to be an uncertain foundation of monetary union: the deep and complex financial interconnections within the euro area implied that policy failure could not be internalised (Bini Smaghi 2010). This 'unintended consequence' of the euro became evident when fiscal problems in Greece, which represented less that 2 per cent of euro area GDP, became systemic. It was discovered that various channels could spread contagion within monetary union, most detrimentally and powerfully via the so-called the bank-sovereign feedback loop (cf. IMF 2010). This feedback loop results from, on the one hand, the strong 'home bias' in sovereign debt holdings in the euro area (Merler and Pisani-Ferry 2012), which leaves domestic banking systems exposed to the direct and indirect effects of sovereign risks; and on the other hand, the large size of these banking systems relative to the balance sheet of the host authority, which makes recapitalisation (or the expectation of it) ruinous for public finances. These effects could be transmitted to other euro area member states through cross-border holdings of sovereign debt (Angeloni and Wolff 2012), through 'yield contagion' based on superficially similar economic conditions (Constâncio 2011), or through increasing counterparty risk (bank-bank contagion).

Fourth, in a situation of rising debt levels, financial instability and contagion, the monetary financing prohibition and the 'no bail-out' clause did not contribute to a self-reinforcing framework, but instead appeared to be destabilising. Without an institution able to provide sufficient liquidity to sovereign bond markets to remove fears of default, some member states in financial difficulties experienced what may have been a self-fulfilling downward spiral (de Grauwe 2011). This led to pressure from observers, market participants and politicians alike for the ECB to provide liquidity to vulnerable sovereigns in sufficient volume to stabilise sovereign debt markets (Wyplosz 2011; Krugman 2011; also many politicians, for example Alain Juppé, French foreign minister,[5] Portuguese President Aibal Cavaco Silva,[6] and indeed David Cameron, British Prime Minister[7]). However, Eurosystem officials strongly resisted this pressure. The rationale was rooted in the founding principles of EMU: purchasing euro area government bonds in sufficient volume to entirely remove risk of default of the most vulnerable sovereigns was not compatible with the spirit of the monetary financing prohibition (Weidmann 2011; Stark 2011).

EMU in Crisis: Options to Fill the 'Gaps'

The euro area's response to this instability could have involved three—somewhat 'stylized'—options. First, inaction; second, for the ECB to relax its resistance to secondary market interventions; or third, for national governments to establish a policy-driven response to calm markets. Historical institutionalism posits that the nature of this response would be constrained by path-dependent processes. In particular, Pierson (1996) finds that the direction of institutional reform will be influenced by sunk costs and the rising price of exit; the resistance of supranational actors; and institutional barriers to reform ('sticky institutions'). Sunk costs and the rising price of exit appear decisive in eliminating inaction as an institutional response. This option would have involved a default or exit of one or some member states and the possibility of a break-up of the euro area. In view of the immense political effort that had gone into establishing a monetary union in Europe since the early 1960s, the 'reputational sunk costs' in avoiding such a scenario were significant. Indeed, a number of key figures who had been involved in the process of designing the euro in the 1990s were still in positions of influence—for example, ECB President Jean-Claude Trichet and German Finance Minister Wolfgang Schäuble. Moreover, the economic costs of this option were projected to be extremely large. In the event of a 'stage managed' Greek exit, the cumulative euro area output loss was estimated to be up to 5 per cent, rising on average to 9 per cent in the event of a break-up (ING 2011). Another study estimated the cost of a 'weak' country exiting to be €9500–€11,500 per person in that country—equating to roughly 40 per cent–50 per cent of GDP in the first year, reducing to €3000–€4000 in subsequent years (UBS 2011). If Germany were to exit the euro, the same study estimated it would cost every German adult between €6000 and €8000 in the first year, or 20 per cent–25 per cent of GDP. Some form of institutional response was therefore preferable for member states than inaction. As Pierson notes, 'rather than reflecting the benefits of institutionalized exchange, continuing integration could easily reflect the rising costs of non-Europe' (Pierson 1996, 145).

Path dependent processes appear to have heavily influenced a second counterfactual—relaxing the interpretation of the monetary financing prohibition. Here the role of supranational actors in resisting attempts by member states to exercise control over their activities appears a powerful explanation (Pierson 1996). Despite considerable pressure from politicians, the ECB, backed up by the force of the prohibition in primary law of monetary financing, refused to be manoeuvred into purchasing government bonds on a similar scale to other major central banks (Figure 3), instead intervening intermittently to maintain the proper functioning of the monetary policy transmission mechanism through the Securities Markets Programme. The rationale for the ECB's position stems from the initial institutional choices in the Maastricht design outlined in the third section, in particular the issue of 'fiscal dominance'. In a situation of high government deficits and debts, the economic rationale resisting 'fiscal dominance' becomes increasingly powerful: were the ECB to intervene on a massive

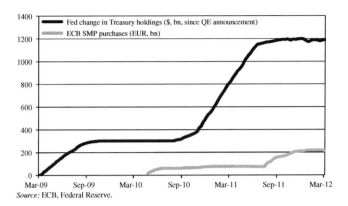

Figure 3. Non-standard purchases of sovereign debt by the ECB and the Federal Reserve

scale as soon as governments faced market pressure, this could create a 'deficit bias' in fiscal policies and reduce incentives to enact fiscal and structural reforms. This would also have had implications for the maintenance of price stability.

The ECB's position also stemmed from the relatively weak democratic foundations for economic and monetary union, which place the ECB in a fundamentally different situation to a central bank in unitary state. When the Federal Reserve or Bank of England purchases its government's debt, it does so in the knowledge that any costs arising from its operations will be internalised by national taxpayers who can hold the government accountable. However, when the ECB purchases the debt of a euro area member state, it creates an implicit risk of redistribution between different sets of national taxpayers. Losses are shared among National Central Banks and paid for by taxpayers across the euro area, either through foregone profits or capital calls. The government responsible for these losses cannot be punished by these taxpayers, and there is insufficient solidarity between euro area countries for such redistribution to be acceptable. The on-going debate about TARGET2 balances in Germany underscores this point (Sinn and Wollmershäuser 2011; Bindseil and Konig 2012). The fact that EMU is not yet a political union places a clear institutional constraint on the ECB's choices, over and above the evident legal provisions.

Therefore, as a result of the resistance of the ECB, and the large costs of exit, the only remaining option to fill the 'gaps' in the institutional framework was for euro area governments to undertake substantial institutional reforms to restore stability—a determined push towards 'governance though governments'. This implied two related processes. First, strengthening economic governance frameworks that would remove the time-inconsistency inherent in budgetary consolidation and credibly 'tie the hands' of future governments (Giavazzi and Pagano 1988). Second, providing liquidity to countries experiencing the greatest market pressure to smooth the adjustment process and remove default risk. However, these processes were also influenced by path dependent institutional constraints which 'close off alternative options and lead to the establishment of institutions that generate self-reinforcing path dependent processes' (Capoccia and Kelemen 2007, 341). The next section discusses how this influenced the policies chosen by member states to address the sovereign debt crisis.

Completing EMU Governance

The central tenet of the response by member states was to redesign or build on *existing* institutions (Salines *et al.* 2012). This has directly addressed the four weaknesses identified in the fourth section. First, reforms have taken place to alter the informational conditions of market discipline. The key problem identified with euro area sovereign debt market—the potential for investors to neglect certain risks and therefore to under-price them—has been addressed through reforms to establish greater transparency over economic conditions within member states. As part of the 'six-pack' of legislation, minimum requirements are imposed for the independence of national statistical authorities with the possibility of sanctions for misreporting (Council Directive 2011/85/EU). The new Macroeconomic Imbalances Procedure draws attention to vulnerabilities in the private sector, including competitiveness trends, private sector credit flows and real estate developments, with the potential for in-depth reviews by the Commission of countries displaying imbalances (Regulation 1174/2011; Regulation 1176/2011). The 'two-pack' of legislation would also enhance transparency by giving the Commission the possibility to place member states under enhanced surveillance if experiencing or threatened with financial difficulties (COM/2011/0819). This would involve stress tests of the banking sector by the European Banking Authority (EBA), monitoring of macroeconomic imbalances and regular review missions by the Commission in liaison with the ECB.

Second, two main developments have taken place to strengthen fiscal governance: reforming the existing SGP and negotiating, as a complement, the Treaty on Stability, Coordination and Governance in the Economic and Monetary Union (the 'Fiscal Compact'). Both the preventive arm of the SGP (Regulation 1175/2011 amending Regulation 1466/97) and the corrective arm (Regulation 1177/2011 amending Regulation 1467/97) have been amended, adding a number of new features that strengthen the automaticity of decision-making and the quality of assessment. For instance, the use of reverse qualified majority voting in the Council (Regulation 1173/2011) strengthens the role of the Commission and 'lowers the bar' for effective peer pressure. The risk that the use of this procedure merely shifts political battles into the College of Commissioners has also been addressed through new working methods to reinforce its independence: any amendments to Commission proposals and recommendations under the new governance framework have to be submitted by written procedure; and a new chief economic analyst will provide an independent assessment. Enforcement of fiscal rules should be strengthened by the requirement, under the Fiscal Compact, to include balanced budget rules in national constitutions (or equivalent). This spreads responsibility for enforcement onto national institutions as well as the Commission and

Council. Under the 'two-pack' of legislation, the Commission will also be able to monitor budget execution (Regulation (EU) No 1173/2011).

Third, incentives for mutual surveillance—going beyond the principle of 'keeping one's own house in order'—have been sharpened by the spillover effects of the crisis. No euro area member state has found itself completely immune from deteriorating economic conditions in others. Moreover, the emergence of a permanent framework for intra-euro area financial assistance creates a new responsibility, and incentive, for national governments and parliaments to monitor economic policies of other member states more closely. The effect of these changing incentives is already visible in the agenda and practice of the Eurogroup, where discussions on economic developments in vulnerable countries have become a regular feature. It is also evident in the keener interest shown by national authorities in strengthening compliance with EU–IMF programmes. For instance, national treasuries have put forward a number of own-initiative proposals—such as the German proposal in January 2012 for an EU Budget Commissioner for Greece—and an increasing number of parliaments make financial assistance conditional on regularly updated debt sustainability analyses.

Fourth, to compensate for the potential for systemic instability created by the ECB's strict adherence to the monetary financing prohibition, member states have gradually developed a framework for providing liquidity to countries in financial difficulties. The European Stability Mechanism (ESM) will be established as a permanent institution under public international law with a paid-in capital of EUR 80 billion and a callable capital of EUR 620 billion. It will dispose of five types of instruments: loans, precautionary programmes, primary market purchases, secondary market purchases, and loans to non-programme countries for bank recapitalisation. This will make the ESM the world's most capitalised international financial institution with a range of instruments that exceed those available to other international lenders such as the IMF.

Looking forward, while enhanced fiscal governance and the ESM represent a significant step in economic union, addressing the deeper channels of contagion that this paper has highlighted—such as the bank-sovereign nexus—requires further progress towards financial union in the euro area. This implies centralised supervision of at least all systemically important financial institutions, if not all institutions, of the euro area, by a single supervisory mechanism, a pan-European deposit insurance, a single framework for bank recapitalisation and resolution, stress tests of large cross-border banking groups, harmonised national regulations with a single rulebook, and a stronger macroprudential watchdog. In June 2012, the euro area Heads of State and Government agreed to establish a single supervisory mechanism involving the ECB, and to allow the ESM to recapitalise directly banks covered by this mechanism. Further progress towards financial union is necessary so that the institutional framework of EMU, after having avoided more or less successfully 'fiscal dominance', will have safeguards in place to also prevent 'financial dominance' (i.e. a situation where monetary policy decisions become dominated by the state of the financial sector).

In August 2012, the Governing Council of the ECB decided to prepare a programme of Outright Monetary Transactions (OMT) in secondary markets for sovereign bonds in the euro area, to be launched if and when the Governing Council so decides, and once a number of conditions are fulfilled. The objective was to repair the monetary policy transmission mechanism so that standard monetary policy could address its primary objective: to maintain price stability. In particular, it aimed to remove redenomination risk which was incompatible with the conduct of a single monetary policy. OMT replaced the Securities Markets Programme and departed from it in a number of its design features, notably the absence of an *ex ante* quantitative limit on bond purchases. This has led some scholars to criticise the ECB, arguing that such non-standard measures are tantamount to monetary financing. Schelkle (forthcoming), for example argues that member states reluctance to establish a permanent fiscal capacity 'forced the ECB to assume a quasi-fiscal role during the crisis'.

Does OMT constitutes a departure in all but name from the ECB's previous refusal to engage in monetary financing? OMT has been specifically designed to avoid either technically or substantively engaging in monetary financing. First, all operations would take place in the secondary market, ensuring that the ECB's counterparties would be private investors, not governments. Second, purchases would be conducted only of bonds with a residual maturity of one to three years, allowing market discipline to operate in full on the long end of the yield curve (which is most important for government financing). Third, to qualify for OMT, a member state would have to request an ESM programme with strong and effective conditionality. This would ensure that ECB operations would always be associated with deficit reduction, rather than financing inflationary deficits.

In these respects, OMT is consistent with the original Maastricht framework described in figure 1. Great care has been taken to ensure the modalities for undertaking OMTs comply with the monetary financing prohibition (as outlined in Article 123 TFEU and clarified by Council Regulation (EC) No 3603/93). Moreover, the strict conditionality attached to OMTs reinforces the positive feedback mechanisms in EMU's institutional design, by covering the necessary macroeconomic, structural, fiscal and financial adjustment needs (ECB 2012b). In addition, the publication of the OMT holdings, the duration, the issuer and the market value, and quarterly review of the conditionality will act as a signalling device to financial markets and enhance the informational conditions for market discipline.

Conclusion

We have argued that the path dependence of the ECB's prohibition on monetary financing was a driving force in strengthening the institutional framework for economic governance in the euro area. By encouraging countries to demonstrate policy credibility, the monetary financing prohibition leads to a gradual strengthening of supranational rules and institutions and a stronger role for the European Commission. By forcing euro area member states to finance mutual assistance through fiscal means rather than relying on monetary policy, it sharpens the incentives for national governments and parliaments to oversee each others' economic policies. The monetary financing prohibition can therefore be seen as a form of 'tough love' that pushes deeper euro area integration and fills the 'gaps' in its original institutional design.

Acknowledgements

The authors would like to thank Nataliya Taleva and Christina Jordan as well as the participants of the College of Europe Conference on economic governance in Bruges on 1 March 2011 for their helpful comments.

Notes

1. Without disregarding the role of agency this paper focuses more heavily on the institutional dynamics of change in the European political economy.
2. Now Art. 123.1. It states 'Overdraft facilities or any other type of credit facility with the European Central Bank or with the central banks of the member states (hereinafter referred to as 'national central banks') in favour of Union institutions, bodies, offices or agencies, central governments, regional, local or other public authorities, other bodies governed by public law, or public undertakings of member states shall be prohibited, as shall the purchase directly from them by the European Central Bank or national central banks of debt instruments'.
3. Now Art. 124 TFEU.
4. Now Art. 125 TFEU.
5. http://www.ft.com/intl/cms/s/0/c4325d02-15de-11e1-8db8-00144feabdc0.html#axzz1qJtxsAg6.
6. http://www.bloomberg.com/news/2011-11-11/ecb-as-lender-of-last-resort-will-resolve-debt-crisis-for-portugal-s-silva.html.
7. http://www.telegraph.co.uk/finance/financialcrisis/8886113/David-Cameron-has-got-it-wrong-on-the-ECB.html.

References

Angeloni, C., and G.B. Wolff. 2012. Are banks affected by their holdings of government debt?, *Bruegel Working Paper 2012/07*, March.
Beechey, M., D. Gruen, and J. Vickery. 2000. The efficient market hypothesis: a survey, Reserve Bank of Australia Research Discussion Paper 2000–01.
Bindseil, U., and P.J. Konig. 2011. The economics of TARGET2 balances. SFB 649 Discussion Paper 2011=035.
Bini Smaghi, L. 2010. ECON Committee Hearing on 'Improving the economic governance and stability framework of the Union, in particular in the euro area', 15 September, http://www.ecb.europa.eu/press/key/date/2010/html/sp100915.en.html (accessed 26 March 2012).
Bini Smaghi, L. 2011. European democracies and decision-making in times of crisis. Speech at the Hellenic Foundation for European and Foreign Policy, Eighth European Seminar 2001, Adjusting to the Crisis Policy Choices and Politics in Europe, Poros, 8 July, http://www.bis.org/review/r110712c.pdf (accessed 27 March 2012).
Buiter, W., G. Corsetti, and N. Roubini. 1993. Excessive deficits: sense and nonsense in the Treaty of Maastricht. *Economic Policy* 8, no. 16: 57–100.
Capoccia, G., and D.R. Kelemen. 2007. The study of critical junctures: theory, narrative, and counterfactuals in historical institutionalism. *World Politics*, April: 341–69.
Constâncio, V. 2011. Contagion and the European debt crisis. Keynote lecture at the Bocconi University/IntesaSanpaolo conference on 'Bank competitiveness in the post-crisis world', 10 October.
De Grauwe, P. 2006. What have we learnt about monetary integration since the Maastricht Treaty. *Journal of Common Market Studies* 44, no. 4: 711–30.
De Grauwe, P. 2011. The governance of a fragile eurozone, *CEPS Working Document No. 346*, May.

Delors, J. 1989. Report on economic and monetary union in the European Community. Presented April 17, by the Committee for the Study of Economic and Monetary Union, EU Commission Working Document.
Dyson, K., and K. Featherstone. 1999. *The road to Maastricht: negotiating economic and monetary union.* Oxford: Oxford University Press.
European Central Bank (ECB). 2006. Fiscal policies and financial markets. *ECB Monthly Bulletin*, February, 71–84.
European Central Bank (ECB). 2008. Ten years of the stability and growth pact. *ECB Monthly Bulletin*, October, 53–65.
European Central Bank (ECB). 2012a. Monetary and fiscal policy interactions in a monetary union. *ECB Monthly Bulletin*, July, 51–64.
European Central Bank (ECB). 2012b. Compliance of outright monetary transactions with the prohibition of monetary financiering. *ECB Monthly Bulletin*, October, 7–10.
Fearon, J.D. 1991. Counterfactuals and hypothesis testing in political science. *World Politics* 43, no. 2: 169–95.
Gennaioli, N., A. Shleifer, and R.W. Vishney. 2010. Neglected risks, financial innovation and financial fragility. *NBER Working Paper*, Working Paper 16068.
Giavazzi, F., and M. Pagano. 1988. The advantage of tying one's hands: EMS discipline and central bank credibility. *European Economic Review* 32, no. 5: 1055–82.
Herdegen, M.J. 1998. Price stability and budgetary restraints in the economic and monetary union: the law as guardian of economic wisdom. *Common Market Law Review* 35, no. 1: 9–32.
International Monetary Fund (IMF). 2010. Global financial stability report: sovereigns, funding, and systemic liquidity, World Economic and Financial Surveys, October 2010
ING (2011), EMU Break-Up: Pay Now, Pay Later, Financial Markets Research, Global Economics, 1 December 2011.
Kydland, F.E., and E.C. Prescott. 1977. Rules rather than discretion: the inconsistency of optimal plans. *Journal of Political Economy* 85, no. 3: pp. 473–492.
Krugman, P. 2011. Incredible Europeans. *New York Times*, 19 November 2011, http://krugman.blogs.nytimes.com/2011/11/19/incredible-europeans (accessed 26 March 2012).
Mahoney, J., and K. Thelen. 2010. *Explaining institutional change, ambiguity, agency and power.* Cambridge: Cambridge University Press.
McNamara, K.R. 1998. *The currency of ideas: monetary politics in the European Union.* New York: Cornell University Press.
Merler, S., and J. Pisani-Ferry. 2012. Who's afraid of sovereign bonds. *Bruegel Policy Contribution*, Issue 2012/02, February.
Münchau, W. 2011. Eurobonds and fiscal union are the only way out. *Financial Times*, 18 September, http://www.ft.com/intl/cms/s/0/9e3d5db2-dfca-11e0-b1db-00144feabdc0.html#axzz1qEGqn3Kb (accessed 26 March 2012).
North, D.C. 1990. *Institutions, institutional change, and economic performance.* New York: Cambridge University Press.
Pierson, P. 1996. The path to European integration: a historical institutionalist analysis. *Comparative Political Studies* 29: 123. Volume 29, No. 2, April 1996, pp. 123–163.
Pierson, P. 2000. Increasing returns, path dependence, and the study of politics. *The American Political Science Review* 94, no. 2: 251–67.
Pierson, P. 2004. *Politics in time: history, institutions, and social analysis.* Princeton, NJ: Princeton University Press.
Pisani-Ferry, J. 2012. The Euro crisis and the new impossible trinity. *Bruegel Policy Contribution*, Issue 2012/01, January.
Roubini, N. 2011. The Eurozone heads for a break up. *Financial Times*, 13 June, http://blogs.ft.com/the-a-list/2011/06/13/the-eurozone-heads-for-break-up/#axzz1qEDfLMdl (accessed 26 March 2013).
Salines, M., G. Glöckler, and Z. Truchlewski. 2012. Existential crisis, incremental response: the eurozone's dual institutional evolution 2007–2011. *Journal of European Public Policy*: 1–17. Volume 19, No.5, June 2012, pp. 665–681.
Schelke, W. Forthcoming. Fiscal integration by default. In Beyond the regulatory polity. *The European integration of core state powers*, ed. Philipp Genschel and M. Jachtenfuchs. Oxford: Oxford University Press. pp. 1–16.
Schoenmaker, D. 2011. The financial trilemma. *Economic Letters.* Volume 111, Issue 1, pp. 57–59.

Schuknecht, L. 2005. Stability and growth pact: issues and lessons from political economy. *International Economics and Economic Policy* 2: June 2005, Volume no.2, issue 1 65–89.

Stark, J. 2011. http://www.reuters.com/article/2011/11/09/ecb-stark-idUSF9E7H801H20111109.

Streeck, W., and K. Thelen. 2005. *Beyond continuity: institutional change in advanced political economies*. Oxford: Oxford University Press.

Sargent, T.J., and N. Wallace. 1981. Some unpleasant monetarist arithmetic. *Federal Reserve Bank of Minneapolis Quarterly Review 5*, no. 3: 1–17.

Sinn, H.W., and T. Wollmershäuser. 2011. Target loans, current account balances and capital flows: the ECB's rescue facility, *CESifo Working Paper No. 2500*, 24 June.

Thelen, K. 1999. Historical institutionalism in comparative politics, *Annual Review of Political Science* 2, no: 369–404.

Turner, A. 2011. Debt and deleveraging: Long term and short term challenges, Speech at the Centre for Financial Studies, Frankfurt, 21 November.

UBS, (2011), Euro break-up, the consequences, UBS Investments Research, Global Economic Perspectives, 6 September 2011.

Weidmann, J. 2011. FT interview transcript, http://www.ft.com/intl/cms/s/0/b3a2d19e-0de4-11e1-9d40-00144feabdc0.html#axzz1q3DHrMIT (accessed 26 March 2012).

Wyplosz, C. 2011. They still don't get it. VoxEU, 25 October 2011, http://www.voxeu.org/index.php?q=node/6845 (accessed 27 March 2012).

Time Will Tell: The EFSF, the ESM, and the Euro Crisis

LEDINA GOCAJ & SOPHIE MEUNIER

ABSTRACT The European Financial Stability Facility (EFSF), a slim and temporary bailout fund created by the European Union in May 2010 to quell a growing sovereign debt crisis in Europe, became the foundation for a permanent, more powerful institution, the European Stability Mechanism (ESM), adopted in March 2011. Did the creation of the EFSF constrain policy-makers and narrow down the path of options subsequently available to them? This paper assesses whether the euro crisis of 2010–2012 provides an instance of historical institutionalism in action, whereby the institutional creation decided at the critical juncture of the initial reaction to the crisis transformed the path of options available at later attempts to tackle the crisis, sometimes with unintended consequences. Through careful process tracing, we analyze the temporal sequences of reactions to the crisis and argue that the creation of the EFSF and ESM created path dependency in the subsequent management of an unrelenting crisis, enshrined intergovernmentalism as the modus operandi, and led to suboptimal solutions.

> Europe will be forged in crises, and will be
> the sum of the solutions adopted for those crises.
> (Jean Monnet, *Mémoires*, 1976)

In early 2010, the Greek sovereign debt crisis triggered a wave of speculation that pushed several euro area economies to the brink of default. The European Financial Stability Facility (EFSF) was the 'shock and awe' solution created in May 2010 to stop the possible contagion of the crisis and convince markets that euro area leaders would stand behind the common currency. Based in Luxembourg and fully operational by August 2010, the EFSF was initially charged with managing €440 billion in member state guarantees. This number was later increased at the same time as negotiations proceeded to transform the EFSF into a permanent bail-out institution, the European Stability Mechanism (ESM), inaugurated in October 2012. Did the enormous financial and political investment in this new institution influence the range of options available to policymakers as the crisis worsened, leading to what some analysts interpret today as a suboptimal solution?

This paper assesses whether the euro crisis of 2010–2012 provides an instance of historical institutionalism (HI) in action, whereby the institutional creation decided at the critical juncture of the initial reaction to the crisis transformed the path of options available at subsequent attempts to tackle the crisis, sometimes with unintended consequences for economic governance in Europe. With a long pedigree albeit under a variety of names, the theory known as 'historical institutionalism' aims to offer a dynamic explanation of how and why institutions evolve (Farrell and Newman 2010, 609–38). HI focuses in particular on the sequencing of events -an initial shock followed by feedback loops, path dependence, and unintended consequences- to explain institutional choice and preference formation. In the case of the European handling of the Greek crisis, the sequence of events - the great initial confusion about the potential implications of the crisis and how to deal with it, the sense of critical urgency in May 2010, the hasty decision to create the EFSF, and then the incremental changes to the institution newly created as the crisis worsened- suggests that this may be an instance of HI in action.

Our ambition is mostly empirical - to tell an accurate account, through careful process-tracing, of whether the creation of this particular institutional structure influenced the subsequent course of events. In so doing, we also hope to shed some theoretical light on institutional development in the EU, in particular the constraining role of path dependency after a critical historical juncture. Our main finding is that the creation of the EFSF narrowed down the range of subsequent options available to member states in responding to the crisis and enshrined an intergovernmental *modus operandi*.The paper starts by analyzing the political compromises that led to the hasty adoption of the EFSF, while the second section explores its initial implementation. The third section follows its eventual transformation into the permanent ESM and the new powers that it gained over the course of 2011.

The Hasty Creation of the EFSF

After the political drama surrounding the failed European constitution in 2005 and the difficult passage of the Lisbon Treaty in 2009, analysts assumed that the post-Lisbon decade would not be one of institutional creation. Yet out of this less than propitious context for institutional creation emerged hastily, and in great confusion, a brand new institution in the EU complex: the EFSF. This section explores the critical juncture of the Spring of 2010 and the various solutions envisioned by euro area leaders for dealing with the crisis and analyzes the conditions in which the EFSF option was selected.

Initial Confusion Over the Greek Crisis

Managing sovereign debt crises was not part of the purview of the European Monetary Union (EMU). The severe crisis that broke out in Greece, which began with the fiscal revisions of October 2008 and worsened through the spring of 2010, had the potential to spread rapidly to the rest of Europe and cause the demise of the euro. Yet the absence of any rules to manage the crisis left member states confused and fumbling for a unified response, further contributing to the volatility of financial markets (Gianviti *et al.* 2010).

A possible Greek default threatened the entire euro area due to the integrated nature of European banking. In February 2010, German and French banks held $119 billion of exposure to Greek borrowers and more than $900 billion to Greece, Portugal, Ireland and Spain; Germany and France held almost half of all European exposures to those countries (Fuhrmans and Moffett 2010). A Greek default could spread panic to German and French banks and the financial system as markets speculated whether they could withstand the losses. It was thus in the interest of all in Europe to find a solution to the sovereign debt crisis.

The Greek Bail-out

European leaders tergiversated for months on how to deal with the spread of the sovereign debt crisis, but events precipitated the eventual political resolution. The first indication that the eurozone could intervene to rescue one of its members was the vague statement on 11 February 2010 from eurozone's leaders, indicating that some intervention was possible in order to 'safeguard financial stability in the euro area as a whole' (European Council 2010b). On 25 March 2010, in response to the Greek crisis, France and Germany, the two countries financing the majority of any bail-out effort at 27.92 per cent and 20.97 per cent respectively,[1] drafted a statement, according to which the euro area member states (EAMS) would contribute coordinated bilateral loans as part of a package with IMF financing (European Council 2011a; Ludlow 2010, 23; Nowotny 2010).

After the markets 'cornered' the EU and the IMF into coming up with a more convincing plan for the day Greece could not go to the markets to roll over its debts, the Eurogroup finance ministers issued a statement on April 11 announcing that the EAMS were ready to provide bilateral loans to Greece, pooled by the Commission in the amount of €30 billion, as part of a package including also €15 billion from the IMF (Ludlow 2010, 24; Eurogroup 2010b). The markets again reacted with a burst of skepticism of Greece's ability to avoid default, despite the EU/IMF funding. On 2 May 2010, the Eurogroup Finance Ministers agreed to activate stability support to Greece after concurring with the Commission and the European Central Bank (ECB) that assistance was necessary to 'safeguard financial stability in the euro area as a whole' (Eurogroup 2010a). The EAMS and the IMF would provide € 80 billion and € 30 billion, respectively, over three years, in the form of bilateral loans centrally pooled by the Commission (Eurogroup 2010a).

The Greek rescue of May 2nd, expected to calm the markets, did not prevent the contagion. European leaders were not simply faced with the reality that the Greek crisis was spreading to other euro zone countries, but also with the possibility that it could plunge the world once again into financial panic.

Contemplating Alternative Options for Dealing with the Crisis

In the spring of 2010, faced with a novel challenge unplanned for by the European treaties, member states contemplated multiple possible options to deal with the crisis that was now spreading beyond Greece:

Provide bilateral loans. One potential solution mirrored the Greek bail-out, which consisted of bilateral loans from EAMS, pooled by the Commission, in addition to IMF funding. Could bilateral loans be used as a stop gap for the rest of the Eurozone? In fact, this option initially appealed to Germany because it appeared as the best way around the no bail-out clause (Renaud-Basso 2011). Bilateral loans were ruled out, however:

> ... because of the amounts we wanted to put on the table [to] show that we stand ready to support any Euro Area member state... bilateral loans would appear too costly, too heavy in terms of balance sheets for governments (Renaud-Basso 2011).

Create a European Monetary Fund (EMF). As early as 2008, when the financial solidity of European banks was increasingly under attack, scholars had proposed a European financial stability fund for euro countries in financial distress, to be on a massive scale of €500–700 billion and a lender of last resort that could issue binding rulings on economic policies (Gros and Micossi 2008, 2–3; Mayer 2009, 140). Talk of an EMF intensified when the German finance minister, Wolfgang Schäuble, called for a fund that could grant emergency liquidity aid to eurozone members to stem the risk of default, but only on 'strict conditionality and a prohibitive price tag' so that the aid is only used as a 'last resort' (Schäuble 2010). While Schäuble did not outline how his proposal would function, the EMF proposal by Daniel Gros and Thomas Mayer envisioned that the fund's main contributions would come from those countries that broke the Maastricht criteria and proposed that a country in need could issue debt guaranteed by EMF funds (Gros and Mayer 2010, 66). The EMF enjoyed support from the Commission and across political parties in Germany ('Krise in Griechenland' 2010). Merkel endorsed Schäuble's EMF proposal, admitting that the EU lacked the tools to deal with the crisis, but said it could not happen because it would require Treaty change and the agreement of all EU member states because of the Maastricht treaty's no-bail-out clause (Ludlow 2010, 15–6; Peel 2010).

Create a European Debt Agency. Yves Leterme, the Belgian Prime Minister at the time, proposed a European Debt Agency in March of 2010 that would issue euro-denominated debt centrally. While old debt would be paid at different interest rates, Leterme proposed a common interest rate for new debt (Leterme 2010). Such an agency would have also required Treaty change.

Create a Commission-backed facility. The Commission proposed creating a stabilization fund under EU authority that would sell bonds backed by guarantees from member states (Charlemagne 2010a; Barber 2010b). EU legal experts warned the Commission that the proposal may be against EU law; but more importantly, Germany would not support it because getting the proposals past its constitutional court might be problematic (Barber 2010b).

Create an intergovernmental Special Purpose Vehicle (SPV). It took the member states months to ponder the options; according to some of the actors and observers, they finally settled on the EFSF, an intergovernmental SPV that would raise money by issuing bonds backed by member state guarantees, as a possible way out of the crisis which emerged, 'really in the middle of the night' (Renaud-Basso 2011).

The EFSF emerged in this atmosphere of confusion, panic, and desperation. According to HI, causal processes are influenced by time and timing (Farrell and Newman 2010). Institutions remain stable, evolving discreetly and incrementally, until comes an exogenous shock. Faced with multiple equilibria and a range of possible paths, confused as to their own preferences, while conscious of a sense of urgency, policy-makers are disoriented. With hindsight, the EAMS' decision of May 2010 was a crossroads, though it may be difficult to discern it as such whilst in the thick of it. This particular historical moment is referred to by historical institutionalists as a 'critical juncture' (Collier and Collier 1991; Pierson 1996, 123–63). In a critical juncture, structural influences on political action are more fluid than in times of institutional equilibrium. Consequently, 'agents face a broader than typical range of feasible options' and 'their choices from among these options are likely to have a significant impact on subsequent outcomes' (Cappoccia and Kelemen 2007, 348).

The EFSF was created at a time that resembles, ex-post, one of these critical junctures. The piecemeal, timid measures European leaders took in early 2010 were interpreted by the markets as too little, too late. In the week after the announcement of the Greek rescue package, the market situation deteriorated for Greece, Spain, and Portugal, forcing European leaders to take action beyond Greece. 'The contagion was something that came up very suddenly', notes Jonathan Yiangou,[2] an economist at the ECB, 'particularly in that week before the 7th of May' (2011). By May 7, interbank lending froze, and tensions in the bond markets and the money markets were at pre-Lehman levels (Ludlow 2010, 28; Yiangou 2011).

The urgency of the need to respond to market before even more destructive speculation on the EAMS could take place when the Asian stock markets opened on Monday created a short period of 'institutional fluidity' characteristic of critical junctures (Cappoccia and Kelemen 2007, 354), as differing viewpoints on what shape the EU response would take were already apparent on May 7. European leaders declared that the Commission would propose a 'European stabilization mechanism to preserve financial stability in Europe', to be voted on in the extraordinary Ecofin Meeting on Sunday, May 9 (European Council 2011b). However, the leaders had not discussed the details of the plan, but the announcement was nevertheless important to signal that they were ready to go beyond bilateral loans and put in place a structural mechanism (Renaud-Basso 2011).

Creating the EFSF

The results of the May 9–10 Ecofin meeting took even seasoned EU analysts by surprise. On May 10, European leaders announced a €750 billion euro area bail-out package, including an unprecedented bail-out institution, the EFSF. By the end of the weekend, European leaders committed €60 billion of EU-backed funds (the European Financial Stabilisation Mechanism (EFSM)), €440 billion of guarantees by euro area countries for a SPV, the EFSF, guaranteed on a pro-rata basis by EAMS and set to expire after three years (European Council 2010a), and €250 billion of IMF money to a bail-out mechanism (European Council 2010a; 'How to run' 2010).

Germany set the parameters of the response and the institution. On one hand, it held the key to the bailout of Greece as the richest country in the eurozone, while its leaders' options were restricted strongly by a public opinion hostile towards any aid to Greece (Tsoukalis 2010). The Merkel government was also constrained by the German Federal Constitutional Court, which could threaten any German participation in aiding Greece or any other eurozone member if it ruled that it went against the EU Treaties. On the other hand, Germany's bargaining power was limited by the exposure of its banks and the understanding that both Chancellor Merkel and the German economy would be damaged by a Greek default (Fuhrmans and Moffett 2010).

Other actors also played important roles. As the second biggest economy of the euro area, France's interests were similar to those of Germany's, given the exposure of French banks to the sovereign debt crisis, but the domestic constraints were different. In a country where the acrimonious debate over the proposed EU constitution had left European institutions unpopular, French president Nicolas Sarkozy suggested that the crisis could be solved by having the Commission mobilize funds and pushing the ECB to take action (Ludlow 2010, 30–2). There are suggestions that an initial proposal to try to increase the own-resources ceiling available (the EU funds), so that the entire deal could be guaranteed by the EU budget, was blocked by the UK (Yiangou 2011). The UK was against pledging funds to any new EU-wide mechanism because it felt the eurozone bail-out was a problem of eurozone countries, even though British banks were heavily exposed to debt holdings in Spain and Ireland (Charlemagne 2010b). Non-EU actors, like the US, worked to encourage a swift and massive EU package, but did not play more than a secondary role in the determination of the final features of the agreement (Ludlow 2010, 28; Barber 2010a, b).

The dynamics behind the deal included a polarized debate on whether the Council or the Commission would lead the new mechanism. During the May 9–10 summit, Germany resisted a more ambitious bail-out effort by the Commission, particularly, creating a stabilization fund under EU authority that would sell bonds and borrow against guarantees from member states (Charlemagne 2010a; Barber 2010b). The SPV structure was the solution to Germany's resistance to Commission control. The SPV, which would sell bonds backed by government guarantees, was eventually proposed by Maarten Verwey, director of foreign relations at the Dutch finance ministry (Barber 2010b). While the Commission would manage the funds when used, the EAMS would strictly oversee this process, and the SPV would be subject to 'national constitutional requirements' (Ludlow 2010, 37). The SPV structure was chosen because 'it was very difficult to use the Commission as the sort of body receiving the guarantee because it raised problems with the non-euro area countries who did want to be parties [and] to be liable to any kind of [rescue]', said Renaud-Basso (2011). The SPV nature also allowed efficiency, as the intergovernmental structure allowed the institution to be set up very quickly (Roche 2011). The Commission would control only the smallest piece of the bail-out, a €60 billion facility, later known as the EFSM, funded by the EU's central budget, and therefore guaranteed by all member states, under Article 122.2 (Charlemagne 2010a).

Additionally, whatever powers over the EFSF were delegated to the Commission were strictly overseen by the member states. The EFSF was an intergovernmental instrument, expected to rely on the Commission for technical work, but ultimately the decisions would be taken by the member states in the Council (Renaud-Basso 2011). More technical aspects also became very political: the legality of the mechanism as concerned the no-bail-out clause, creating a balance-sheet-heavy fund versus a guarantee-based facility, and distinguishing illiquidity from insolvency are issues that were discussed, but by no means settled, with the EFSF.

Implementing the EFSF

What came to be the EFSF is a complex institution, whose mandate is to safeguard financial stability in Europe by raising funds in capital markets to finance loans for the euro area member states. This section explores the initial implementation of the EFSF.

Implementing the EFSF

The set-up of the EFSF reflects Germany's effort to control the institution and keep it out of the EU's 'technocratic' management. The EFSF is a corporation under Luxembourgish law, and therefore technically neither in the Commission, nor in the Council. Participating member states are the shareholders and sit on the board, with observers from the Commission and ECB (Gianviti *et al.* 2010, 29). Designed as a temporary institution, it has a limited tenure of three years until June 2013. Registered as a limited company in June 2010, the institution is housed on the second floor of a rather inconspicuous building on John F. Kennedy Avenue in Luxembourg and initially had twelve employees. Klaus Regling, former German Director-General for economic and financial affairs at the Commission, is the CEO ('Klaus Regling' 2010; EFSF 2011b). The number two, Christophe Frankel, CFO and deputy CEO, is, of course, French ('Klaus Regling' 2010). The EFSF is supported by two institutions that assure member state control: the German Debt Management Office (DMO), which provides front office support for debt issuance, cash and risk management; and the European Investment Bank (EIB), a bank owned by the member states which provides back office support, including accounting, documentation and infrastructure.

The EFSF became fully functioning on 4 August 2010, after more than 90 per cent of the total guarantee commitment was confirmed by the member states. It could initially issue bonds backed by a total of €440 billion on a pro rata based on the share of the paid-up capital to the ECB. Germany is by far the largest contributing member state, with an initial share of €119,390.07 million. France and Italy provide the second and third largest sums, initially at €89,657.45 million and €78,784.72 million, respectively (EFSF 2011d). In case a country steps out of EFSF commitments, as happened with Ireland, the contribution key is adjusted among the remaining guarantors.

Initially, a country could only request EFSF financial support when it lost access to capital markets or 'has to pay excessively high interest rates' (EFSF 2011a). After a formal request for aid, a program was negotiated by the Commission, in liaison with the ECB, and the IMF. The euro area finance ministers approved the final decision before the EFSF was allowed to act. The Commission negotiated the Memorandum of Understanding (MoU) with the country seeking aid but the Eurogroup Working Group (within the Council's Ecofin) approved the final MoU before signing and the main terms of the loan facility agreement after a proposal from the Commission (EFSF 2010).

The EFSF package was at first welcomed by investors, but the euphoria was short-lived. A week after the announcement, market analysts worried that a Greek default was still possible, that Europe had written an insurance policy instead of pumping money into the system, and that the cost of bail-outs would drag down the rest of the EAMS (Bowley 2010). By 14 May 2010, the Euro fell to $1.2385, its lowest level against the dollar since November 2008 (Bowley 2010). Two months after its creation, *The Economist* reported that 'if the SPV was designed to calm nerves, it hasn't worked yet' ('Klaus Regling' 2010).

Politics trumped economics in the design of the EFSF, which was supposed to lend at a punitive interest rate to discourage 'bad behavior', to emphasize its *ultima ratio* nature, and to avoid anything that looked like a Eurobond (Munchau 2011). These political reasons did not translate well into economics, as the interest rate given to Greece and, later, Ireland only exacerbated their situation. The interest rate was the market rate plus a charge of 300 basis points for maturities of up to three years and an additional 100 basis points for longer maturities. In addition, a service fee of 50 basis points would be added to cover operational costs. 'That's a mistake that clearly comes from the German both political and legal issue of making sure it's not considered a subsidy', observes Pisani-Ferry (2011).

Despite the Irish bail-out facilitated by a successful EFSF bond auction in January 2011, borrowing costs for Portugal, Spain and Italy rose sharply and the euro fell. The situation worried markets and EU leaders because if Portugal, Spain or Italy required a bailout in the following months, the EFSF's limited lending capacity would not have been enough (Atkins 2010). The political decision to ensure the EFSF's AAA rating made both the capacity much lower than the nominal amount first agreed to and enhanced Germany's role in the EFSF as the largest AAA guarantor. By late 2010, it became apparent that the lending capacity of the EFSF was nearly half of its nominal amount. The EU was once again grossly underprepared to deal with the bourgeoning crisis and EAMS leaders had to scramble to come up with a politically and economically viable decision.

From the EFSF to the ESM

A combination of misunderstandings about the long-term nature of the sovereign debt crisis, continuing contagion, heightened threat of Greek default in the autumn of 2010, and an institution conceived in haste resulted in calls for transforming the slim, temporary EFSF into something more permanent. This section examines the grand bargain that led to the overhaul of the EFSF and the creation of the ESM in 2011.

Creating the ESM

Academic and political debates began early on about changes to the EFSF, in particular raising the lending ceiling, lowering the interest rate, making the institution permanent or altering its structure (Alcidi 2011). Germany was adamantly opposed to expanding the EFSF's powers but supported a Treaty change to set up a permanent rescue mechanism that would allow a method for orderly default (Barysch 2010; Castle 2011; Spiegel and Pignal 2011). At the same time, the ECB was uncustomarily forward in its desire for the EFSF to start buying bonds, to increase the size of the fund, and decrease interest rates (Peel and Atkins 2011). Trichet called for flexibility in the use of the EFSF to recapitalize banks as early as July 2010, before the institution was operational (BBVA 2010).

Countries on the receiving end of bail-out programs also called for change: Portugal criticized the delays in making the EFSF more flexible while Ireland started a campaign to lower interest rates (Wise 2011). The post-EFSF bargaining period also exhibited a more vocal role for the Commission, whose officials, such as Jose Manuel Barroso and Olli Rehn, spoke out in favor of lowering interest rates, arguing that high interest rates that discourage countries from seeking aid are unnecessary because governments are already reluctant to embrace EU bail-outs for political reasons (Spiegel and Peel 2011). Klaus Regling, the EFSF's head, pushed for an expansion of the fund's lending capacity, telling a closed committee session in the German parliament that AAA countries like Germany would have to increase their guarantees to the EFSF to do so (Rinke and Nomiyama 2011). France also supported greater powers for the EFSF (Spiegel *et al*. 2011).

The EFSF's increased powers and move to a permanent mechanism were formalized at the March 24/25 Council summit, where leaders agreed to raise the lending capacity of the EFSF/ESM to an effective €500 billion, lowered interest rates by 100 basis points, and gave the EFSF/ESM bond buying powers in primary markets (European Council 2011a). The new ESM, which was initially planned to take over the role of the EFSF and EFSM after June 2013[3] (European Council 2011a), would be a permanent mechanism, despite the fact that certain countries, Germany in particular, had been avoiding this outcome for so long. This permanence was pushed simultaneously by a need to respond to financial markets, a belief that it would prevent moral hazard, a show of ongoing political will to defend the euro area (Proissl 2011), and a desire to provide clarity for what would happen after 2013 (Renaud-Basso 2011).

Despite these changes, the ESM was met with skepticism, many pointing to serious weaknesses in its design and even the risk of accelerating the crisis (Manasse 2011). The skeptics were right, as the EU had to come up with yet another Greek bail-out and enhancement of EFSF/ESM powers on July 2011, allowing the institutions to recapitalize banks and intervene in secondary markets, actions unthinkable just a few months earlier (European Council 2011c).

On 9 December 2011, the EAMS issued a statement recognizing the increased 'market tensions' and formally agreeing to leverage the EFSF through the two options: one, new Partial Protection Certificates issued together with the beneficiary member state's bonds, providing a 20–30 per cent protection of the initial amount of the bond, and two, the establishment of Co-Investment Funds to buy the bonds of beneficiary member states in the primary and/or secondary markets, agreed upon on November 29 (European Council 2011d; EFSF 2011c).

The ESM as the Result of Path Dependence

Historical institutionalism aims to explain how a policy outcome at a particular critical juncture triggers feedback mechanisms that reinforce the recurrence of a particular political pattern and restrict the policy options available later on in the historical sequence. The 'path not taken or the political alternatives that were once quite plausible may become irretrievable lost' because the costs of switching have become very high (Pierson and Skocpol 2002, 693–721). Previously available alternatives become more difficult to achieve (Pierson 1996, 145–6). This is especially true when an institution has self-reinforcing qualities that create complementary relationships with other institutions and 'thus enhance the value associated with specific designs' (Fioretos 2011, 377).

The creation and existence of the EFSF structured the subsequent terms of the debate. The sunk political costs of creating the EFSF significantly constrained the actions of the member states and other European actors. Negative market reactions forced member states to come up with a permanent mechanism faster than some, especially Germany, wanted to. Leaders may have chosen to adopt the EFSF framework for the ESM for the same reason Ewald Nowotny, President of the National Bank of Austria and member of the ECB's governing council, supported IMF involvement in the early spring of 2010: the markets know what to expect, something that is crucial in securing a positive response (Nowotny 2010). Creating a new structure that would both be accepted by other members and convince markets in such a short time would have been costly and risky. Additionally, all member states had already passed the EFSF through their parliaments — making an amended EFSF easier to pass again than an entirely new bail out plan or institution. Many of the operational mechanisms had already been determined and put to use with the EFSF, especially the role of the Commission, ECB, and other important institutional links, such as the German DMO and the EIB.

Similar to the HI framework that expects initial decisions to lock into suboptimal institutional arrangements (Fioretos 2011, 380; Pierson 1996, 145–6), the EFSF/ESM structure seems to be suboptimal in dealing with an unrelenting crisis. Since the EFSF gets its AAA credit rating from its shareholders, it is vulnerable to their own downgrades: when France was downgraded on 13 January 2012, so was the EFSF. A downgrade also limits its lending capacity because the cash buffers the rating agencies require to be kept from the proceeds of each EFSF bond issuance are increased automatically. Despite a successful first auction in January 2011, the most recent EFSF bond auctions have been weak, indicating a lack of investor demand (Pisani 2011). The yield on the 10-year EFSF bond in November 2011 was 3.59, almost double the rate in January 2011 (Pisani 2011). Due to the large amount of guarantees given to the EFSF/ESM by the member states and the immense institutional investment in the EFSF/ESM over the past two years, the EAMS may have few options other than continuing to prop up the institution with various new powers and leveraging schemes.

Initially, the short run emphases on sovereignty, rather than long term emphasis on effective crisis management, may have pushed EAMS leaders to an intergovernmental solution. The SPV structure was chosen to avoid the difficulties associated with using the Commission as the receiving body for the guarantees (Renaud-Basso 2011). Additionally, adds Frankel, European countries are reluctant to create new institutions: 'the individual countries don't want... any loss of sovereignty', explaining that it is politically difficult to add another institution to the complex EU structure (Frankel 2011). Merkel was also concerned with the Constitutional Court's ruling on the Lisbon Treaty in 2009 that required Bundestag approval of any significant EU initiative (Ludlow 2010, 36). In particular, the June 2009 ruling, explains Proissl, 'limited the margins of the German government to transfer any sort of sovereignty, especially in fiscal affairs' (2011).

Did these considerations cause leaders to discount long-term economic considerations? The EFSF was initially set up as a temporary intergovernmental institution, in a miscalculated judgement of the long term nature of the crisis, and was not originally thought out as the basis for a sovereign debt management regime in the EU. Today, many analysts argue that both the EFSF and ESM lack the main characteristic that is necessary to end this sovereign debt crisis: the mutualization of debt at a supranational level or essentially 'a move to a full fiscal union' ('Europe's sovereign-debt crisis' 2011). Especially because the ESM, the permanent institution, locks in a intergovernmental process to distribute funds by requiring unanimity by its board of members (the participating member states), it is unlikely to convince investors. 'The ESM is meant to be a permanent fixture but it does not look like a lasting response to the crisis', judged *The Economist* ('CAC flap' 2012).

Another option available during the May 9/10 weekend was the a more ambitious bail-out effort proposed by the Commission and fiercely opposed by Germany: creating a Eurozone rescue fund under EU authority that would sell bonds and borrow against guarantees from member states (Charlemagne 2010a; Barber 2010b). Barber quotes Olli Rehn, Commissioner for Economic and Monetary Affairs and the Euro, as saying that 'if Germany had endorsed the Commission's proposals, they would have flown. But the Germans made the point that there might be problems getting the proposals past their constitutional court' (Barber 2010b).

A counterfactual thought experiment supports our assertion that the importance of contingency during the critical juncture significantly impacted the new institutional equilibrium. The conditions under which the EFSF emerged as the preferred solution reeks of bounded rationality: the information available to the actors was limited and their decision may have seemed rational then, but not be in the long run. Indeed, the political and economic consequences of the new institutional mechanism had not been really considered: 'It was not a very long term, thought-through plan to have an SPV' (Renaud-Basso 2011). What if, instead of the miscalculation of the nature of the crisis and the severe deterioration of the markets the weekend of May 9/10, the EAMS had instead began the fast-track treaty change in early 2010 rather than late 2010? A fast-track treaty change could have allayed German concerns about their constitutional court; in fact, only months laters, a treaty change allowing a euro area bail out institution was agreed by the Council on 17 December 2010, precisely to address the German Constitutional Court's concerns with the EFSF. This would have made the Commission's proposal much more palatable to Germany,[4] and the decisions that led to the creation of purely intergovernmental EFSF would have been improbable. In fact, there is evidence that Merkel may have agreed to this supranational, rather than purely intergovernmental, effort had treaty change dismissed the spector of the constitutional court: in early 2010, Merkel endorsed Schäuble's European Monetary Fund (EMF) proposal, but said it would be impossible without treaty change (Ludlow 2010, 15–6; Peel 2010).

Conclusion

Historical institutionalist scholarship generally presents three characteristics: 'big real world puzzles', temporality, and context (Meunier and McNamara 2007, 4). Our present inquiry shares many of these commonalities. First, the evolution of the EFSF, Europe's front line against the sovereign debt crisis, is certainly a major policy issue with the potential for catastrophic consequences if not addressed properly. It is also a puzzle because it is unclear why EAMS leaders chose to make the EFSF, an incredibly complex structure often called a 'CDO', or Collateralized Debt Obligation, by its critics, the base for a permanent bail-out structure in Europe. In addition, we find that the temporal sequence of creation and evolution of the EFSF fits the framework usually highlighted by historical institutionalist studies: a new institutional response emerged from a confusing situation with no guidance from the existing institutions and a multiplicity of possible options, yet a clear sense of urgency. The creation of the EFSF then determined and narrowed down the subsequent options possible, in particular the creation of the ESM.

HI has been used to explain the process of European integration.[5] It argues that once gaps in member state control of the institutional evolution are created, they cannot be entirely corrected because of the large sunk costs that make reversal of decisions impractical. This explains the gradual supranationalization of many policies in the EU. However, the handling of the Greek crisis suggests that we may be faced with an HI story in reverse: instead of locking in European integration, the creation of the EFSF locked in intergovernmentalism as the *modus operandi* for dealing with the sovereign debt crisis — and future crises.

It is not clear whether the member states would have preferred to put in place another, more supranational system, had they started from scratch today, instead of being constrained by the sunk costs associated with the prior design of the EFSF. Our inquiry is limited by the short time period we are analyzing and by a problem of multicollinearity in the counterfactual analysis of the critical juncture, that is beyond the scope of this paper. Research should try to address this concerns in light of the rapidly unfolding institutional change in Europe.

Acknowledgements

The authors would like to thank Jean-Pierre Landau, Jeffry Frieden, Christine Landfried, the participants of the College of Europe Conference on economic governance in Bruges on 1 March 2011 and the participants of the panel 'Assessing the Eurozone Crisis' of the IPSA World Congress in Madrid on 8 July 2012 for their comments.

Notes

1. Pro rata based on the share of the paid-up capital to the ECB, see Ludlow (2010, 23).
2. The views expressed by Yiangou are in a personal capacity and do not necessarily reflect those of the ECB.
3. The ESM was officially inaugurated in October 2012.
4. Assuming, for the sake of this thought experiment, that the mechanism would have been limited to the EAMS to avoid UK opposition.
5. See Pierson (1996).

References

Alcidi, C. 2011. Interview by Ledina Gocaj, CEPS, Brussels, January 24.
Atkins, R. et al. 2010. Five potential weapons for the Eurozone. The Financial Times, December 1. http://www.ft.com/intl/cms/s/0/d6e13bae-fd83-11df-a049-00144feab49a.html.

Barber, T. 2010a. How Washington pushed Europe to save the euro. *The Financial Times*, October 10 http://www.ft.com/intl/cms/s/0/8ed137b4-d2f0-11df-9ae9-00144feabdc0.html.
Barber, T. 2010b. The euro: dinner on the edge of the abyss. *The Financial Times*, October 10 http://www.ft.com/intl/cms/s/0/190b32ae-d49a-11df-b230-00144feabdc0.html.
Barysch, K. 2010. *Why Berlin wants a eurozone bankruptcy act.* Center for European Reform, November 18.
BBVA Research. 2010. Europe ECB Watch. Madrid, July 8.
Bowley, G. 2010. Wall St. Slides, Fearing Return to a Recession. The New York Times, May 14.
'CAC flap'. 2012. *The Economist.* February 3 http://www.economist.com/blogs/freeexchange/2012/02/european-stability-mechanism.
Cappoccia, G., and R.D. Kelemen. 2007. The study of critical junctures: theory, narrative, and counterfactuals in historical institutionalism. *World Politics* 59, no. 3: 341–96.
Castle, S. 2011. European officials want to expand bailout fund. *The New York Times*, February 14 http://www.nytimes.com/2011/02/15/business/global/15iht-euro15.html.
'Charlemagne, financial fortress Europe'. 2010a. *The Economist.* May 13 http://www.economist.com/node/16116909.
'Charlemagne, perfidious Albion again'. 2010b. *The Economist.* May 20 http://www.economist.com/node/16163218.
Clancy, R. 2010. Weathering the storm. The challanges facing the euro, the eurozone crisis. Investment International and Barclays Wealth, Barclayswealth.com http://www.barclayswealth.com/Images/Mark-Richards-interview112010.pdf (accessed March 1 2011).
Collier, R.B., and D. Collier. 1991. *Shaping the political arena: critical junctures, the labor movement, and regime dynamics in Latin America.* Princeton: Princeton University Press.
EFSF. 2011a. An Introduction to the European financial stability facility. Presentation provided to the author, which may not be publically available, EFSF headquarters, Luxembourg, January.
EFSF. 2011b. European financial stability facility, about, http://www.efsf.europa.eu/about/index.html (accessed 27 February 2012).
EFSF. 2011c. Maximising the capacity of the EFSF. Terms and conditions – 29 november 2011, *efsf.europa.eu* (accessed 29 November 2012).
EFSF. 2011d. The European financial stability facility – FAQ, http://www.efsf.europa.eu/attachment/faq_en.pdf (accessed 27 February 2012).
EFSF. 2010. EFSF framework agreement between euro area member states and EFSF, efsf.europa.eu (7 June 2012).
Eurogroup. 2010a. Statement by the Eurogroup, May 2.
Eurogroup. 2010b. Statement on the support to Greece by euro area members states, Brussels, April 11.
European Commission. 2010. Report on the Greek government deficit and debt statistics, Brussels, January 8.
European Council. 2010a. Press release, extraordinary council meeting, economic and financial affairs, Brussels, May 9/10.
European Council. 2010b. Statement by the heads of state and government, February 11.
European Council. 2010c. Statement by the heads of state and government of the euro area, March 25.
European Council. 2011a. Conclusions of the European Council, Brussels, March 24/25.
European Council. 2011b. Statement by the heads of state and government, May 7, *The European Council* in 2010, January.
European Council. 2011c. Statement by the heads of state and government, July 21.
European Council. 2011d. Statement by the heads of state and government, December 9.
'Europe's sovereign-debt crisis; scaling the summit'. 2011. *The Economist*, December 10 http://www.economist.com/node/21541414.
Farrell, H., and A. Newman. 2010. Making global markets: historical institutionalism in international political economy. *Review of International Political* Economy October: 609–38.
Fioretos, O. 2011. Historical institutionalism in international relations. *International Organization* 65, no. 2: 367–99.
Frankel, C. 2011. Interview by Ledina Gocaj, EFSF headquarters, Luxembourg, January 28.
Fuhrmans, V., and S. Moffett. 2010. Exposure to Greece weighs on French, German banks. *Wall Street Journal*, February 17 http://online.wsj.com/article/SB10001424052748703798904575069712153415820.html.

Gianviti, F., A.O. Krueger, J. Pisani-Ferry, A. Sapir, and J. Von Hagen. 2010. A European mechanism for sovereign debt crisis resolution: a proposal, *Bruegel Blueprint Series*, Volume X.

Gros, D., and T. Mayer. 2010. How to deal with the threat of sovereign default in Europe: towards a Euro(pean) monetary fund. *Intereconomics* 45, no. 2: 64–8.

Gros, D., and S. Micossi. 2008. A call for a European financial stability fund. *CEPS Commentary*, October.

'How to run the euro'. 2010. *The Economist*, September 23 http://www.economist.com/node/17093339.

Leterme, Y. 2010. Pour une agence européene de la dette, *Le Monde*, March 5 http://www.lemonde.fr/idees/article/2010/03/05/pour-une-agence-europeenne-de-la-dette-par-yves-leterme_1314894_3232.html.

Ludlow, P. 2010. In the last resort, the euro crisis and the European Council, Spring 2010. *EuroComment* 7, no. 7/8, http://www.eurocomment.be/?p=182#more-182.

'Klaus Regling, chief bail out officer'. 2010. *The Economist*, July 1 http://www.economist.com/node/16485600.

'Krise in Griechenland; EU stützt Ruf nach Euro-Währungsfonds'. 2010. *Spiegel Online*, March 7 http://www.spiegel.de/politik/ausland/krise-in-griechenland-eu-stuetzt-ruf-nach-euro-waehrungsfonds-a-682223.html.

Manasse, P. 2011. The trouble with the European stability mechanism, *VoxEU.org*, April 5 http://www.voxeu.org/article/trouble-european-stability-mechanism.

Mayer, T. 2009. The case for a European monetary fund. *Intereconomics* May/June: 138–141.

Meunier, S., and K. McNamara. 2007. *Making history: European integration and institutional change at fifty*, Vol. 8. New York: Oxford University Press.

Monnet, Jean. 1976. *Mémoires*. Paris: Fayard.

Munchau, W. 2011. Interview by Ledina Gocaj, Eurointelligence headquarters, January 27.

Nowotny, E. 2010. The financial crisis: lessons learned. Talk given at Princeton University, Princeton, April 27.

Peel, Q. 2010. EMF plan needs new EU Treaty, says Merkel. *The Financial Times*, March 9 http://www.ft.com/intl/cms/s/0/2b0933f4-2b1a-11df-93d8-00144feabdc0.html.

Peel, Q., and R. Atkins. 2011. March deadline for stability accord. *The Financial Times*, January 13 http://www.ft.com/intl/cms/s/0/4c4469f4-1f4c-11e0-8c1c-00144feab49a.html.

Pierson, P. 1996. The path to European integration: a historical institutionalist analysis. *Comparative Political Studies* 29, no. 2: 123–63.

Pierson, P., and T. Skocpol. 2002. 'Historical institutionalism in contemporary political science'. In Political Science: State of the Discipline, eds. I. Katznelson and H. Milner, 692–721. New York: W.W.Norton.

Pisani, B. 2011. Why EFSF auction was so weak. *CNBC.com*, November 7 http://www.cnbc.com/id/45195376/Why_EFSF_Auction_Was_So_Weak.

Pisani-Ferry, J. 2011. Interview by Ledina Gocaj, Bruegel headquarters, Brussels, January 27.

Proissl, W. 2011. Interview by Ledina Gocaj, Frankfurt, January 27.

Renaud-Basso, O. 2011. Interview by Ledina Gocaj, European Council. Brussels, January 25.

Rinke, A., and C. Nomiyama. 2011. Regling pushes Germany to expand EFSF sources. *Reuters*.com, February 9 http://www.reuters.com/article/2011/02/09/efsf-germany-idUSLDE7182FJ20110209.

Schäuble, W. 2010. Why Europe's monetary union faces its biggest crisis. *The Financial Times*, March 11 http://www.ft.com/intl/cms/s/0/2a205b88-2d41-11df-9c5b-00144feabdc0.html.

Spiegel, P., and Q. Peel. 2011. EU leaders wrestle over revamped rescue fund. *The Financial Times*, January 30 http://www.ft.com/intl/cms/s/0/a357f7e2-2c9e-11e0-83bd-00144feab49a.html.

Spiegel, P., and S. Pignal. 2011. EU efforts to boost rescue fund rejected. *The Financial Times*, February 15 http://www.ft.com/cms/s/0/c8205bda-392a-11e0-97ca-00144feabdc0.html.

Spiegel, P., V. Mallet, and P. Hollinger. 2011. Wider powers for eurozone bail-out fund. *The Financial Times*, February 3 http://www.ft.com/intl/cms/s/0/0dce13ee-2fca-11e0-91f8-00144feabdc0.html.

Tsoukalis, L. 2010. Interview by Ledina Gocaj, Princeton, NJ, October 26.

Wise, P. 2011. Portugal calls for EU rescue fund flexibility. *The Financial Times*, February 15 http://www.ft.com/intl/cms/s/0/88daf832-38fc-11e0-b0f6-00144feabdc0.html.

Yiangou, J. 2011. Interview by Ledina Gocaj, European Central Bank, Frankfurt, January 25.

Fiscal Policy Coordination and the Future of the Community Method

MICHELE CHANG

Department of European Political and Administrative Studies, College of Europe Dijver, Brugge, Belgium

ABSTRACT The global financial and sovereign debt crises led to the creation of numerous new agreements and institutions to contain the current crisis and prevent future ones. These measures reinforce the historical trend towards the predominance of intergovernmental decision-making in economic and monetary union (EMU), going so far as to re-intergovernmentalize cooperation that had previously been decided upon by the Community method. Using principal–agent analysis, this contribution looks at fiscal policy cooperation since the outbreak of the sovereign debt crisis and considers how the impact of re-intergovernmentalization is manifested largely in the policy process rather than the policy outcome. However, this is still cause for concern given the precarious nature of EMU's legitimacy and the loss of efficiency that delegation typically provides.

In an address to the students of the College of Europe, German Chancellor Angela Merkl outlined an approach she dubbed the 'Union method' (Merkel 2010). She expressed skepticism towards the divide between intergovernmentalists (the Council, European Council and member states) and 'the representatives in the European Parliament and in the European Commission [who] see themselves as the sole true champions of the community method' (Merkel 2010, 6). While 'a particular solution is not, after all, automatically better simply because it has been put in place or implemented by EU institutions' (Merkel 2010, 6), even legislation that can decided according to the community method has been prone to a large degree of interference by the member states, to a degree that one can consider a re-intergovernmentalization of policy.

In December 2011 the 'six-pack' reforms on economic government went into force. Analysts had long warned of the dangers of Economic and Monetary Union (EMU) without a corresponding political union, and the reform package constituted a major step in bolstering fiscal cooperation between states. Technically, the six-pack was decided upon according to the 'community method', one of the few Eurozone crisis response mechanisms to do so. Nevertheless the six-pack confirmed the weakness of the community method in EMU as the Van Rompuy Task Force (VRTF) entered into the fray at the behest of the European Council. The Commission's authority as agenda-setter was stretched almost beyond recognition as its proposals seemingly served as a rough draft for the VRTF's proposals that were being released the following month. The European Parliament then flexed its muscles and saved the reform package from being watered down, reasserting the community method and the premium placed on the input of supranational institutions. Shortly after its entry into force, however, a new treaty (the Treaty on Stability, Coordination and Governance (TSCG)) was agreed upon that brought fiscal policy coordination back into an intergovernmental agreement.

This article uses a principal–agent (P–A) framework to analyze the six-pack and demonstrate how the community method has been subverted in the name of economic crisis management in a way that impacts policy processes but not necessarily policy outcomes. The insights yielded from a principal–agent analysis of fiscal policy coordination run counter to some of the prevailing wisdom on the need for the independence of institutions and the elasticity of delegation (policy outcome). The P–A literature also points to some of the dangers that can arise in the legitimacy of policy process, something that has exacerbated the EU's democratic deficit since the onset of the crisis (see also Francisco Torres' contribution in this volume for the legitimacy issues faced by the ECB).

The first part lays out the analytical framework regarding principal–agent theory and how it relates to the community method. The subsequent sections apply it to the negotiations of the six-pack and TSCG, arguing that both the Van Rompuy Task Force and the TSCG acted as control mechanisms to reassert member state authority in the face of potential agency drift by the Commission and the Parliament. The conclusion considers the implications of the bypassing of the community method in monetary integration.

The Community Method, Delegation and EMU

The community method refers to the legislative process in which policy is initiated by the Commission and then decided upon by the Council (using qualified majority voting) and the European Parliament under the ordinary legislative procedure as equal partners and subject to the judgment of the European Court of Justice (ECJ). A defining feature of EU cooperation is the significant role played by supranational institutions, as international organizations typically lack supranational institutions with strong powers.

Within this context the Commission enjoys numerous functions, including policy proposals, enforcement and managerial functions (Nugent 2000; Chang & Monar 2013). Temple Lang and Eamonn (2005, 1028) defend the necessity of:

> ... a fully representative and independent Commission in order to create an institutional structure in which large and small member states could co-exist satisfactorily... The key feature that made the Community effective and which made it acceptable even to member states that were outvoted.

In addition, the European Parliament serves as a democratic check on the decisions taken, and the ECJ ensures its uniform application. This system has made the European Union something that falls short of a nation state but goes well beyond an international organization, serving as a model for the potential of regional integration in political and economic terms.

However the community method has been supplemented with looser forms of cooperation in politically sensitive areas that substantially limit the powers of supranational institutions and thus restrict the delegation of powers: 'When the member states... want to ensure [that] cooperation remains entirely under their control... they create new silos to contain this cooperation' (Warleigh-Lack & Drachenberg 2010, 211), thus giving rise to new forms of governance, including the former pillar system of the Maastricht Treaty and the open method of coordination. As Kenneth Dyson's contribution notes, the EU lacks a supranational 'supreme emergency' authority, and EMU has been dominated by intergovernmental institutions, save for the European Central Bank. For example, the forerunner of monetary union, the European Monetary System, originated from a Franco–German bargain rather than a Commission proposal (Ludlow 1982). Puetter (2012) argues that the crisis has reinforced the decentralized nature of EMU's economic pillar, and the lack of consensus on the way forward has made the EU dependent on 'deliberative intergovernmentalism'. Eurozone states delegate monetary policy to the ECB, which has exclusive competence, and member states have exhibited great reluctance to grant more policymaking authority to supranational institutions in order to complete EMU. Nevertheless the Parliament has enjoyed a steady expansion of powers over the last few decades as an increasing number of policies fall under the ordinary legislative procedure.

What is the impact of the reluctance of member states to delegate authority to supranational institutions? Or to claw back some powers that were already delegated? The first part of the answer lies in the reasons behind delegation. Principal–agent theory argues that delegation can improve the policy process by enhancing the credibility of a policy through the use of a neutral actor as an arbiter between conflicting interests and provide more credible regulation and enforcement of agreements. Delegation therefore can lead to more desirable policies by allowing the agent to utilize fully its technical expertise (Pollack 2003). This rationalization of delegation that renders both superior policy processes (supranational agents as neutral) and outcomes (supranational agents as providing technocratic expertise) has been used extensively to justify central bank independence, for example (Cukierman 1992).

However delegation includes risk, as supranational agents 'possess powers and preferences distinct from those of their member state principals' (Pollack 2003, 3). For example, the prospect of the agent gaining an informational advantage that could be used against the principal, or the risk of an agent 'concealing actions' from the principal. If the agent's preferences deviate from that of the principal, 'agency loss' could occur. In order to minimize these risks, principals can limit the agent's room for maneuver both before and after the agent fulfills its delegated task. *Ex ante*, the principal can limit the acceptable range of policy options from which the agent can select. For example, the principal can engage in monitoring as the agent fulfills its tasks, either by using police patrols and continuously monitoring the agent, or by using fire alarms and relying on third parties to inform the principal of agency slack (Kiewiet & McCubbins 1991).

The presence of multiple principles increases such risk (Nielson & Tierney 2003), as does competing interests among the principals (Dűr and Elsig 2011), both of which are present in the case of EU delegation. It is further complicated by the plethora of EU institutions, as member states are represented by the European Council as well as the Ecofin council in the case of fiscal policy coordination. Therefore the benefits of delegation (improved policy process and outcomes) can be muted by the use of instruments that limit the ability of the agents to fulfill their delegated tasks.

Within EMU the Commission functions as a 'delegated monitor but enjoys few if any powers of representation, initiation and execution in relation to EU economic governance' (Hodson 2009, 461). While the six-pack is an exception to this characterization, the TSCG conforms to it (unnecessarily so, as will be explained later). What was the impact of delegation (or the lack thereof) in the case of the six-pack (which used the community method) and the TSCG (which did not)? One might expect a relatively weak policy, considering the interference of the member states in the policymaking process and that delegation theories emphasize the danger of government actors manipulating policy for short-term political gain (hence the delegation to technocratic institutions). The next section looks at the proposal, ratification procedure and outcomes of these two policies to see whether and how the member states were able to achieve their objective of strengthening fiscal policy coordination (policy outcome) by delegating authority under the community method in the first instance and bypassing the community method in the second but at the cost of policy process and legitimacy.

Institutionalizing Fiscal Policy Coordination through the Community and Union Methods

The Six-pack: Whose Proposal Was It? Who Cares?[1]

As the crisis in Greece unfolded in March 2010, the European Council (2010a) requested proposals from the Commission to strengthen European economic governance by June 2010 within the parameters set by the TFEU. The same European Council conclusions charged European Council President Herman Van Rompuy with forming 'a task force... to present to the Council, before the end of this year, the measures needed to reach the objective of an improved crisis resolution framework and better budgetary discipline, exploring all options to reinforce the legal framework'. While the European Council conclusions only specified the task force would contain 'representatives of the member states, the rotating presidency and the ECB', the formation took the shape of Ecofin members with Van Rompuy at the helm.

The roles of both the Task Force and the Commission were soon clarified in May 2010 when a joint letter from French President Nicolas Sarkozy and German Chancellor Angela Merkl was sent to European Commission President Barroso and Van Rompuy, instructing that they reinforce the euro's economic governance, and that 'all contributions from the European Commission and the member states should be evaluated by the working group'.[2] This letter not only established the parameters of their tasks, but it established the VRTF as the authoritative body to which the Commission was expected to report.

Therefore one can view the European Council as the principal, the Commission as an agent, and the VRTF as another agent of the European Council that was placed in charge of the Commission, thus making it akin to a police patrol system of avoiding shirking and deviating from the interests of the principal. Normally such a request from the European Council for a proposal from the Commission would lead to discussions within the latter, particularly within DG ECFIN, with a dialogue emerging between the appropriate actors in the Council (e.g., the Eurogroup and the Eurogroup working group). This allows for an exchange of ideas as well as gives the Commission a sense of what would or would not be an acceptable proposal to the Council, thus allowing the Commission to craft a more strategic proposal as well as utilize its technocratic expertise in setting the agenda. By appointing the VRTF to preside over the Commission proposal, it robbed the latter of its normal function as agenda-setter. Although in practice the Commission would have consulted with most of the same actors anyway, the appointment of the VRTF still held some significance. First, it served as the first important platform for the new European Council president, which he would later build upon and establish himself as a key player in the reform of Eurozone economic governance (and continue its intergovernmental bent). Second, it forced the Commission to share the spotlight in an issue that it would normally be the sole agenda-setter, at least officially. In fact, the Commission had claimed credit for the content of its previous round of reforms of fiscal policy coordination (Heipertz & Verdun 2010), making its reduced margin for maneuver in the six-pack's round of SGP reforms even more significant and contributing to the perception of the declining role of the Commission. Finally, in augmenting its existing control mechanism over its agent (the Commission) with a form of police patrolling (VRTF), the principal (the European Council) expended additional resources that potentially undercut some of the benefits of delegation to the Commission, including the perceived credibility of the policy process (now subject to even closer member state control) and potentially the policy outcome.

Soon afterward the European Commission (2010a) issued its first communication on 12 May 2010, which presented a three-pronged approach to reforming the economic governance system. Based on Article 136 of the TFEU, the Commission proposed a reform of the SGP, creating a macroeconomic surveillance mechanism that would include competitiveness, and enabling more timely economic policy coordination through the construction of a European Semester. The VRTF met on 21 May and decided on four main objectives. First, the SGP should be strengthened. Second, the diverging competitiveness within the EU needed to be addressed. Third, a crisis resolution mechanism should be established. Fourth, the EU needed to augment its economic governance system. The first two elements matched the Commission's proposals, which are referred to in the VRTF press release. Van Rompuy (2010) announced the target of October 2010, two months ahead of the December deadline originally set by the Council. When the VRTF met again in June, they had incorporated the European Semester into their discussion. In addition, the references to diverging competitiveness had taken the shape of budgetary and macroeconomic surveillance, similar to what had already been elaborated upon by the Commission. Moreover, in an effort 'to define a new set of sanctions — more progressive and consistent... we have asked the Commission to come forward with proposals'. The VRTF had now become a principal itself and delegated a task to the Commission as both organizations worked on their proposals together as well as separately.

On 8 June the Ecofin Council (Council 2010a, 13) welcomed the proposals of both the Commission and the Task Force, but only the Task Force was referenced when commenting on the proposed new surveillance function. On the other hand, the conclusions of the European Council (2010b) meeting on 17 June referenced both the VRTF and the Commission proposals and agreed with the suggested strengthening of the SGP, creation of a scoreboard and a new macroeconomic surveillance framework. In addition, it noted that 'the European Council invites the Task Force and the Commission to rapidly develop further and make operational these orientations', and acknowledged the October deadline that the VRTF had set for itself (European Council 2010b). When the Commission issued a follow-up communication on 30 June, it set for itself a September deadline (European Commission 2010b) in an effort to recapture the initiative that had been coopted by the VRTF.[3]

The VRTF's meeting on 12 July introduced the possibility of automatic sanctioning of member states. Soon afterwards, the first of a series of instructions from member state governments increased the principals' control over their agents (VRTF and the Commission) even further, decreasing their freedom of that did not respect the rules.[4] The letter weakened the Commission and VRTF proposals in terms of the ability of the EU to impinge on the budgetary sovereignty of the member states, urging greater flexibility 'to take account of national budgetary procedures'. However the suspension of voting rights had been proposed by neither the Commission nor the VRTF and was viewed as a hardening of Germany's stance. This interference can be construed as another version of police patrolling over the Commission's and VRTF's activities, carrying with it the implied threat of not passing member state approval should either body deviate too strongly from it.

In September 2010 both Ecofin (Council 2010b, 6) and the European Council (2010c) referenced the European semester and credited the VRTF, even though the proposal originated with the Commission's communication in May. The Commission's proposals were to be released at the end of the month. In anticipation of the reform package that he 'chiefly supports', German Finance Minister Schäuble sent a letter to Van Rompuy and all of the EU finance ministers (i.e., most of the VRTF) in which he went further than the July letter with Lagarde by suggesting that CAP and development funds be suspended in addition to a country's voting rights in the Council. Battle lines were being drawn as Germany, the Netherlands, the UK and the Commission came out in favor of automatic fines as France and Italy advocated for more discretion (Spiegel and Hall 2010).

On 29 September 2010 the Commission reforms on economic governance were released (see Table 1).

Intergovernmental meddling in the economic governance reform proposals reached its apex with the Deauville deal. Lingering differences between France and Germany remained, as Germany supported the idea of automatic sanctions under the SGP and the excessive imbalances pro-

Table 1. The Commission's six-pack proposals

Proposals related to fiscal policy	Proposals related to macroeconomic imbalances

COM (2010) 526 final
  Regulation amending 1466/97, OLP Introducing 'prudent fiscal policy-making' in monitoring public finances with the Commission able to give a warning in case of a significant deviation
	COM (2010) 527 final
	  New regulation, OLP Creating excessive imbalances procedure (EIP) to prevent and correct macroeconomic imbalances

COM (201) 522 final
  Regulation amending 1467/97, consultation with ECB Placing debt levels on equal footing with deficits in triggering the corrective arm of the Stability and Growth Pact
	COM (2010) 525 final
	  New regulation, OLP Enforce EIP based on a reverse qualified majority vote of Eurozone members

COM (2010) 524 final New regulation, OLP Giving financial sanctions for the SGP with a reverse voting mechanism to guarantee better enforcement	
COM (2010) 523 final Directive giving minimum requirements for national budgetary frameworks, consultation	

Source: European Commission (2010c).

cedure against French resistance (Peel *et al.* 2010). On 18 October Merkel agreed to Sarkozy's request to place sanctioning to a Council vote (under QMV) rather than having it occur automatically. In exchange, Sarkozy agreed to a treaty change that would strip rule-breaking states of their voting rights as well as establish a permanent crisis mechanism to replace the EFSF once its operations ended in 2013.[5] The Deauville deal was roundly criticized by member states that were excluded from the 'Merkozy' agreement. One source complained of the sidelining of the Commission: 'we find it very questionable to put this possibility totally to Mr Van Rompuy... what's the future of the community method?' (Peel *et al.* 2010). After Deauville, the VRTF met one last time. As expected, German representative Jörg Asmussen changed his position regarding automatic sanctions, in line with the agreement made by Merkel and Sarkozy (Chaffin and Spiegel & B. Hall. 2010). However the recommendations issued by the VRTF on 18 October 2010 still included the automatic sanctioning that required a qualified majority vote against it to stop the procedure (see Table 2). In addition, the VRTF proposals included a crisis resolution mechanism and the creation of an independent institution that could assess domestic fiscal policies.

The European Council endorsed the Task Force's report and advocated that a 'fast track' approach be taken so that an agreement could be reached 'by summer 2011 on the Commission's legislative proposals, noting that the Task Force report does not cover all issues addressed in these proposals and vice versa' (European Council 2010d). Subsequent European Council conclusions, however, credited the VRTF with authorship of the economic governance reforms, rather than the Commission (European Council 2010d, e).

In summary, the proposals of the VRTF and the European Commission contained many of the same elements. The idea of strengthening the SGP by making building up the importance of the debt criterion and giving the sanctioning process more automaticity appeared in both, as did measures relating to macroeconomic surveillance, incorporating European fiscal rules into national legislation, and the creation of a European semester. Although the reverse qualified majority was not part of the Deauville agreement, the idea of greater automaticity appealed to an important contingent of national governments, including Germany. Principal–agent theory acknowledges the greater likelihood of agency slack when the principals (in this instance, the member states) are divided. Nevertheless the Commission proposals (the ones officially submitted to the Parliament for legislation) still had to meet the approval of the Council and the European Parliament. From the perspective of policy output, the addition of the VRTF as a police patrol did not seem to substantially change the Commission proposals, particularly in light of the attempt to constrain them after the Deauville deal. From the standpoint of policy process, however, the Commission had been marginalized in an area over which it had previously enjoyed a stronger agenda-setting role.

Table 2. Summary of the Van Rompuy Task Force proposals on economic governance

Proposals related to fiscal policy	Proposals related to macroeconomic surveillance	Proposals related to economic coordination	Proposals related to crisis management	Proposals related to stronger institutions
More financial and political sanctions in the SGP	Early warning system that would detect real estate bubbles and strong divergences in competitiveness	European Semester	Create a credible crisis resolution mechanism for the euro area in the medium term	Set up national-level institutions that would give independent analysis of domestic finances
Greater focus on the debt criterion Sanctions activated earlier				

Bringing Back Intergovernmentalism: The Treaty on Stability, Coordination and Governance

For four out of the six legislative proposals in the six-pack, the European Parliament had co-decision. Sharon Bowles, Chair of the Economic and Monetary Affairs Committee, argued that 'two are not co-decision but we are in the position to sell this to the Council as a package… they need to negotiate with us on the package as a whole'.[6] Principal–agent theory has been less successful at explaining the delegation power enjoyed by the European Parliament (Pollack 2003, 9), as the reasons for delegation differ (democratic legitimacy instead of credibility). Nevertheless the challenges faced by the member states as principals (whether in the European Council formation or through national representatives) in preventing shirking and deviations from its preferences (individually or collectively) remain. The strides made by the Parliament despite the protests of some of the member states can help explain why such institutions were bypassed for the subsequent round of institutionalization of fiscal policy coordination, the TSCG.

On 19 April 2011 the Parliament responded to the six-pack with over 2000 amendments. The automaticity of the sanctions against profligate states remained the most divisive issue between the member states and the Parliament, as certain member states supported the status quo of sanctions remaining a political decision. Nevertheless, states like the Netherlands openly supported the Parliament's position, as did the president of the European Central Bank (Chaffin 2011).

In advance of the European Council's June summit, the European Parliament adopted its official position.[7] The most important categories that emerged from the vote related to sanctioning, transparency and legal codification. On sanctioning, the Parliament agreed to use reverse qualified majority voting so that warnings and sanctions are less prone to political interference, particularly when a government does not rectify macroeconomic imbalances; member states paying an interest bearing deposit sanction of 0.1 per cent GDP for not correcting macroeconomic imbalances; and the introduction of a fine of 0.5 per cent GDP for fraudulent deficit and debt statistics. On transparency, more texts would be made public, and both the European and national parliaments would ensure that national governments were held accountable; statistical bodies would be more independent; and the Commission would have more power when it comes to garnering information in its surveillance of member state finances. Legal codification included incorporating the European semester into legal text. The Parliament's documents contained a clause that 'reduces the power of the Deauville deal coined by France and Germany to keep a firm grip on Commission assessments of non-compliance'.[8]

These disagreements prevented an agreement from being reached by June 2011, the Council's original objective. The two main issues were the Council's refusal to accept the reversed qualified majority system in the preventive arm of the SGP and the symmetry principle in the macroeconomic imbalances procedure that would have made both deficit and surplus countries subject to censure (Goulard 2011). On the other hand, the member states had made some concessions, including supporting the Parliament's proposal to sanction countries submitting false economic data. Member states also acquiesced to the Parliament's insistence that sanctioning for noncompliance begin earlier: member states that do not implement required economic reforms would need to pay a preliminary penalty into an interest-bearing account prior to being fined. Remaining controversies included the level of automaticity of sanctioning as well as the Parliament's desire to have the right to summon noncompliant governments before a parliamentary committee (Spiegel *et al.* 2011a).

As negotiations between the Parliament and Council continued, further plans for economic governance were being made by France and Germany. In July 2011 a letter from Merkel and Sarkozy that was addressed to Herman Van Rompuy stated that the Eurozone summits (of heads of state and governments) provided 'the cornerstone of the enhanced economic governance of the euro area',[9] voicing the primacy of the principals/member states. The same letter outlined other objectives for euro area governance reform, including 'all member states of the euro area will incorporate a balanced budget fiscal rule into their national legislation by summer 2012'. The *Financial Times* noted the 'seemingly anti-Commission tenor of the plan' (Spiegel *et al.* 2011b). German representatives indicated the desire to strengthen intergovernmental elements by providing Van Rompuy with a new secretariat in his capacity of leader of the Euro Summits and a reinforcement of the Eurogroup's activities. Moreover the EFSF/ESM would be 'equipped with new analytical capacities... to complement the analysis and recommendations provided by the European Commission, the European Central Bank, and the International Monetary Fund'.[10] The institutional capacity of the intergovernmental institutions of European economic governance continued to be augmented as the

Parliament fought for the strengthening of community institutions like the Commission in the six-pack.

Thus among the most significant changes in the final proposal were:[11]

- The inclusion of the European semester into legal texts, giving 'the procedure more weight much more weight and bite'.
- Granting more powers to the Commission, which can request more information than envisaged in the original proposals and conduct spot checks on member states.
- A new fine (0.2 per cent GDP) for Eurozone members giving fraudulent data.
- A sanction of 0.1 per cent GDP in form of an interest-bearing deposit for Eurozone countries that to not implement recommendations to rectify a macroeconomic imbalance.
- Safeguarding social bargaining processes and wage setting agreements when delivering recommendations.
- Public hearings of finance ministers in front of the European Parliament 'to participate in an exchange of views'.
- Surveillance of macroeconomic imbalances for deficit and surplus countries, which would allow the Commission to give early warnings to member states in danger of creating asset bubbles[12] and investigate surplus countries.

Greater automaticity was introduced for Commission recommendations. If the Council does not adopt a Commission recommendation (or does not vote on it), after one month the Commission can put forward the same decision again and it would be adopted automatically unless a majority of euro area countries reject it within 10 days (and the vote of the member state concerned would not count). Thus the Commission could demand that the member state take specific actions as well as levy sanctions, which can only be overturned by a qualified majority vote in the Council.[13] The Haglund report noted that 'reversed qualified majority voting in the Council should be used wherever possible under the TFEU'.[14]

Before the six-pack even went into force in December 2011, EU leaders made plans for a 'fiscal compact' to 'build on and enhance' the six-pack measures that strengthen the SGP and economic policy coordination (Euro Area 2011). The Treaty on Stability, Coordination and Governance in the Economic and Monetary Union includes the following measures:

- Balanced or in surplus government budgets, with an annual structural deficit below 0.5 per cent of nominal GDP.
- Introduction of the aforementioned into national legal systems.
- The Commission creating a calendar of convergence for member states on reaching their reference level.
- Countries under the EDP give the Council and the Commission an 'economic partnership programme' that includes structural reforms. The Council and Commission endorse the plan and then monitor its implementation.

- National debt issuance of member states reported by member states *ex ante*.
- Reinforced EDP with 'automatic consequences' for breaches of 3 per cent unless a reversed qualified majority vote in the Council occurs.
- A numerical criterion for debt reduction (1/20 rule) for countries exceeding 60 per cent.

The UK and the Czech Republic declined to participate, making it an intergovernmental treaty with 25 signatories of the EU. The TSCG was seen as a quid pro quo for the early start of the European Stability Mechanism (Peel 2012), as ECB President Mario Draghi had implied that greater ECB assistance would need to be accompanied by 'new fiscal compact' in a speech to the European Parliament in November 2011 (Draghi 2011).

There are a number of issues with the fiscal compact that have generated controversy, first and foremost that it takes place outside of the framework of the existing treaties. The original cause was the refusal of the UK to sign on to the pact. The European Parliament has been particularly vocal in its objections to the treaty that marginalizes the Parliament to introduce measures that could have been written into existing legislation (Quatremer 2012). Moreover, the very necessity of the treaty has been questioned, as it 'provides little enhancement with respect to the Stability and Growth Pact and includes measures that are either too vague or likely to be ineffective. It also fails to address the current crisis' (Marcellino 2012). The six-pack had gone a considerable way in delegating further authority to European institutions, and the TSCG continued to do so. Nevertheless the policy outcome of greater delegation belies the extent to which the policy process increasingly moved away from the Community method and towards a Union method. This raises questions on the need for delegation in order to bolster policy credibility, going against some of the expectations of principal–agent theory on credibility (though not on legitimacy).

Conclusion

Weary of ceding further sovereignty to the EU after giving up national currencies and monetary policy under EMU, economic integration proceeded at a slow pace until the sovereign debt crisis demanded that that the EU take action. However the EU still lacked a clear blueprint on the way forward. The six-pack proposals on economic reform were decided upon under the Community method. According to principal–agent theory, this gave the supranational institutions the chance to pursue their own interests and institutionalize their influence in the evolving system of economic governance.

But the potential for agency slack was thwarted by the use of police patrols by the member states. Public letters with instructions for those constructing the legislation were continually used. In addition, more extreme versions were introduced with task force and an intergovernmental treaty to re-intergovernmentalize legislation that could have been done within the context of the existing treaties and the community method. In an address in Toulon, Sarkozy (2011) talked of the need to rebuild Europe, rejecting one based on 'supranationalism... and old quarrels between partisans of a Europe of nations and a federal Europe'. Instead European integration would occur through intergovernmentalism.

While recourse to a Union method may be necessary and appropriate for new mechanisms and instruments like the ESM or policies that had previously fallen under the open method of coordination, the re-intergovernmentalization of policies that fall under the existing treaties is a separate issue. One could argue that new Union-method instruments are necessary and even desirable in the absence of a consensus and a legal basis for further action. This questions previous assumptions on the need for delegation in order to achieve better policy outcomes. Moreover the fact that the policy outcomes of the six-pack and TSCG resulted in a strengthening of cooperation (and even of supranational institutions) seems to indicate that the policy process is a secondary concern for the principals. A useful avenue for further research would be the reasons for this, which would likely point to the domestic politics of the member states, particularly Germany.

Undercutting legislation that does fall under the community method, however is pernicious and destructive to European cooperation more broadly. It undercuts the achievements already made under the community method and threatens to allow the EU to take a step backwards from a highly developed institution that goes far beyond what most international organizations can accomplish. In the short-run, the re-intergovernmentalization of policy makes the policy itself less credible if it is prone to meddling and political manipulation (which intergovernmental policies have tended to be, though they were not in the fiscal policy coordination reforms). It also diverts scarce resources, as government representatives (particularly heads of state and government) take on tasks that had previously been done by more specialized actors, thus compromising some of the credibility and efficiency that delegation had offered. In the long-run, reverting policies from the community method to the Union method could contribute to the unraveling of both.

Acknowledgements

I would like to thank Alessandro Fusacchia, Gabriel Glöckler, Mitchell Smith and Guntram Wolff for their comments and insights into the policy-making process. I also thank the anonymous reviewer and the participants of the workshop Redefining European Economic Governance held in Bruges for their helpful comments. Finally I thank the College of Europe for its support of this project. All errors remain my own.

Notes

1. For an extended analysis of the six-pack, see Chang (2013).
2. http://www.elysee.fr/president/root/bank_objects/06.05_lettre_franco_allemande.pdf.
3. Interview, Guntram Wolff, Deputy Director, Bruegel (formerly of the European Commission)
4. http://www.minefe.gouv.fr/actus/pdf/100721franco-german.pdf.
5. http://www.elysee.fr/president/root/bank_objects/Franco-german_declaration.pdf.
6. http://www.europarl.europa.eu/pdfs/news/public/focus/20110429FCS18371/20110429FCS18371_en.pdf.

7. http://www.europarl.europa.eu/pdfs/news/public/focus/20110429FCS18371/20110429FCS18371_en.pdf.
8. http://www.europarl.europa.eu/news/en/pressroom/content/20110622IPR22350/html/Economic-governance-Parliament-seals-its-position-ahead-of-European-Council.
9. http://media.ft.com/cms/1e93f294-c8df-11e0-a2c8-00144feabdc0.pdf.
10. http://www.bundesregierung.de/Content/EN/_Anlagen/2011-08-17-dt-franz-brief-eng.pdf?__blob=publicationFile.
11. http://www.europarl.europa.eu/news/en/headlines/content/20110429FCS18371/1/html/Parliament-gives-green-light-to-future-economic-governance-plans; http://www.europarl.europa.eu/pdfs/news/expert/background/20110920BKG27073/20110920BKG27073_en.pdf.
12. http://www.ft.com/cms/s/0/9ba25e22-e9c0-11e0-bb3e-00144feab49a.html#ixzz1mOUOPt2A.
13. http://www.europarl.europa.eu/pdfs/news/expert/background/20110920BKG27073/20110920BKG27073_en.pdf.
14. http://www.europarl.europa.eu/sides/getDoc.do?pubRef=-//EP//NONSGML+REPORT+A7-2011-0182+0+DOC+PDF+V0//EN.

References

Chaffin, J. 2011. Pillar of EU economic reform faces collapse. *Financial Times*, 16 June. http://www.ft.com/intl/cms/s/0/70a93d66-983b-11e0-ae45-00144feab49a.html (accessed on 16 March 2013).

Chaffin, J., and P. Spiegel. 2010. Franco–German bail-out pact divides EU. *Financial Times*, 24 October. http://www.ft.com/intl/cms/s/0/56984290-df96-11df-bed9-00144feabdc0.html (accessed on 16 March 2013).

Chang, M. 2013. Constructing the Commission's six-pack proposals: political leadership thwarted? In *The European Commission in the post-Lisbon era of crises: between political leadership and policy management*, eds. M. Chang and J. Monar, 15–21. Brussels: Peter Lang.

Chang, M., and J. Monar. 2013. *The European Commission in the post-Lisbon era of crises: between political leadership and policy management*. Brussels: Peter Lang.

Council of Economic and Financial Affairs (Ecofin). 2010a. Press release 10689/10, 8 June.

Council of Economic and Financial Affairs (Ecofin). 2010b. Press release 13161/10, 7 September.

Cukierman, A. 1992. *Central bank strategy, credibility and independence*. Cambridge, MA: MIT Press.

Draghi, M. 2011. Hearing before the plenary of the European Parliament on the occasion of the adoption of the resolution on the ECB's 2010 annual report, 1 December.

Dür, A., and M. Elsig. 2011. Principals, agents, and the European Union's foreign economic policies. *Journal of European Public Policy* 18, no. 3: 323–38.

Euro Area Heads of State and Government. 2011. Statement on a reinforced architecture for economic and monetary union, 9 December, www.consilium.europa.eu/uedocs/cms_data/docs/pressdata/en/ec/126658.pdf (accessed 16 March 2013).

European Commission. 2010a. Communication on reinforcing economic policy cooperation, 12 May, COM (2010) 250.

European Commission. 2010b. Communication on enhancing economic policy coordination for stability, growth and jobs and tools for stronger EU economic governance, 30 June, COM (2010) 367/2.

European Commission. 2010c. Press release IP/10/1199, EU economic governance: the Commission delivers a comprehensive package of legislative measures, Brussels, 29 September.

European Council. 2010a. Conclusions. EUCO 7/10. 25–26 March.

European Council. 2010b. Conclusions, 17 June.

European Council. 2010c. Conclusions, 16 September.

European Council. 2010d. Conclusions, 28–29 October.

European Council. 2010e. Conclusions, 16–17 December.

Goulard, S. 2011. The economic governance 'package', http://sylvie-goulard.eu/articles2011/230611-presentation-paquet-EN.pdf (accessed 16 March 2013).

Heipertz, M., and A. Verdun. 2010. *Ruling Europe: theory and politics of the stability and growth pact*. Cambridge: Cambridge University Press.

Hodson, D. 2009. Reforming EU economic governance: a view from (and on) the principal–agent approach. *Comparative European Politics* 7, 4: 455–75.

Kiewiet, D.R., and M. McCubbins. 1991. *The logic of delegation: congressional parties and the appropriations process*. Chicago: University of Chicago Press.

Leipold, A. 2010. Good governance for the euro area: proposals for economic stability. *The Lisbon Council E-Brief* (8).

Ludlow, P. 1982. *The making of the European monetary system*. London: Butterworth Scientific.

Marcellino, M. 2012. Why we don't need the new fiscal treaty. *Eurointelligence.com*, http://www.eurointelligence.com/eurointelligence-news/comment/singleview/article/why-we-dont-need-the-new-fiscal-treaty.html (accessed 16 March 2013).

Merkel, A. 2010. Speech given at the opening ceremony of the 61st academic year of the College of Europe in Bruges on 2 November, www.bruessel.diplo.de/contentblob/2959854/Daten/945677/DD_RedeMerkelEuropakollegEN.pdf (accessed 16 March 2013).

Nielson, D., and M. Tierney. 2003. Delegation to international organizations: agency theory and World Bank environmental reform. *International organization* 57, no. 2: 241–76.

Nugent, N. 2000. *The European Commission*. Basingstoke: Palgrave Macmillan.

Peel, Q. 2012. Germany and Europe: a very federal formula. *Financial Times*, 9 February. http://www.ft.com/intl/cms/s/0/31519b4a-5307-11e1-950d-00144feabdc0.html (accessed 16 March 2013).

Peel, Q., G. Parker, J. Chaffin, and B. Hall. 2010. Germany confident of 'crisis resolution' deal. *Financial Times*, 19 October. http://www.ft.com/intl/cms/s/0/6816b234-db6f-11df-ae99-00144feabdc0.html (accessed 16 March 2013).

Pollack, M. 2003. *The engines of European integration: delegation, agency and agenda setting in the EU*. New York: Oxford University Press.

Puetter, U. 2012. Europe's deliberative intergovernmentalism: the role of the Council and European Council in EU economic governance. *Journal of European Public Policy* 19, no. 2: 161–78.

Quatremer, J. 2012. Cohn-Bendit: L'Europe négocie un traité dont elle n'a pas besoin. *La Libération*, 23 January. http://www.liberation.fr/economie/01012385071-l-europe-negocie-un-traite-dont-elle-n-a-pas-besoin (accessed 16 March 2013).

Sarkozy, N. 2011. Discours à Toulon, 1 December. Speech available on http://www.youtube.com/watch?v=GbKV5MItfqU (accessed 16 March 2013).

Spiegel, P., and B. Hall. 2010. Germany backs tough EU deficit rules. *Financial Times*, 26 September. http://www.ft.com/intl/cms/s/0/ff448198-c992-11df-b3d6-00144feab49a.html. Accessed 16 March 2013

Spiegel, P., J. Chaffin, A. Barker, and J. Fontanella-Khan. 2011a. Do or die time for the Hungarian presidency. *Financial Times*, 10 June. http://blogs.ft.com/brusselsblog/2011/06/do-or-die-time-for-the-hungarian-presidency/ (accessed 16 March 2013).

Spiegel, P., J. Chaffin, A. Barker, and J. Fontanella-Khan. 2011b. Is the Sarko–Merkel plan anti-Commission? *Financial Times*, 18 August. http://blogs.ft.com/brusselsblog/2011/08/is-the-sarko-merkel-plan-anti-commission/ (accessed 16 March 2013).

Temple Lang, J., and E. Gallagher. 2005. The Commission, the 'Community method' and the smaller member states. *Fordham International Law Journal* 29, no. 5: 1009–33.

Van Rompuy, H. 2010. Remarks following the first meeting of the task force on economic governance, 21 May, PCE 102/10.

Warleigh-Lack, A., and R. Drachenberg. 2010. Policy-making in the European Union. In *European Union politics*, eds. M. Cini and N. Borragan, 209–24. Oxford: Oxford University Press.

The Politics of Risk-sharing: Fiscal Federalism and the Greek Debt Crisis

NIKOLAOS ZAHARIADIS

Department of Government 410 HHB, South University of Alabama at Birmingham, Birmingham, USA

ABSTRACT Focusing on the ability of financial markets to discipline state economic performance, EU fiscal federalism specifies three conditions that need to be met for it to work effectively: clear market signals, no bailout, and corrective action driven by central rules and implemented by domestic populations. While some conditions have obviously not been met in the European response to the Greek sovereign debt crisis (2009–2012), evidence suggests the explanatory power of fiscal federalism is surprisingly robust. The study raises concerns with risk-sharing in EU economic governance and has implications for theories of EU institution-building.

'If a crisis emerges in one country, there is a solution… Don't fear for this moment—we are equipped politically, intellectually and economically to face this crisis scenario', declared Commissioner Joaquin Almunia in March 2009 responding to talk of an impending crisis in the eurozone (quoted in Manolopoulos 2011, 220). Upon winning Greek elections seven months later, Prime Minister George Papandreou informed stunned Greek voters that the government's budget was in far worse shape than everyone was led to believe, but the government had the resources and a plan to deal with it. We now know there were neither resources nor rescue plan in Greece or the European Union (EU).

This contribution assesses the effects of the EU's structure of economic governance on the European response to the Greek sovereign debt crisis (2009–2012). Economic governance here is limited to a framework (philosophy and architecture) for the conduct of macroeconomic policy (Begg 2008, 5). Fiscal federalism is the particular institutional expression of EU economic governance, which uses financial market pressure to discipline state performance under specific conditions (Hallerberg 2011). The conditions stress clear market signals, no obligation to bailout member states, and responsive corrective mechanisms. Hallerberg argues the crisis occurred because the conditions were not met, but I demonstrate fiscal federalism as practiced in Europe is a more robust explanation; the crisis persists because some of the conditions are actually met.

Examining the Greek crisis (2009–2012) is important because Greece is one of the triggers to Europe's financial crisis. It demonstrates in most vivid terms that budget decisions in a smaller euro zone economy have implications for all eurozone countries. Although it is not the only country being bailed out, it is an important barometer about the do's and don'ts of bailouts. Being part of the eurozone it represents a possible future for some countries, such as Spain, Italy, Germany, US, and France, whose leaders have openly implored their citizens to accept reforms and avoid promises that would give them 'a one-way ticket to Greece' (Erlanger 2012; Kounalaki 2012). In this sense, Greece serves as the catalyst to expose some institutional weaknesses in European economic governance. At the same time, fiscal federalism is useful because a single framework aids in diagnosing the crisis and illuminating the European predicament. As practiced, EU fiscal federalism paints a zero-sum narrative. It institutionalizes collective responsibility and also provides incentives that decrease the likelihood of national fiscal accountability. Institutional efforts to recalibrate the balance risk undermining collective solidarity.

Fiscal Federalism and Risk Management

Economic and Monetary Union (EMU) is a risk-sharing system in the sense that the likelihood of economic catastrophe in the system is lower relative to that in any one country. Hence premiums to finance economic growth should be lower and the volume of finance higher than otherwise. However, risk-sharing necessitates a pattern of actor behavior that minimizes risk individually and collectively.

Fiscal Federalism and Market Discipline

As long as governments have to finance their deficits in the open market, they need to contend with the risk of borrowing at increasingly higher premiums. When EU governments decided to share macroeconomic and monetary policies through EMU, they accepted the inevitability of sharing this type of risk. However, information and behavioral asymmetries necessitated the construction of institutions that would provide incentives to mitigate national risk and avoid the free-rider problem. In cases where risk is pooled, individual governments might be tempted to behave irresponsibly. The marginal cost of irresponsibility is not borne by the irresponsible party but rather is shared among all members of EMU, raising premiums for all by a little rather than for one by a lot. Under what conditions and institutional arrangements can markets impose fiscal discipline in a monetary union?

Hallerberg (2011) identifies three important conditions for market discipline to work under EU's fiscal federalism. He argues the sovereign debt crisis occurred because the conditions were not met and suggests alternatives that may guide the EU response. I provide evidence which shows he understates his case. The explanatory power of fiscal federalism is quite robust. While some of the conditions were clearly not met, the EU's response has been guided to a surprising extent by the principles of fiscal federalism.

First, markets need to have accurate and timely information about state finances. Information needs to be clear and independently gathered. In this way, national authorities may claim ownership of the targets and credibility of signals. This is very important because once governments politically negotiate caps in budget deficits they have an incentive to cheat. Enjoying a monopoly in collecting and processing information, they have incentives to send signals that do not raise concerns. This is the role played by bond markets. The latter provide continuous and easily accessible information about state finances. When states run high budget deficits or exceed previously agreed upon targets, markets react by making it more expensive for governments to borrow; premiums on government bonds rise to more accurately reflect the increased risk of investing in government bonds. Stability and Growth Pact (SGP) targets of no more than 3 per cent government deficit and no more than 60 per cent public debts are supposed to provide clear benchmarks for markets, governments, and populations to trigger fiscal discipline. Of course pooling risk also assumes a relative symmetry of shocks, a condition that does not quite describe EMU (Wyplosz 2006). Nevertheless, clear and timely signals about finances are essential.

Second, valuation needs to accurately reflect the market's assessment of the sustainability of state finances. The essence of this condition refers to pre-specified monitoring and corrective mechanisms, such as fiscal punishment. Compliance is publicly assessed by the Commission and enforced by the Council. If governments are found to be in violation of agreed targets, they must submit plans that contain credible commitments to correct imbalances. What happens if governments do not comply? The newly enacted Fiscal Compact calls for a two-stage approach which uses reverse qualified majority unlike the previous excessive deficit procedure, i.e., sanctions are automatic unless members in the Council reverse the decision by qualified majority.

- An interest-bearing deposit can be imposed after one failure to comply with the recommended corrective action
- After a second compliance failure, this interest-bearing deposit can be converted into a fine (up to 0.1 per cent of GDP). Sanctions

can also be imposed for failing twice to submit a sufficient corrective action plan.

Embedded in this condition is the problem of moral hazard. The system contains incentives for governments to cheat unless market discipline is strictly enforced. How can markets value accurately the probability of default? How credible is this probability when talking about sovereign EU members? The more countries are insured against sovereign default through a risk-sharing scheme such as EMU, the less incentive they have to maximize growth and the more risks they will individually take (Persson and Tabellini 1996). EMU designers understood this problem and attempted to solve it by including a 'no-obligation-for-transfers' clause in the Treaty (article 125 of the Treaty on the Functioning of the European Union). Valuation of state finances was also based on future (in)ability of states to finance debt on a mark-to-market basis (with some reasonable assumptions about available liquidity). Examples from nineteenth century American federalism show when the central government refuses to bailout profligate sub-national governments, the pain caused by the economic recession led state populations to demand balanced budgets and better handling of state finances (Wibbels 2003).

Paradoxically, the political nature and endogeneity of risk may also increase the probability of a rescue under the threat of contagion. The eurozone is a system where monetary institutions are strongly and tightly connected to each other. There is significant transfer of capital across national borders, making financial systems highly interdependent and vulnerable to local disturbances. Indeed, when the British and later Irish government decided to take over their failing banks, other eurozone governments speedily moved to support their own systems largely to avoid negative spillovers of capital from financial institutions subject to a variety of risks in their territories to risk-free British and Irish institutions where deposits were now guaranteed by taxpayers (Quaglia 2009; European Commission 2009, 62). Risk endogeneity accelerates the downward spiral (Dowd 2009, 161). When asset prices begin to fall and trader positions reach their limits, most risk management strategies call for traders to sell. Sales exacerbate the situation leading to more sales, which cause asset prices to plummet closing the loop. Institutional attempts to limit endogeneity through coordination (Torres, this volume) may also have the opposite effect by tightening structural links among risky investments.

Third, national populations need to interpret market discipline as a signal about their governments' competence, punishing those that face market pressure. This is because systemic shocks are likely in a system where national policies are not entirely verifiable (Persson and Tabellini 1996). In order to do so, populations must be informed and accept centrally defined fiscal rules. Indicators of SGP surveillance are centrally monitored and publicized but individual budgets and sanctions are politically determined. Until the Fiscal Compact, the Commission monitored and recommended, but the Council decided on when the rules are broken and what needs to be done about it. In essence, the 'no transfers union' clause legitimates this paradox. As former German Chancellor Schröder aptly argues:

'[national] decision-making authority in... budget policy [is] the compensation for giving up sovereignty in monetary policy' (Marsh 2011, 286). It is politically palatable and reassuring to weary taxpayers of creditor countries. By definition a crisis implies individual countries have exceeded their resources in terms of meeting the needs of their populations created by a damaging event. This condition enables mobilization of resources across jurisdictional levels.[1]

Publication of compliance at regular intervals is important to voters. A publicly available scorecard will inform domestic populations as well as EU allies about progress, as the newly enacted Macroeconomic Imbalance Procedure demonstrates. The idea is to provide incentives for voters to check on national governments and other EU allies through public and politically independent means and if need be, punish those policy-makers or governments who cheat. If governments do not comply with signals, voter well-being is reduced by higher premiums on debt. Policy-makers are assumed to be motivated by re-election and voters are assumed to be guided by rewarding (or punishing) those who most increase (or decrease) their economic welfare (Hallerberg 2011).

The process works in the form of a two-stage feedback loop with clear goals and reasonable lag between feedback and response (Deutsch 1966, 189). Markets send a signal that some governments do not comply with the fiscal targets specified in EMU. Populations receive this signal and demand their government correct imbalances. If not, populations use the democratic vote to punish those policy-makers or governments who do not comply.

In short, the fiscal federalist approach spelled out in Hallerberg (2011) yields three expectations. States will meet their fiscal targets *via* market discipline if there is clear and timely information, if no bailout is expected, and if corrective action is guided by pre-specified central rules and enforced by domestic populations. Expectations are probed in three areas: the perceived causes of the Greek crisis, the first bailout, and the design and political repercussions of the second bailout plan. The first probes the expectation of clear and timely signals. The second assesses the question of moral hazard. The third examines the logic of corrective mechanisms and the role of domestic populations.

What Kind of Crisis Is It?

The fiscal federalist approach expects accurate and timely market signals. Evidence suggests some signals were clear and timely but others were missed. Although viewed with alarm in private, international institutions and the Greek government downplayed the risk of economic collapse. It was feared the cost of major reform might destabilize the country's fragile economy and combined with the adverse economic climate at the time might precipitate the very disaster they were trying to avoid. In March 2009 the Commission publicly censured Greece for excessive deficit in 2007 but still noted the country's past strong economic growth (Manolopoulos 2011, 138). Greece's vulnerable fiscal position was stressed with alarm in the International Monetary Fund's (IMF) early warning exercise and the 2009 country report, but the conservative government at the time ignored the recommendations for painful reforms partly because of its one-seat majority in parliament and the opposition's negative response (Ellis 2011). The issue would be settled in the general elections scheduled for October 2009. At the same time, the Greek government continued to borrow heavily to cover its yawning current account deficit while engaging in costly populist measures such as the buyback of old cars at significantly subsidized discounts.

Greece was running a combination of higher budget deficits and accumulated public debt than other eurozone members (see Fig. 1). Theodore Pagkalos, the government's vice-premier, admitted in a TV interview this was the cause of the crisis (New Folders 2011). But that was not the whole story because the deficit did not increase appreciably since Greece's entry in the eurozone in 2001 except for 2009. Besides, other eurozone countries, such as Ireland and Portugal, were running similarly high deficits but they had lower public debt ratios.[2] There was more to it than

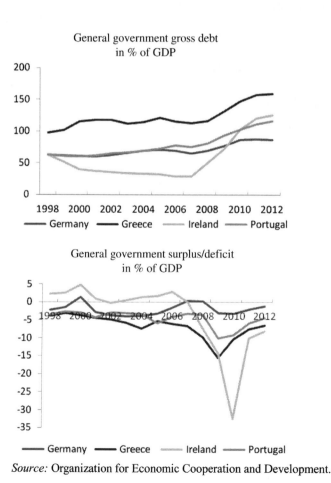

Source: Organization for Economic Cooperation and Development.

Figure 1. General government gross debt in % of GDP

that. Prime Minister Papandreou initially blamed currency speculators. In a speech to the Brookings Institution he said:

> We will have a very hard time implementing our reform program if the gains from our austerity measures are swallowed up by prohibitive interest rates… If Europe and America jointly step in to shore up global financial regulation—and to finally ensure enforcement of regulations—we can curtail such activities. (Davis 2010)

But it was clear from the increasing bond spreads speculators were betting Greece underestimated its problems and overestimated the EU's willingness to rescue the Greek economy. Currency speculation exacerbated the crisis (the euro reached unprecedented heights relative to major currencies by October 2009), but it is implausible that CDS speculation on such a small fraction of Greek debt ($9 billion as of March 2010) could influence bond rates for the remainder. It is more likely that investor appetite for risky credit vehicles and falling liquidity diminished substantially since the emergence of the global financial crisis in 2008. As investors pulled their money to safer investments, bond and CDS spreads temporarily soared in late 2008 (following the collapse of Lehman Brothers) in Greece and climbed again since late 2009 (Fontana and Scheicher 2010, 29).

Still, there are two other culprits, neither of which was monitored by SGP rules at the time: rising externally held debt and private indebtedness. In other words, the signals were there but no one was paying attention. Data from the Bank of Greece show that in 1994 roughly 85 per cent of Greek public debt was held by domestic investors (banks, insurance and pension funds, and others) (Manolopoulos 2011, 114). By 2009 debt holdings completely reversed with almost 82.5 per cent held by foreign investors, 93.5 per cent of which were claims by European banks. The difference between domestically and externally held debt is significant. Domestically held public debt can be recycled back into the economy because repayment and interest stay within national borders. Externally held debt essentially gives away future income to support today's standard of living. At the end of 2011, the country's gross external debt (public and private sectors) was estimated to be 192.2 per cent of GDP with a gross external financing need of 111.2 per cent (IMF 2012, 74, 97). Fig. 2 goes one step further to show the composition of the externally held debt by country and sector. Only two sources, France and Germany, own 41 per cent of the external debt, concentrating creditor power in the hands of both governments. More importantly, foreign claims on the Greek non-bank private sector are more than 50 per cent of the total, implying the private sector may be in worse shape than the public sector.

Figure 3 confirms this claim. Indebtedness in Greek households has gone up significantly in the last 15 years. Financial liabilities in households stood at 14.1 per cent of GDP in 1998. By 2001, the year Greece entered the eurozone, they rose to 23.4 per cent. By 2010 the figure reached 65.8 per cent of GDP. This increase is due to financial liberalization in the

Notes: (1) ultimate risk basis.
Source: Bank of International Settlements.

Figure 2. Foreign claims on Greek debt[1] (December 2010)

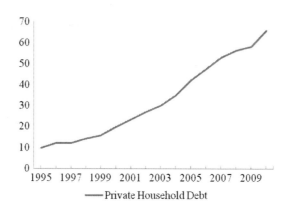

Figure 3. Greek household debt as% of GDP

1990s and monetary integration; both factors contributed significantly to credit expansion and a sharp fall in private savings. Comparing Figures 1 and 3, we see private household debt increased almost 360 per cent from 1998 to 2010 while public debt rose 'only' by 50 per cent. Simply put, Greeks borrowed heavily, mainly from foreign sources, to finance largely private consumption. SGP surveillance did not monitor these indicators though it does now through the Integrated Economic Policy Guidelines adopted in 2010; neither could the Commission issue an excessive deficit warning. Yet, they appear to be at the heart of Greece's deteriorating economic position.

In the meantime, Greeks were saddled with one more problem: corruption and distrust run rampant in Greek administration. Those two elements affect Greek relations with external actors and between Greek citizens and the state, clouding the wisdom of relying solely on market signals. Former Prime Minister George Papandreou admitted this much: 'We developed a lot of corruption at the highest levels and we did not take the structural measures to change our economy, to move our economy, to make it more competitive' (Elliott 2010). Suspicion over Greek data was heightened in 2004 when the incoming conservative government alerted Eurostat that major defense purchases in the beginning of the decade artificially lowered the budget deficit used to qualify for EMU because they were accounted on the date of delivery rather than purchase (Zahariadis 2013). The incoming Socialists complained similarly in 2009. Government books have since been audited and numbers recalculated with Eurostat finally giving its stamp of approval in 2010. The Commission found severe irregularities in data collection, no respect for accounting rules, lack of coordination between the three responsible bodies—Elstat (the Greek Statistics Office), the General Accounting Office, and the Ministry of Finance—non-transparent or improperly documented bookkeeping by many Greek public institutions, and lack of individual accountability, leaving 'the quality of fiscal statistics subject to political pressures and electoral cycles' (European Commission 2010, 4). Interestingly, in September 2011 members of Elstat accused its director and government officials of artificially inflating the budget deficit in 2009 (which Eurostat approved) to make it look bigger than it otherwise would have been for political gain (Lazaridis 2011)! Market signals just didn't work.

Moral Hazard and the First Bailout

In an insightful essay, Otmar Issing (2010), a former member of the ECB's executive board, argues that a Greek bail-out means the end of the euro because it violates EU treaties and opens the gate for more aid to other members. Fiscal federalism adamantly insists on no bailouts. Monetary union is based on two pillars: stability of the euro guaranteed by an independent European central bank, and fiscal health delivered by individual member states. By accepting the rules of monetary union, member states also accept the consequences. Because EMU does not oblige any sovereign member to bailout others; transferring public funds from those who obeyed the rules to those who didn't 'would create hostility toward Brussels and between euro area countries' (11). To quote Guido Westerwelle, Germany's Foreign Minister, it would be intolerable to 'throw German and EU money out of the window and thereby reduce the pressure on Greece to reform' (Evans-Pritchard 2010).

The argument raises the specter of moral hazard. On the one hand, helping a fellow government in need encourages the same profligate behavior that one is trying to discourage because it minimizes adverse consequences. On the other hand, not helping exacerbates the magnitude of the problem through the risk of contagion (Zahariadis 2012). Fiscal federalism reinforces discipline through market consequences but eurozone members were not prepared to face them. Credibility, and to an extent commitment, were lacking (Schelkle 2006).

Markets were unconvinced Greece could reform on its own. Papandreou then turned to his EU partners for support. Ecofin responded that it was Greece's problem. As Featherstone (2011, 202) observes, 'it required Greece (under Article 126(9)) to cut its deficit and correct its divergences, thereby 'removing the risk of jeopardizing the proper functioning of EMU'. While endorsing the Greek austerity program, political divisions and the lack of details failed to pacify investors. The problem was particularly acute for German Chancellor Angela Merkel, whose Christian Democrats (and her Free Democrat partners) faced tough upcoming state elections. Merkel postponed making a decision on the Greek package for several weeks until panic in financial markets forced her hand. The drawn-out, derisive debate in the German press fuelled speculation that Germany wanted to avoid it all together.

Finally, EU leaders agreed on 25 March on a pledge to provide €25 (later raised to €45) billion to Greece, if needed, *via* bilateral three-year loans from other eurozone member states and the IMF. Papandreou and several EU leaders favored a Europe-only solution, but Germany wanted IMF participation, fearing it would end up footing the bill. IMF involvement amounted to a perceived 'historic' defeat for the euro (Manolopoulos 2011, 225), but the IMF's presence also blocked a challenge in Germany's constitutional court and deflected some blame from the impending pain to the Washington-based 'villain'. EU governments fiercely opposed a central (EU) response fearing political backlash at home. The risk of systemic calamity outweighed the cost of bailout, putting creditors in the uncomfortable position of having to save Greece in order to save their own banks.

Upon witnessing its credit rating reduced to junk status, Greece informed its partners on 23 April 2010 it was activating the rescue package, invoking article 122(2), which allows aid in case of emergency. The Memorandum of Understanding (MoU) involved the gigantic amount of €110 billion over three years (€80 billion in bilateral loans and €30 by the IMF), monitored and disbursed quarterly on the basis of progress on specific indicators assessed by the IMF, the ECB, and the European Commission (the so-called troika). The point was to temporarily help Greece generate primary surplus to meet obligations to external creditors at a reasonable interest rate. In return, Greece agreed to a series of painful measures designed to reduce its public sector, cut salaries and pensions, and increase tax revenues.

The Greek and EU responses clearly defied fiscal federalist predictions. Despite calls for no bailouts, it quickly became apparent the cost of not bailing out Greece outweighed the benefit of sticking to the rules. Because a Greek default would also infect its creditors (largely French, German, and British banks), EU intervention became necessary.

The Second Bailout

Greece implemented some of the MoU reforms but failed to meet the agreed targets. Fiscal federalism calls for domestic populations to punish the non-complying governments in order to maintain economic welfare. Although the evidence is mixed, fiscal federalism receives considerable support.

By early 2011, the government had lost its appetite for reforms for two reasons. First, the issue with the Greek crisis was not so much the design of ineffective solutions as it was the persistent address of the wrong problems. The MoU addressed the problem of contagion by shoring up foreign and Greek creditors. Creditor governments limited the risk of contagion and the Greek government deflected attention from its own inadequacies (Zahariadis 2012). But the government was losing control of implementation as more and more workers went on strike, demanding an end to austerity. Second, the urgency caused by the crisis conflicted with the need for political gain. Greeks were hard pressed by creditors to slash expenditures and shore up revenues. However, electoral concerns impeded the government's ability to deliver on both fronts. Client groups which depend on state handouts or guarantees, such as pharmacists, lawyers, civil engineers, taxi owners and others in closed professions, resisted changes. Figures from the IMF (2012) paint a bleak picture. Real GDP declined more than 20 per cent since 2009 significantly exceeding projections. Despite lower government expenditures—the Greek government actually achieved the highest reduction in general government deficit in the eurozone by 5 per cent of GDP in 2010 for a total of 8.25 per cent of GDP between 2009 and 2011—state revenues collapsed because of lack of political will and strikes by tax collectors. The 10-year bond spread between Greek and German bonds remains at an astronomical 35 per cent, having fallen to 5 per cent in May 2010 and skyrocketed since then (IMF 2012, 56). As a result, the government consistently missed the MoU targets.

To put an effective end to the specter of Greek default, a deal was crafted in July 2011 for a second bailout package. The terms were dictated almost entirely by Greece's private and public debtors. The matter was revisited in the summit of 26–27 October (and put into place in March 2012). Greece would get €130 billion of fresh loans, €30 billion of which would go to prop up domestic Greek banks. While providing additional capital to banks, the agreed 50 per cent haircut on private holders of Greek debt would likely leave insolvent Greek public sector bond holders (such as social insurance funds and municipalities) who already faced both losses on their own funds deposited with the Greek Central Bank and increased demands on their resources due to the economic crisis. Consistent with the fiscal federalist expectation, implementation was centralized according to fiscal rules spelled out in the bailout package. While Greece would retain nominal implementation powers, EU advisors would be dispatched to monitor and assess compliance 'on the ground' (Chaffin and Hope 2011). The Task Force, established in 2011 to provide administrative and technical expertise to Greece, would assess priorities and assist in implementing a restructuring program that invited numerous French, Dutch, and German experts and companies to reform Greek public services and revenue collection (IMF 2012). If all went well, the Greek government would bring its public debt ratio back to the 2009 levels (125 per cent of GDP) by 2021 while generating primary surpluses.

In the meantime, all eurozone governments agreed among others to pass a balanced budget provision by the end of 2012, keep budget deficit and public debt within SGP provisions, subject their annual budgets to scrutiny by the Commission and the Council, and accept stiff penalties by the European Court. The so-called 'Six-Pack' measures aim to ensure fiscal discipline, stabilize the EU economy, and prevent a new crisis. Passed at the insistence of several creditor countries led by Germany, they are so unrealistic that when they entered into force in December 2011, 23 of 27 EU members, Germany included, could not meet them (European Commission 2011). Fiscal federalism appears to have inspired the EU's new institutional architecture but there is a major drawback. Despite efforts to strengthen financial discipline and state performance, the problem of credibility remains. How credible can the sanctions envisioned in the new institutional arrangement be if the overwhelming majority of member states cannot meet their own goals?

The cacophony and hesitation among Europe's politicians have made matters worse, while centralization of powers in Brussels creates a vacuum of democratic accountability, which may undermine the long-term viability of fiscal federalism. The crisis has metastasized to other countries, Spain, Italy, and even France amidst speculation that Greece should be expelled from the eurozone. Charles Dallara, head of Institute of International Finance, the global consortium of banks and investment houses, openly worried about the lack of EU leadership: the euro's successes 'are being masked and undermined by parochialism and nationalism' (Beattie 2011). Prime Minister Papandreou was publicly rebuked by German and French leaders when he put the deal to a Greek referendum. He subsequently resigned demonstrating that democracy in economic governance may be sacrificed in the name of effective centralized response. As Commissioner Olli Rehn readily admits, 'we need leadership... [but] without democratic legitimacy, all the best intentions are doomed to fail' (Spiegel 2011). And yet when Papandreou sought legitimacy through a referendum in November 2011, he was roundly condemned by the same leaders who admit lack of legitimacy.

Two rounds of Greek general elections in May and June 2012 have produced a weak coalition government. Voters punished the two profligate parties ruling Greece since 1974, confirming fiscal federalism's expectations. Moreover, the parties that gained most were indeed those which promised a return to economic well-being, further strengthening the explanation. However, the vote does not appear to be in favor of fiscal discipline by markets in the name of economic prosperity. Quite the contrary, it was a protest vote against economic austerity brought about by fiscal consolidation. Alexis Tsipras (2012), the biggest winner of the elections, rejects austerity as 'suicide' and calls for renegotiation and a new bailout.

Crisis, Response, and Economic Governance

Fiscal federalism has been used to assess fiscal discipline in Europe's economic governance. Signals were unclear, hindering an early and timely diagnosis of the crisis. Despite explicit constitutional prohibition of bailouts, the threat of default was not credible. As a result, market discipline proved inadequate. Nevertheless, evidence from the design and political repercussions of the second bailout corroborates some of fiscal federalism's expectations. Failures have been punished by domestic populations. Implementation rules, timetables, and expectations are increasingly set in Brussels though designed in some national capitals. Despite efforts for more Europe (see Yiangou, O'Keeffe, and Glöckler, this volume), the end result appears to be greater movement toward a more visible form of national involvement. But it's not quite what Puetter (2012) calls deliberative intergovernmentalism. National governments have greater visibility, but deliberation is not among equals. EU response to the crisis has been guided by a curious mix of uploading national preferences to lock in structural inequalities.

The crisis has exposed the weakness of risk-sharing enshrined in EMU (Dyson and Featherstone 1999) and has revived old enmities and suspicions that EMU was supposed to put to rest. Rifts may eventually undermine the neofunctional imperative behind EU integration. The logic of converging expectations underlying neofunctionalism necessitates the launch of treaties that 'appeal to a large enough constituency to establish a converging pattern of support' (Haas 1968, 290). Support is increasingly lacking as investors and many voters throughout the EU remain unconvinced of political talk of economic solidarity. German taxpayers are resentful of being asked to bailout less solvent EU allies to shore up markets which are becoming increasingly marginal to German exports. Anger against austerity dictated from abroad has reached the boiling point in Greece. Similar sentiment, though less intense, exists throughout the EU. As Blyth and Matthijs (2012) boldly claim, 'the structure—twenty-seven radically different member states and no leader—remains the main obstacle'.

Seeking to address the deficiencies of EU's fiscal federalism (clearer signals and corrective measures), the new structure of economic governance raises the visibility of national power but also potentially plants the seed for undermining collective solidarity. Structural economic asymmetries within EMU have left debtor countries—Greece, Ireland, Portugal, Spain, Italy, and now France—struggling with two major problems. First, they have borne the brunt of adjusting to the crisis by implementing major austerity measures amidst tight monetary policy. The response plans have left the 'no-obligation-for transfers' principle intact without making the threat of default any more credible. Tighter integration and more risk-sharing make the next bailout more rather than less plausible because of high opportunity costs. While adherence to this clause in addition to balanced budget rules (despite exceptions contained therein) pacify weary publics in creditor countries, debtors are left with no growth, more long-term pain, and increasingly less popular support. Second, bank bailouts have conveniently been accomplished by blaming only profligate debtors. They deflect attention from private greed and legitimize huge wealth transfers to private investors. For example, Peter Böfinger, an economic advisor to the German government, has admitted billions in eurozone bailouts are going primarily to German banks: 'It is not primarily about the problem countries, but our own banks, which are heavily involved with loans there' (Schultz and Wittrock 2011). Taxpayers have been saddled with gargantuan debt: benefits are concentrated largely to banks and other financial institutions but costs are spread throughout the EU.

European leaders throughout the crisis have argued the euro will survive because there is considerable political will to do so. This is probably true, but the economic misery and political uncertainty increasingly engulfing the eurozone beg the question: at what price?

Acknowledgements

The author wishes to thank Michele Chang, the College of Europe, and officers of EUSA's political economy section. Special thanks to participants of the workshop on European Economic Governance organized in Bruges for reminding me how to blend social science and collegiality.

Notes

1. Evidence of the effectiveness of the SGP is generally mixed but positive. Some (e.g., Ioannou and Stracca 2011) find it has not had a statistically significant effect on fiscal improvements of the primary balance (deficit/surplus before interest), but others (e.g., Buiter 2006, 699) argue it has made a contribution to fiscal sustainability but only where its prescriptions were incentive-compatible for the target country.
2. Stein (2011) finds Greece and Portugal suffer from high government debt while Ireland and Spain turned private toxic assets into a government problem. While there may be different causes, it is clear both are now connected.

References

Beattie, A. 2011. Europe's successes undermined by 'parochialism', *Financial Times*, 14 September, http://www.ft.com/intl/cms/s/0/393be280-dedf-11e0-9130-00144feabdc0.html?ftcamp=rss&ftcamp=crm/email/2011915/nbe/BrusselsBrief/product#axzz1dhjJyctT (accessed 14 September 2011).

Begg, I. 2008. *Economic governance in an enlarged euro area, DG for Economic and Financial Affairs Economic Papers 311*. Brussels: European Commission.

Blyth, M., and M. Matthijs. 2012. The world waits for Germany. *Foreign Affairs*, 8 June, http://www.foreignaffairs.com/articles/137697/mark-blyth-and-matthias-matthijs/the-world-waits-for-germany?page=show (accessed 20 June 2012).

Buiter, W.H. 2006. The 'sense and nonsense of Maastricht' revisited: what have we learnt about stabilization in EMU? *Journal of Common Market Studies* 44, no. 4: 687–710.

Chaffin, J., and K. Hope. 2011. Greeks hostile as EU Task Force starts work. *Financial Times*, 31 October, http://www.ft.com/intl/cms/s/0/ec030304-03cd-11e1-bbc5-00144feabdc0.html#axzz1vV79xfUr (accessed 14 December 2011).

Davis, B. 2010. Greece seeks US support for reining in speculation. The Wall Street Journal, 8 March, http://online.wsj.com/article/NA_WSJ_PUB:SB10001424052748704869304575109670804279964.html (accessed 20 March 2010).

Dowd, K. 2009. Moral hazard and the financial crisis. *Cato Journal* 29, no. 1: 141–66.

Dyson, K., and K. Featherstone. 1999. *The road to Maastricht: negotiating economic and monetary union*. Oxford: Oxford University Press.

Elliott, L. 2010. No EU bailout for Greece as PM promises to 'put our house in order'. *The Guardian*, 28 January, http://www.guardian.co.uk/business/2010/jan/28/greece-papandreou-eurozone (accessed 20 March 2010).

Ellis, A. 2011. IMF's warning in 2009 that was ignored by Greece. *Kathimerini*, 7 November, http://www.ekathimerini.gr/4dcgi/_w_articles_politics_100073_07/11/2011_461917 (in Greek) (accessed 14 December 2011).

Erlanger, S. 2012. Sarkozy and his rivals trade attacks as vote nears. *New York Times*, 5 April, http://www.nytimes.com/2012/04/06/world/europe/sarkozy-and-hollande-trade-attacks.html?_r=1&ref=france (accessed 15 June 2012).

European, Commission. 2009. *Economic crisis in Europe: causes, consequences, and responses*, European Economy/7. Luxembourg: Office for Official Publications of the European Communities.

European Commission. 2010. *Report on Greek government deficit and debt statistics*, http://epp.eurostat.ec.europa.eu/cache/ITY_PUBLIC/COM_2010_REPORT_GREEK/EN/COM_2010_REPORT_GREEK-EN.PDF (accessed 20 September 2010).

European Commission. 2011. EU economic governance 'six-pack' enters into force, 12 December, http://europa.eu/rapid/pressReleasesAction.do?reference=MEMO/11/898 (accessed 15 March 2012).

Evans-Pritchard, A. 2010. Europe agrees IMF–EU rescue for Greece. *Daily Telegraph*, 25 March, http://www.telegraph.co.uk/finance/financetopics/financialcrisis/7521433/Europe-agrees-IMF-EU-rescue-for-Greece.html (accessed 25 April 2010).

Featherstone, K. 2011. The Greek sovereign debt crisis and EMU: a failing state in a skewed regime. *Journal of Common Market Studies* 49, no. 2: 193–217.

Fontana, A., and M. Scheicher. 2010. *An analysis of Euro area sovereign CDS and their relation with government bonds*, ECB Working Paper 1271. Frankfurt: European Central Bank.

Haas, E.B. 1968. *The uniting of Europe*. Stanford: Stanford University Press.

Hallerberg, M. 2011. Fiscal federalism reforms in the European Union and the Greek crisis. *European Union Politics* 12, no. 1: 127–42.

International Monetary Fund. 2012. *Greece: request for extended arrangement under the Extended Fund Facility*. Country Report No. 12/57, Washington, DC: IMF.

Ioannou, D., and L. Stracca. 2011. *Have Euro area and EU economic governance worked? Just the facts*. ECB Working Paper 1344, Frankfurt: European Central Bank.

Issing, O. 2010. A Greek bail-out would be a disaster for Europe. *Financial, Times*, 16 February, p. 11.

Kounalaki, X. 2012. Foreign leaders verbally attack Greece. *Kathimerini*, 20 April, http://news.kathimerini.gr/4dcgi/_w_articles_ell_100032_20/04/2012_479464 (in Greek) (accessed 15 June 2012).

Lazaridis, E. 2011. Conflict in the independent statistical authority. *To Vima*, 5 October, http://www.tovima.gr/opinions/article/?aid=423380&wordsinarticle=Γεωργαντ (in Greek) (accessed 14 December 2011).

Manolopoulos, J. 2011. *Greece's 'odious' debt*. London and New York: Anthem Press.

Marsh, D. 2011. *The Euro*. New Haven, CT: Yale University Press.

New Folders. 2011. Theodore Pagkalos. *Skai TV*, 3 October, http://folders.skai.gr/main/theme?id=247&locale=en (in Greek) (accessed 14 December 2011).

Persson, T., and G. Tabellini. 1996. Federal fiscal constitutions: risk sharing and moral hazard. *Econometrica* 64, no. 3: 623–46.

Puetter, U. 2012. Europe's Deliberative intergovernmentalism: the role of the Council and European Council in EU economic governance. *Journal of European Public Policy* 19, no. 2: 161–78.

Quaglia, L. 2009. The 'British plan' as a pace-setter: the Europeanization of banking rescue plans in the EU. *Journal of Common Market Studies* 47, no. 5: 1063–83.

Schelkle, W. 2006. The theory and practice of economic governance in EMU revisited: what have we learnt about commitment and credibility? *Journal of Common Market Studies* 44, no. 4: 669–85.

Schultz, S., and P. Wittrock. 2011. Parade of ego-Europeans. *Spiegel Online*, 12 May, http://www.spiegel.de/wirtschaft/soziales/0,1518,762097,00.html (accessed 15 June 2012).

Spiegel, P. 2011. Brussels' new-found aggression raises hackles. *Financial Times*, 7 November, http://www.ft.com/intl/cms/s/0/a3cc10fc-0964-11e1-a2bb-00144feabdc0.html#axzz1daViK5yq (accessed 20 December 2011).

Stein, J.L. 2011. The diversity of debt crises in Europe. *Cato Journal* 31, no. 2: 199–215.

Tsipras, A. 2012. Press conference. *To Vima* (in Greek) 21 May, http://www.tovima.gr/politics/article/?aid=458783 (in Greek) (accessed 22 May 2012).

Wibbels, E. 2003. Bailouts, budget constraints, and leviathans: comparative federalism and lessons from the early United States. *Comparative Political Studies* 36, no. 5: 475–508.

Wyplosz, C. 2006. European Monetary Union: the dark sides of a major success. *Economic Policy* 21, no. 46: 207–61.

Zahariadis, N. 2012. Complexity, coupling, and policy effectiveness: the European response to the Greek sovereign debt crisis. *Journal of Public Policy* 32, no. 2: 99–116.

Zahariadis, N. 2013. National fiscal profligacy and European institutional adolescence: the Greek trigger to Europe's sovereign debt crisis. *Government and Opposition* 48, no. 1: 33–54.

The EMU's Legitimacy and the ECB as a Strategic Political Player in the Crisis Context

FRANCISCO TORRES

European Studies Centre, St. Antony's College, Oxford University, and Robert Schuman Centre for Advanced Research, European University Institute, Florence

ABSTRACT   The sovereign debt crisis made it clear that, to be sustainable and serve its initial purpose (notably price stability), EMU would require enhanced policy coordination, increased sovereignty- and risk-sharing and further centralisation at the EU level of various competencies. In the crisis context, the ECB has emerged as an anchor of stability and confidence within a highly fragmented political system. It started to focus on the sustainability of EMU as its foremost objective, engaging in more active (and non-standard) policies and wider economic policy debates than otherwise required from a traditional central bank. This article departs from a gap in the literature with respect to the legitimacy of delegations to a supranational and independent institution like the ECB. It adopts an interdisciplinary view, bringing together various concepts (broad categories) of legitimacy and various types constraints that the common monetary authorities face. The framework is applied to examine the ECB's rationale to act strategically and its quest to legitimate its strategic political role through a renewed monetary dialogue with the EP.

Introduction

After the first decade of Economic and Monetary Union (EMU), it became clear that its very incompleteness had allowed for the building up of disequilibria and that it had brought to the forefront institutional fragilities, which led to the sovereign debt crisis. During EMU's first 10 years, the lack of national reforms in some member states and the incapacity of financial markets to distinguish between Eurozone sovereigns paved the way for increasing intra-EMU macroeconomic imbalances. The fact that economic, financial and fiscal governance institutions were unable to account for increasing policy interdependence left EMU institutions, already affected by the 2008–2009 global financial crisis, incapable to deal with the parallel and still on-going sovereign debt crisis. In response to the financial crisis, the EU moved towards enhanced (albeit not yet sufficient) coordinated financial supervision. As a response to the second and more important crisis, new mechanisms of economic governance and stronger fiscal and macroeconomic surveillance mechanisms (the European Semester, the 2011 EU economic governance package, dubbed 'six-pack', the Euro Plus Pact) have been established in an incremental way in an attempt to sustain EMU and, eventually, prepare a leap forward in integration in economic but also fiscal (Treaty on Stability, Coordination and Governance, TSCG), financial (EU banking union, the European Stability Mechanism, ESM) and political (possibly a new IGC to revise the EU treaties) terms.

EMU's input legitimacy resides in the act of delegation of monetary policy to the ECB, by means of a European treaty agreed upon by all governments of the member states and ratified by all national parliaments. However, the initial act of delegation was not complete because EMU itself was an open ended political compromise (in the economic union part). It would therefore at some point require enhanced policy coordination, increased sovereignty- and risk-sharing and further centralisation at the EU level of various competencies in order to keep it functioning and hence fulfil its initial purpose. The Stability and Growth Pact (SGP) and the Lisbon Strategy, which have been subject either to parliamentary approval and/or enacted on the basis of a voluntary open policy coordination mechanism among member states, are cases in point. However, those two exercises in economic policy coordination (the Lisbon Strategy being continued by the Europe 2020 Strategy since 2010) have proved insufficient for ensuring the sustainability of EMU in the crises context. New institutions (such as the European System of Financial Supervisors, ESFS, the European Financial Stabilisation Facility, EFSF, and the ESM) and non-standard policies (the Securities Market Programme, SMP, the Long Term Refinancing Operations, LTRO, and Outright Monetary Transactions, OMT) have been created and enacted or at least envisaged for that purpose. Those institutions depict already an increasing centralisation of previously national competencies, which, together with new non-standard policies of the ECB (arguably of a quasi-fiscal nature), may well change the nature and the degree of economic and political integration agreed upon at Maastricht. Although new acts of delegation will benefit from input legitimacy, via parliamentary approval, they might well require internal constitutional changes and/or new treaty changes voted and ratified by all member states in order to function in a permanent and efficient way rather than in an *ad hoc* manner.[1] In addition, for EMU's long-term sustainability its legitimacy would have to go beyond the act of delegation and encompass EMU's functioning.[2]

This article departs from a gap in the literature with respect to the legitimacy (and accountability and/or responsiveness) of delegations to a supranational and independent institution, like the one of monetary policy to the ECB. It brings together various types of constraints faced by the common monetary authorities, presented in the second section, and various concepts (broad categories) of legitimacy—input, output and throughput legitimacy—examined in the third section. The fourth section applies that framework to examine the ECB's incomplete contract and rationale to act strategically. The fifth section analyses the building up of a common-interest bound accountability by the European Parliament (EP) and the ECB as an informal institution and how it has been used by the latter in order to legitimate its strategic role. The sixth section concludes.

Central Bank Independence and Accountability: The ECB as Special Case

From a rational-choice perspective, principal–agent accounts of delegation stress the rationality of member state principals in delegating powers to supranational organisations, mainly to allow their respective governments to 'reduce the transaction costs of policy-making, in particular through the monitoring of member state compliance, the filling-in of incomplete contracts, and the speedy and efficient adoption of implementing regulations' (Pollack 2012). This approach seems to apply to the relationship between the EU's member states as principals and EU supranational bodies like the Commission as agents, where the former establish *ex ante* the scope of the agencies' activities and the latter are accountable (and therefore subject to sanctioning and/or reward) *ex post*. However, it seems unable to account for the delegation of monetary policy to a new type of agency like the ECB, which is independent from its principal.[3] As stressed by Dyson (2009), central banks (not as independent as the ECB, one may add) are in general embedded in more common principal–agent relations (in Westminster type of states) with an emphasis on parliamentary sovereignty whereas in the post-war German tradition, transferred to the ECB, the central bank was seen as a disinterested trustee for a specific public interest.[4]

A 'political economics' approach to the theory and practice of economic policy allows for distinguishing two types of constraints that policy-makers face: credibility constraints and political constraints.[5] Credibility constraints are related to the temptation of policy-makers to deviate from pre-announced plans, without disagreement over the ultimate policy goals. The concept derives from work on time-inconsistency and rules and reputation (commitment technologies) and does not encompass political conflict. Enforceable rules lead to the implementation of pre-set objectives. That kind of implementation fits well into the category of policy-making at the EU level that Schmidt (2012) characterised as 'policy without politics', which presupposes relying on output legitimacy, that is, governing *for* the people on the basis of previously accepted and selected objectives. Such a form of legitimation is particularly relevant for the case of regulatory institutions.

Conversely, political constraints regard conflicts of interest over those goals or, to use Drazen's (2001) terminology, ex-post preference heterogeneity.[6] The idea of binding political constraints stems from the political business cycle literature, where governments have opportunistic incentives to adopt certain policies, from the theory of public choice, where there are conflicting policy preferences among different interest groups and/or from the so-called agency and/or principal drift in principal–agent relations.

The recognition of the existence of credibility constraints, or political transaction costs *à la* Majone, has resulted in a very particular institutional design of EMU (the establishment of an independent European central bank with the primary objective of price stability), which is characterised by a change in the nature of delegation (Torres 2006) or by a fiduciary mode of delegation (Majone 2001; Maggetti 2010) of monetary policy. This different form of delegation features a substantial differentiation between the initial principal and the agency's preferences and behaviour.

In contrast, political constraints are more difficult to address and involve the question of the accountability of the monetary authorities. That is why economists also acknowledge that, from a normative perspective, legitimacy cannot be reduced only to performance (De Grauwe 2011; Geraats 2010; Geraats *et al.* 2008; Buiter 2008, 2012). They implicitly or explicitly address output legitimacy concerns (stressing that there is little to be done except increasing transparency as a means of sustaining the monetary authorities' credibility and defending their independence) and in some cases even hint at some form of enhanced (procedural) informal accountability (the need for political control over monetary policy). As far as the ECB is concerned, they tend to disregard both the above-referred change in the nature of delegation and the Bank's strategic role in shaping EMU's completion. The latter has become particularly important since the eruption of the sovereign debt crisis.

Buiter (2008) defends that truly operationally independent central banks such as the ECB lack any substantive accountability, which increases the risk of political backlashes against their independence. As put by Jones (2009, 1093), the ECB 'cannot ignore the possibility of unfavourable political reactions' when politicians have to choose between defending the ECB and pleasing public opinion and their electorates. Even if taken in opposite and contradictory directions, attacks on the ECB affect its credibility and hence its output legitimacy.

Therefore, the ECB has a strong interest in finding ways to be perceived, on the one hand, as accountable and transparent (and within a wider EMU *cum* EU governance system, responsive) and, on the other hand, as acting effectively on behalf of the interest of European or Eurozone citizens (output legitimacy).

Bridging the Gap Between Delegation and Delivering Results: Throughput Legitimacy

Initial legitimate principals expect agents to carry out policies that are consistent with their initial preferences in the steady state of supranational regulation. However, the agent's actions may differ from the principal's preferences because either the principal's or the agent's preferences or indeed both may change. Output legitimacy ('government *for* the people'), the indirect legitimacy via the performance in attaining objectives (namely the objectives established in the treaties), is then not sufficient to sustain EMU.

Against the background of possible disagreements with respect to European monetary governance, there is a need for some type of procedural legitimacy. In fact, there is an optimal degree of politicisation to deal with political constraints.[7] Yet, there are few possibilities of resorting to input legitimacy ('government *by* the people') beyond the act of delegation. To a limited extent, input legitimacy is still exercised along the process, notably through the process whereby national governments appoint the members of the ECB's decision-making bodies (ECB 2002). This process has also evolved and since the Lisbon treaty members of the ECB's Executive Board are appointed by the European Council, acting by qualified majority and no longer by common accord, on a recommendation from the Council of the EU. However, one-time acts of legitimisation cannot *per se* replace mechanisms of democratic accountability.

For EMU's sustainability, and beyond input and output legitimacy, ECB's policies should therefore also be perceived as much as possible as 'government *with* the people'. This intermediate type of legitimacy (throughput legitimacy), in between the input and the output types of legitimacy (Schmidt 2012), is related to the quality of the decision-making process itself (Risse and Kleine 2007). It is compatible with the type of independent agency in question, that is, the common monetary authority of a multi-level polity like the EU. Throughput legitimacy is practised as an informal dialogue between the ECB and other EU organisational actors such as the EP, the EU Council and the European Council, the European Commission and, through effective communication also with society at large.

Table 1 systematises the above discussion on policy constraints and EMU's legitimacy. It sets the various types of constraints affecting policies against the various types of legitimacy considered (coined by and discussed in Scharpf 1999; Lord and Magnette 2004; Risse and Kleine 2007; Schmidt 2012) and the means (and phases) of addressing them.

Why Does the ECB Act Strategically?

Traditional principal–agent notions of accountability applied to EU institutions do not consider the political and dynamic nature of the process of monetary integration. In the context of EMU, the ECB is not a mere agency responsible for the implementation of monetary policy but also an

Table 1. Policy constraints and EMU's legitimacy

Types of constraints affecting policies	Types of legitimacy to address the two types of constraints	Means and phases of implementation
Credibility constraints (related to the temptation of policy makers to deviate from pre-announced plans; time-inconsistency)	Output legitimacy (government *for* the people): rests on the effectiveness of policy achievements and is especially relevant for the case of non-majoritarian institutions	Through the performance in attaining its proposed objectives (namely the objectives established in the treaties) all along the process
Political constraints (regarding conflicts of interest over the ultimate goals of policy; ex-post preference heterogeneity)	Input legitimacy (government *by* the people): rests on popular representation and participation and is especially relevant for the case of majoritarian institutions	Available mainly at the initial (constitutional) phase of setting EMU's policy objectives and through the act of delegation of monetary policy to the ECB; also, indirectly, through the process of nomination of the ECB Executive Board and the Governing Council
EU multi-level governance	Throughput legitimacy (government *with* the people; responsiveness): rests on the quality of the decision-making process itself and/or on interest intermediation and is relevant for both majoritarian and non-majoritarian institutions involved in multi-level governance. Bridge between the input legitimate act of delegation of monetary policy to the ECB and the (procedural) phase of implementation of EMU's objectives	Through informal dialogue between the ECB, the EP, the EU Council and the European Council, the European Commission and effective communication with society at large all along the process; legitimates strategic role of the ECB, adopted to assure EMU's sustainability

actor in the political equilibrium of the entire EU *cum* EMU governance construct. Such a strategic role is particularly important in a crisis setting.

As Bartolini (2006) notes, a governance system cannot be accountable in *strictu sensu*. He argues that a wider—that is, less strict—notion of accountability, such as the notion of responsiveness, appears more suitable in the context of governance than a traditional notion of accountability. It is even more adequate given the continuous change in the nature of economic governance in the EU. The type of legitimacy with which complex channels of responsiveness seem more compatible is throughput legitimacy.

Furthermore, EMU's economic side had been left incomplete at Maastricht and that incompleteness, with the sovereign debt crisis, has come to negatively affect monetary policy and the very sustainability of EMU. On the one hand, monetary policy has to face up to member state governments with independent and often uncoordinated if not contradictory economic policies.[8] On the other hand, spill-overs from the financial, fiscal and economic areas of the union into its monetary side have come to challenge the ECB's independence through renewed political pressures on the monetary authorities and have put at stake EMU's stability (Torres 2012). As a result, the ECB—which operates under an incomplete contract, since EMU was created as and still is an incomplete and open-ended mechanism—does not seem to take its independence for granted.

The ECB responded to the crisis providing liquidity (including through non-standard measures)[9] but also as the only European institution that could step in to avert major credit incidents: intergovernmental funds were either not in place, not operational for buying government bonds or simply not sufficient for countries such as Italy and Spain from summer 2011 onwards. For the same reason, it also engaged in the building up of new institutions such as (the modalities of) a EU banking union and agreed to take on supervisory powers. Moreover, in August and September 2012, the ECB announced that it would impose strict conditionality on member states, that is, governments would have to 'stand ready to activate the EFSF/ESM in the bond market with strict and effective conditionality in line with the established guidelines' (ECB 2012a) upon OMTs in secondary sovereign bond markets, aiming 'at safeguarding an appropriate monetary policy transmission and the singleness of the monetary policy' (ECB 2012b). OMTs substitute the SMP in order to address the severe malfunctioning in the price formation process in the bond markets of euro area countries (which may hinder the effective working of monetary policy). The start, continuation, suspension and termination (once their objectives are achieved or in case of non-compliance) of macroeconomic adjustment or precautionary programmes is to be decided by the Governing Council in full discretion and acting in accordance with its monetary policy mandate (ECB 2012b).

The ECB became also more vocal with respect to other policy domains classified by Buiter (2008) as an unwarranted invasion from the point of view of the Bank's legitimacy—such as product and labour market reforms, privatisations, 'true oversight' of national budgets, centralisation of financial supervision, a framework for bank resolution, among others. Even Buiter (2008), however, in his criticism of central bank (in particular ECB) intrusions into wider economic policy debates well beyond their mandates and competences, acknowledges that in one specific situation such a posture is justifiable, namely when an independent central bank's independence is threatened.

For the ECB, this 'invasion of other policy domains'—by calling for sound economic policy management, in particular in the fiscal domain, for structural reforms and for reinforced economic governance in general—is motivated by the fact that the euro area is at the epicentre of the sovereign debt crisis. Considering what the ECB has emphasised on many occasions, as for instance in Padoa-Schioppa (2000), Trichet (2011) and Draghi (2012), those 'intrusions' are driven by a sense of mission of an institution that perceives itself as an anchor of stability and confidence within a highly fragmented political system.

For the ECB (2011b), individual member states' economic policies should contribute to the achievement of the objectives of the Union (Article 120 of the TFEU[10]) and be regarded as a matter of common concern to be coordinated within the Council (Article 121(1) of the TFEU). EMU then implies the need to transfer national sovereignty in economic policy-making to the supranational level, given that price and financial stability-oriented monetary policies alone are insufficient to sustain EMU.[11]

Moreover, the ECB functions in a state of 'institutional loneliness', within a complex structure of EU multi-level governance.[12] With the crisis, it became also a guardian of EMU since the EU's political system *per se* seems incapable of providing timely and consistent solutions to a governance problem. It therefore interprets its engagement in exceptional measures and its strategic role as within its mandate (Draghi 2012).[13]

The wider interpretation of the ECB's mission (its inflation and burden-sharing impacts across member states) is not uncontroversial even within the ECB, both within its Executive Board and its Governing Council. Their respective members have publicly emphasised their disagreements over particular aspects of the ECB's role, namely in the case of the SMP and other non-conventional measures, and on how the ECB can best preserve its independence. Those divisions within the bank's Governing Council affect the overall political equilibrium of the EMU construct but they also reflect the strategic political role that the ECB plays vis-à-vis the Council and individual Eurozone states. Different positions on non-standard measures within the ECB's Governing Council, namely of a member of the Executive Board and a national central bank governor of the same nationality, are also the result of a successful strategic interaction (suitable equilibrium for both parts) with a particular Eurozone member, notably Germany. The ECB has therefore strategically engaged in conditioning reform in some Eurozone members, notably Italy and Spain and arguably France (not to mention the countries under the supervision of the Troika, of which the ECB is part), gaining in this way the support of other members, such as Germany, for some of its more controversial (with potential significant redistributive effects) policies aimed at sustaining EMU.

In sum, it is due to the perceived threat to its independence that the ECB tends to act strategically, especially with respect to the Council but also with respect to specific states.[14] On the other hand, for the ECB, EMU needs to be completed (on its economic side) in order to fulfil its objectives and to be sustainable and therefore it engages in wider economic policy debates. The ECB derives its legitimacy not only from delivering price stability (and, without prejudice to that primary objective, from supporting the general economic policies in the Union—art. 127 of the TFEU) but also from acting as a guardian of EMU objectives, doing 'whatever it takes to preserve the euro'. The ECB aims at guaranteeing what may be termed its foremost objective: the sustainability of EMU as such. This implicit objective, not addressed in the literature on EMU's legitimacy, leads the Bank to behave strategically and engage in exceptional measures and in wider economic policy debates.

Legitimating the ECB's Strategic Role Through a Common-interest Bound Accountability

According to Majone (2005b) and Maggetti (2010), principals can transfer their powers but not their legitimacy to an independent agency and therefore the latter must rely on other external sources of legitimacy.

As for EMU, one can argue that member states did not only transfer their responsibility over monetary policy to the ECB but that, at the same time, they have created the conditions for the gradual emergence of another legitimate principal as far as monetary policy is concerned, the EP.[15] In this particular case, (initial) principals transferred their powers to a common independent agency, the ECB, and their legitimacy to another source of legitimacy, the EP, external to the agency but internal to the democratic system of the Union. The legitimacy of the Parliament is clearly stated in Article 10.2 of the TEU: 'Citizens are directly represented at Union level in the European Parliament'. The ECB being a supranational institution, a transfer of legitimacy of the initial (national) principals of (national) independent central banks to a supranational representative institution comes as a logical development.

The Treaty of Maastricht gave the EP significant competencies.[16] As stressed by Jabko (2009, 402–3) and Torres (2011), the ECB's interest in acquiring legitimacy and the Parliament's desire to get a greater say in the conduct of economic policy within the EU, especially with respect to Eurozone governance, has greatly contributed to the convergence of the two supranational actors on 'the rules of the accountability game'.[17] In fact, precisely because of their common supranational nature, already during EMU's first decade—in good years—the two institutions had converged a great deal with respect to the ECB's independence and accountability and to the role of monetary policy within the wider EU *cum* EMU governance framework. The ECB itself explicitly recognises that legitimacy, as part of a mutual-interest strategic collaboration: 'the EP, as the institution which derives its legitimacy directly from the citizens of the EU, plays a key institutional role in holding the ECB to account'.[18]

However, their strategic collaboration has considerably widened in scope during the financial and sovereign debt crises, in favour of a new economic governance institutional architecture (Torres 2011). This is the case of the successes achieved by the Parliament in strengthening the Stability and Growth Pact by reverse qualified majority voting (RQMV), which implies the need for a qualified majority of member states to block warnings and sanctions against debt offenders.[19] It also succeeded in raising budgetary surveillance in general and in pushing for more EU-level economic policy coordination.

Another example of this collaboration between the EP and the ECB (emphasized by former ECB president Trichet in his last hearing at the Committee on Economic and Monetary Affairs of the European Parliament in October 2011) was the new architecture of financial supervision, which the Parliament had regularly called for throughout the first decade of 2000, pointing out significant failures in the supervision of ever more integrated European financial markets. Following the European Commission's initiative with respect to the financial supervisory package, the Parliament, counting on the ECB's support, worked towards strengthening the powers of the new supervisory authorities.

Moreover, the ECB has encouraged the EP, in the new framework of economic governance (adopted in October 2011 and in force since December 2011), to use the symmetric tool of 'economic dialogue' to promote economic integration with the 'required legitimacy', which, by enhancing transparency in the process of fiscal and macroeconomic surveillance, would lead to better results (Trichet 2011).[20] The new financial supervisory framework and the new 'EU *cum* EMU governance' package are two examples of collaboration that are especially worth analysing within the continuous monetary and economic dialogues. This is because through the enacting of the review clause in 2013 and in 2014, the European Parliament, on the basis of its track record, has two more occasions to move further. The examples fit into a type of strategic interaction whose role in determining political outcomes is also stressed by rational choice institutionalism.

In his last hearing at the EP, ECB president Trichet (2011) also stressed that, while the ECB was the guardian of the currency of the European citizens, the European Parliament was the heart of the living democracy in Europe and that the fact that the ECB was fully independent in its actions to protect the currency was not incompatible with the EP's request for the ECB reporting to it. In fact, the European Parliament is *a priori* less conditioned by domestic (debt biased) vested interests and political business cycles than the Council. The domestic oppositions to national governments are also represented in the EP and may well have different views on the issue under discussion.[21]

The strategic cooperation between the ECB and the EP roots in what they, as supranational institutions, perceive as the common interest of the people of Europe versus the various (and at times irreconcilable) interests of the EU member states. It demonstrates the ECB's interest in not only acquiring more democratic legitimacy with the Parliament but also in influencing the coordination of economic policies within the EU and to move (leap forward) to a new economic governance institutional architecture (a desire shared with the Parliament). Beyond aligned objectives of principal (the EP) and agent (the ECB) in the making, there are converging interests between the two institutions with respect to the EU economic governance institutional architecture. The two institutions can make use of their cooperation to condition the position of the Council of the EU, of the European Council and of the Commission, going beyond (but in that way also contributing to) securing their independence and role of principal in the making, respectively. They can also shape the development of the economic side of EMU with a view to not having to face various uncoordinated and at times contradictory fiscal and economic policies by Eurozone members, which totally escape the democratic oversight of the Parliament and affect (through negative spill-overs) the credibility and independence of the ECB.

Conclusion

This article departed from the observation that there is a gap in the literature with respect to the analysis of the legitimacy of the ECB. The literature does not provide a framework for analysing the legitimacy of monetary policy at the Eurozone level, especially for the case of the EU *cum* EMU complex governance structure and in times of crisis.

The article put forward a framework that brought together broad categories of legitimacy and various types of constraints that the common monetary authorities face. The framework was applied to examine the ECB's rationale to act strategically and its quest to legitimate its strategic political role through a renewed monetary dialogue with the EP.

The ECB acts strategically because of the perceived threat to its independence from an incomplete EMU (on its economic side) and seeks to derive its legitimacy not only from delivering price (and financial) stability but also from acting as a guardian of EMU objectives, doing 'whatever it takes to preserve the euro'. In that sense, it aims at guaranteeing what may be termed its foremost objective: the sustainability of EMU as such. This implicit objective leads the Bank to engage in exceptional policies, beyond standard monetary tools, and wider economic policy debates, pushing for 'a gradual and structured effort to complete EMU' (Draghi 2012).

The article also explained the ECB's engagement in the building up of a common–interest bound accountability with the EP as a means of legitimating its policies and of promoting the completion of EMU to protect its independence. This 'accountable independence' has operated in the context of the monetary dialogue between the two institutions, which has become especially productive since the beginning of the crises.

Acknowledgements

The author (on leave from Universidade Católica, Lisbon) would like to thank the editors of this special issue, an anonymous referee, Iain Hardie, Adrienne Heritier, David Howarth Jorge Braga de Macedo, Waltraud Schelkle, Chiara Zilioli and other participants in earlier workshops in Bruges, Edinburgh, Oxford, Florence and Porto for very valuable comments and discussions.

Notes

1. See ruling of Germany's Federal Constitutional Court of 7 September 2011 (2 BvR 987/10, 1485/10 and 1099/10). It established the decision-making rights of the German parliament in any rescue package, and by analogy in any further centralization of competencies that could exceed

the capacity of the federal budget and the contingency on reforms by the receiving country. In September 2012, the *Bundesverfassungsgericht* opened the way for Germany's ratification of the ESM but specified additional conditions, reinforcing the rights of the national parliament.
2. As put by Magnette (2000, 331), the initial act of delegation makes the ECB a legal institution but 'legality does not produce legitimacy on its own'.
3. Political science approaches to principal–agent problems in the EU, encompassing the main theories of and approaches to European integration, do in general not address the case of a fully independent agency like the ECB. See Kassim and Menon (2005).
4. See Keohane and Nye (2003), Buiter (2008) and Dyson (2009) for a discussion of these issues for the specific case of the ECB and the classical debate between Buiter (1999) and Issing (1999). For the ECB (2002, 48), the notion of 'being accountable' entails being held responsible for one's decisions but only implies an *ex post* explanation and justification.
5. See Persson and Tabellini (1990, 2000), Drazen (2000) and, for a link between constitutional systems and economic policy, Persson and Tabellini (2003).
6. Ex-post preference heterogeneity is equivalent to the spill-over effects of the legitimation of EU supranational governance (in this case monetary policy) to national level democracy and legitimacy. This question is also related to wider considerations on the qualitative change in the nature of EU and international governance.
7. Such optimal degree of politicisation parallels Rogoff's (1985) optimal degree of commitment in monetary policy as a means of dealing with credibility constraints.
8. Unlike in the cases of the US Fed or the Bank of England, the ECB faces a situation that potentially puts at risk the entire monetary construct and stability of the Union. In another sense, its role is reduced as compared to the one of other central banks that are also assumed lenders of last resort. However, one can argue that, with the financial and sovereign debt crises, the ECB is catching up.
9. The ECB (2011a, 58) recognises that the benefits of non-standard measures increase with the severity of economic shocks whereas their costs (strains induced on central bank operations and the risk exposure of its balance sheet) will tend to exceed their benefits in normal times.
10. Besides having to 'conduct their economic policies with a view to contributing to the achievement of the objectives of the Union, as defined in Article 3 of the Treaty on European Union, and in the context of the broad guidelines referred to in Article 121(2)', the member states and the Union shall also, according to article 120 of the TFEU, 'act in accordance with the principle of an open market economy with free competition, favouring an efficient allocation of resources, and in compliance with the principles set out in Article 119'.
11. This is consistent with ECB president Draghi's first address to the European Parliament on 1 December 2011, pressuring the European Council for a fundamental restatement of EMU's fiscal rules.
12. The ECB, as a strong central bank in a weak polity or in a polity in the making suffered from what Padoa-Schioppa (2000, 37) termed institutional loneliness. See also Jabko (2009, 401) and Dyson (2009), who refers to the ECB as an isolated central bank in an institutionally fuzzy polity.
13. As put by the ECB president (Draghi 2012): 'The ECB is not a political institution. But it is committed to its responsibilities as an institution of the European Union... The banknotes that we issue bear the European flag and are a powerful symbol of European identity'.
14. See Kirkegaard (2011) for various examples of the ECB strategy aimed at 'getting recalcitrant Eurozone policy-makers to do things they otherwise would not do'. Acting strategically, the ECB has also been able to get either explicit or implicit support from creditor countries for some of its more controversial non-conventional measures.
15. This is even more so with respect to new tasks that shall be attributed to the ECB, notably financial supervision.
16. Notably, articles 284(3) and 283(2) of the TFEU, formerly articles 109-B (3) and 109(2b) of the Treaty establishing the European Community (TEC). See Torres (2006) for a detailed analysis.
17. 'Inventing a European tradition of accountable independence' in the words of Magnette (2000, 339).
18. See http://www.ecb.int/ecb/orga/accountability/html/index.en.html, last consulted on 29 August 2012. This more recent formulation goes beyond the ECB's views on accountability (with respect to the EP) in 2002 (ECB 2002, 45).

19. The fact that RQMV was agreed by France and Germany in December 2011 to be enshrined in the treaties in forthcoming revisions is a good example of a potential recursive relationship (in the terminology coined by Farrell and Héritier 2003) between formal and informal (in this case the role of monetary dialogue in advancing EMU cum EU governance) institutions.
20. A European Parliament resolution, adopted on 1 December 2011 on the European Semester for Economic Policy Coordination (2011/2071(INI)), called for the Annual Sustainable Growth Guidelines to be subject to a co-decision procedure that should be introduced by the next Treaty change.
21. It is not to be expected that say the German or Portuguese opposition would come to rescue their respective countries from an early warning under the excessive deficit procedure as it happened in the Council (Heipertz and Verdun 2010; Schuknecht et al. 2011).

References

Bartolini, S. 2006. Comment on Torres and Schmidtke. In *EMU rules: the political and economic consequences of European monetary integration*, ed. F. Torres, A. Verdun, and H. Zimmermann, 83–5. Baden-Baden: Nomos Verlagsgesellschaft.

Buiter, W. 1999. Alice in Euroland. *Journal of Common Market Studies* 37, no. 2: 181–209.

Buiter, W. 2008. Monetary economics and the political economy of central banking: inflation targeting and central bank independence revisited. Paper presented at the Central Bank of Argentina conference on 'Monetary policy under uncertainty', June 4–5, in Buenos Aires.

Buiter, W. 2012. The role of central banks in financial stability: how has it changed? *CEPR Discussion Paper No. 8780*, January.

De Grauwe, P. 2011. The European Central Bank: lender of last resort in the government bond markets? *CESifo Working Paper No. 3569*, September.

Draghi, M. 2012. The future of the euro: stability through change. Contribution from the President of the ECB, published in 'Die Zeit', 29 August.

Drazen, A. 2000. *Political economy in macroeconomics*. Princeton, NJ: Princeton University Press.

Drazen, A. 2001. How does politics affect economic outcomes? Insights from 'new' political economy. *The Political Economist*, Newsletter of the Political Economy Section of the American Political Science Association, Winter.

Dyson, K. 2009. The age of the euro: a structural break? Europeanization, convergence, and power in central banking. In *Central banks in the age of the euro*, ed. K. Dyson and M. Marcussen. Oxford: Oxford University Press, 1–52.

European Central Bank. 2002. The accountability of the ECB, *Monthly Bulletin*, November, 45–57.

European Central Bank. 2011a. The ECB's non-standard measures – impact and phasing-out, *Monthly Bulletin*, July, 55–69.

European Central Bank. 2011b. The reform of economic governance in the euro area – essential elements, *Monthly Bulletin*, March, 99–119.

European Central Bank. 2012a. ECB President introductory statement to the press conference, Frankfurt am Main, 2 August.

European Central Bank. 2012b. Technical features of outright monetary transactions, press release, Frankfurt am Main, 6 September.

Farrell, Henry., and Adrienne Héritier. 2003. Formal and informal institutions under codecision: continuous constitutional-building in europe. *Governance* 16, no. 4: 577–600.

Geraats, P. 2010. ECB credibility and transparency. In *The Euro. The first decade*, ed. M. Buti, S. Deroose, V. Gaspar, and J.N. Martins. Cambridge: Cambridge University Press.

Geraats, P., F. Giavazzi, and C. Wyplosz. 2008. *Transparency and governance. Monitoring the European Central Bank*, 6, London: CEPR.

Heipertz, M., and A. Verdun. 2010. *Ruling Europe. The politics of the stability and growth pact*. Cambridge: Cambridge University Press, 193–229.

Issing, Otmar. 1999. The eurosystem is transparent and accountable, or Willem in Wonderland. *Journal of Common Market Studies* 37, no. 3: 503–19.

Jabko, N. 2009. Transparency and accountability. In *Central banks in the age of the euro. Europeanization, convergence and power*, ed. K. Dyson and M. Marcussen. Oxford: Oxford University Press, 391–406.

Jones, E. 2009. Output legitimacy and the global financial crisis: perceptions matter. *Journal of Common Market Studies* 47, no. 5: 1081–101.

Kassim, H., and A. Menon. 2005. The principal–agent approach and the study of the European Union. In *The political economy of European integration. Theory and analysis*, ed. E. Jones and A. Verdun, 39–53. London and New York: Routledge.

Keohane, R., and J. Nye. 2009. Redefining accountability for global governance. In *Governance in a global economy: political authority in transition*, ed. M. Kahler and D. Lake. Princeton, NJ: Princeton University Press, 386–411.

Kirkegaard, J. 2011. The next strategic target; De Gaulle's EU legacy, VoxEU, 30 November.

Lord, C., and P. Magnette. 2004. E pluribus unum? Creative disagreement about legitimacy in the EU. *Journal of Common Market Studies* 42, no. 1: 183–202.

Magnette, P. 2000. Towards 'accountable independence'? Parliamentary controls of the European Central Bank and the rise of a new democratic model. *European Law Journal* 6, no. 4: 326–40.

Maggetti, M. 2010. Legitimacy and accountability of independent regulatory agencies: a critical review. *Living Reviews in Democracy* 2, http://www.livingreviews.org/lrd-2010-4, accessed on 29 September 2011

Majone, G. 2001. Non-majoritarian institutions and the limits of democratic governance: a political transaction-cost approach. *Journal of Institutional and Theoretical Economics* 157, no. 1: 57–78.

Majone, Giandomenico (2005), Delegation of powers and the fiduciary principle, in CONNEX Workshop, Paris.

Padoa-Schioppa, Tommaso (2000), "An Institutional Glossary of the Eurosystem", Center for European Integration Studies (ZEI), Working Paper B-16, University of Bonn, 23–37.

Persson, T., and G. Tabellini. 1990. *Macroeconomics, credibility and politics*. London: Harword Academic Publishers.

Persson, T., and G. Tabellini. 2000. *Political economics: explaining economic policy*. Cambridge, MA: MIT Press.

Persson, T., and G. Tabellini. 2003. *The economic effects of constitutions*. Munich Lectures in Economics. Cambridge, MA: MIT Press.

Pollack, M. 2012. Realist, intergovernmentalist, and institutionalist approaches. In *The handbook on the European Union*, ed. E. Jones, A. Menon, and S. Weatherill, 3–17. Oxford: Oxford University Press.

Risse, T., and M. Kleine. 2007. Assessing the legitimacy of European treaty revisions. *Journal of Common Market Studies* 45, no. 1: 69–80.

Rogoff, Kenneth. 1985. The optimal degree of commitment to an intermediate monetary target. *The quarterly journal of economics* 100, no. 4: 1169–89.

Scharpf, F. 1999. *Governing in Europe. Effective and democratic?* Oxford: Oxford University Press.

Schmidt, V.A. 2012. Democracy and legitimacy in the European Union. In *The handbook on the European Union*, ed. E. Jones, A. Menon, and S. Weatherill, Oxford: Oxford University Press, 3–17.

Schuknecht, Ludger, Philippe Moutot, Philipp Rother and Jürgen Stark (2011), The stability and growth pact – crisis and reform, european central bank occasional paper 129, September.

Torres, F. 2006. On the efficiency-legitimacy trade-off in EMU. In *EMU rules: the political and economic consequences of European monetary integration*, ed. F. Torres, A. Verdun, and H. Zimmermann, 31–49. Baden-Baden: Nomos Verlagsgesellschaft.

Torres, F. 2011. The sustainability and completion of EMU, unpublished manuscript.

Torres, F. 2011. *The political economy of monetary governance: the role of preferences, policies and strategies*. Lisbon: UCP.

Torres, F. 2012. Completing EMU through an 'Eurozone Economic Governance Compact'. Paper presented at the conference 'European economic governance', College of Europe, 1 March, in Bruges.

Trichet, J.-C. 2011. Introductory statement. Hearing at the Committee on Economic and Monetary Affairs of the European Parliament, Brussels, 4 October.

The Little Engine that Wouldn't: Supranational Entrepreneurship and the Barroso Commission

DERMOT HODSON

Department of Politics, School of Social Sciences, History and Philosophy, Birkbeck, University of London, Malet Street, London, UK

ABSTRACT This paper seeks to evaluate and explain the degree of supranational entrepreneurship shown by the European Commission following the global financial crisis. Focusing on the period 2007–2011, it finds that the Commission used its right of initiative and/or mobilised ideas and information to pursue a supranational European Union (EU) economic policy in few cases. These findings are explained with reference to strategic entrepreneurship, that is the Commission's reluctance to support integrationist initiatives unless they stand a chance of success, and by the fact that partisanship took precedence for the EU executive over the pursuit of integration in some cases. The Commission could yet capitalise on the crisis but its actions in this period call for greater attention by scholars to preference formation by supranational actors as well as a reconsideration of what it means for the EU executive to lead.

Introduction

'Please, Little Blue Engine,' cried all the dolls and toys.
'Won't you pull our train over the mountain?' (Watty Piper)

Whether supranational entrepreneurship can succeed is a recurring question in debates about European integration, with Sandholtz and Zysman (1989) and Moravcsik (1999) differing over Jacques Delors' influence, just as Haas (1958) and Hoffmann (1964) had done in relation to Jean Monnet. Scholars typically see the European Commission as being 'in decline' after Delors (Peterson 2012, 97). Both Jacques Santer and Romano Prodi were criticised for weak leadership (Cini 2008), while José Manuel Barroso is seen as a pragmatist rather than a pioneer (Cini 2005). For all such declinism, the idea that the Commission can show leadership in general (see Sandholtz and Stone Sweet 2012) and in relation to specific areas of policy-making (Howarth 2008; Parker and Karlsson 2010) still resonates with some scholars.

Theories of supranational entrepreneurship tend to emphasise structure over agency. Pollack (1997) sees the Commission's capacity for entrepreneurship as contingent on member states' uncertainty about optimal policy choices. Distributional consequences also matter for Pollack, who sees member states as turning to the Commission for information and ideas on further integration in cases where the costs of common policies are low. Commission entrepreneurship also depends, he argues, on the support of significant non-governmental actors. For Moravcsik (1999), supranational entrepreneurship will succeed if the Commission can solve collective action problems before national governments. Failures of organisation and representation will favour entrepreneurship, he argues, when the Commission is better informed than governments about interest groups that support integrationist initiatives. Failures of aggregation will work similarly, Moravcsik argues, when the Commission backs such initiatives before governments form a coherent negotiating position.

There is limited space for agency in these accounts since both assume the Commission would engage in entrepreneurship if structural conditions allow. For Pollack (2005, 36), the Commission is an engine of integration because its officials are hardwired to support 'more Europe' for reasons of self-interest or ideology. This point is consistent with Moravcsik (1999, 271n) who assumes that the Commission 'tend[s] to favor more ambitious schemes for further institutional and substantive integration'. Recent research gives reason to question these assumptions. That the EU executive has become more partisan is suggested by Hix (2008), who finds that the median-voter in the Barroso Commission is to the right of the median-voters in the Santer and Prodi administrations. This is due, he argues, to changes introduced by the Nice Treaty, which allowed a qualified majority of (centre-right) governments to propose Barroso as President in June 2004 and ended the practice whereby large countries nominated Commissioners from both the left and right. What these changes mean for supranational entrepreneurship Hix does not say, but his findings surely imply that partisanship can take precedence over the pursuit of further integration.

This paper uses the reform of EU economic policy following the 2007–2008 global financial crisis as a case study in supranational entrepreneurship. As economic crises go, the EU has faced no greater challenge, severe liquidity shortages starting in mid 2007 followed by a systemic banking crisis in late 2008. These events led to a severe recession in the euro area in 2009 followed by surge in government borrowing. By early 2010,

Greece was close to defaulting, with Ireland and Portugal facing a similar fate soon after. Although the crisis had clearly yet to run its course by the end of 2011, it had already served as a catalyst for policy change, with member states agreeing on, inter alia, a coordinated bank rescue, a joint fiscal stimulus package, new legislation on financial regulation and economic surveillance and the creation of ad-hoc and permanent crisis resolution mechanisms. For all this policy activism, this paper finds little evidence that the Barroso Commission used its right of initiative or mobilised information or ideas to further integration following the global financial crisis. This lack of entrepreneurship is explained with reference to both structure and agency. In the case of the former, the Commission acted strategically by steering clear of integrationist initiatives that were opposed by member states. As regards the latter, José Manuel Barroso's defence of fiscal conservatism and light-touch financial regulation over further integration fits with the centre-right orientation of his administration.

The remainder of this paper is divided into three sections. The first section considers different definitions of supranational entrepreneurship and, on this basis, evaluates the degree of entrepreneurship displayed by the Commission during the period 2007–2011. The second seeks to explain the Commission's cautious response to the global financial crisis with reference to the role of structure and agency. The final section considers the wider implications of these findings and considers whether the Commission could yet emerge as an entrepreneur in response to the crisis.

Evaluating Commission Entrepreneurship Following the Crisis

Traditional theories of supranational entrepreneurship can be traced in spirit, if not in name, to Haas (1964, 153). Here Haas highlighted the Commission's tendency to upgrade the common interest—i.e., seek additional powers for itself at the expense of member states—in negotiations over shared policy problems. While Haas (1964) saw the Commission's right of initiative as the supreme instrument of supranational entrepreneurship, contemporary scholars tend to focus on informal agenda setting, with the latter involving the mobilisation of information and ideas in support of further integration rather than specific legislative proposals (Pollack 1997; Moravcsik 1999). Taking these definitions as its point of departure, this section evaluates the extent to which the Commission sought to 'upgrade the common interest' and/or engage in informal agenda setting in relation to EU economic policy from mid 2007 to the end of 2011. Following Musgrave (1959), this investigation focuses on the classic functions of economic policy: regulation, stabilisation, allocation and redistribution.

Regulation

The Commission's regulatory response to the financial crisis was cautious at first. It was not until the banking turmoil took hold in Autumn 2008 that the EU executive tabled a revised directive on deposit insurance and a new regulation on credit rating agencies. The remainder of José Manuel Barroso's first term saw new proposals on the regulation of hedge funds and capital requirements and the reform of EU financial supervision. Barroso's second term, which began in February 2010, saw a surge in regulatory reforms with the Commission adopting 20 proposals for new or revised regulation by the end of 2011, including a further tightening of the rules on deposit insurance, credit rating agencies, hedge funds and capital requirements along with proposals for new and revised legislation on over-the-counter derivatives, short-selling, market abuse and accounting standards.

The Commission's willingness to use its right of initiative in this context chimes with Haas (1964), but it is questionable whether such proposals seek to empower the Commission at the expense of governments. A case in point is the proposal on the European Systemic Risk Board (ESRB), with the Commission seeking a place on the new body's General Board but leaving it to the European Central Bank (ECB) and the 27 governors of the national central banks of EU member states to choose a chair from their ranks. Nor did the Commission seek binding powers for this new body. National authorities are under no legal obligation to follow ESRB recommendations with non-compliers required only to give reasons for their decision under a so-called 'ask and explain' mechanism.

Turning to informal conceptions of entrepreneurship, the Commission was also cautious about mobilising information and ideas in favour of financial re-regulation during the period in question. Whereas French President Nicolas Sarkozy waited just six days after worldwide liquidity shortages came to light in August 2007 before publicly calling for greater financial transparency, stronger financial supervision and a reevaluation of the role of credit rating agencies (Gauthier-Villars 2007), José Manuel Barroso waited until January 2008 before making substantive public remarks about the regulatory implications of the crisis. Even then, Barroso sounded a conservative rather than radical note, urging EU leaders to steer clear of 'futile attempts to stem financial globalisation' at a meeting of EU G8 members in London (Commission. 2008a). The Commission President stuck to this line even after the turbulent events of Autumn 2008, warning against 'grand initiatives that have no chance of being followed through' (Barroso 2008).

If the Commission showed any ideational leadership at this time it was in relation to EU financial supervision. Significant in this respect was Barroso's decision in November 2008 to invite Jacques de Larosière to lead a high-level group on EU financial supervision. Although the group's recommendations were not implemented in full—EU finance ministers, for example, diluted attempts to give the new supervisory agencies binding powers of dispute resolution in the event of disagreement between national authorities—they nonetheless served as a blueprint for the legislative package proposed by the Commission in September 2009 and adopted by the Council of Ministers and the European Parliament in November 2010.

In spite of this reform and others, financial regulation was by no means championed in the Commission's post-crisis vision. In his 2010 State of the Union address, for example, Barroso (2010) acknowledged the necessity of 'proper regulation and proper supervision' while insisting on the importance of 'a strong and sound financial sector ... that serves the real economy'. More tangible evidence of the Commission's reticence regarding financial re-regulation can be found in the Single Market Act. This package of twelve proposals for 'new, greener and more inclusive growth' in the light of the crisis launched in July 2011 called for common rules on venture-capital funds but otherwise made no reference to financial market policies (Commission 2011a).

Stabilisation

When it came to economic stabilisation, the Commission was willing to propose new legislation over the period 2007–2011 in only some instances. The Commission's most decisive step in this regard was the so-called 'six-pack', a set of six legislative proposals presented in September 2010 with a view to reinforcing EMU's fiscal rules and widening the scope of economic surveillance. Also important in this regard was the so-called 'two-pack', a set of proposals put forward in November 2011 calling for closer scrutiny of member states' draft budgets and more intrusive surveillance for euro area members facing financial instability. Significant though such proposals were, it is debatable whether they upgrade the Commission's power over economic stabilisation to any significant degree. The 'two-pack', for example, called for the Commission to be given the power to issue ex-ante opinions on member states' future budgetary plans, while leaving the final say over such plans in the hands of national governments and parliaments.

Of the many ideas inspired by the euro area's sovereign debt difficulties, Eurobonds are perhaps the most integrationist, involving as they would the joint issuance and/or guarantee of national government debt. The Commission, for its part, was a late convert to this particular cause and even then a somewhat reluctant one. When asked about Eurobonds in an appearance before the European Parliament in December 2009, José Manuel Barroso said only that such an idea was not being proposed at the present juncture (European Parliament 2009). Commissioner for Economic and Monetary Affairs Olli Rehn took a small step further in December 2010, describing Eurobonds as 'intellectually attractive'. By September 2011, the Commission's thinking on this issue had shifted but not radically so, with José Manuel Barroso telling MEPs that the Commission would present 'options for the introduction of Eurobonds' (Barroso 2011). The Commission seemed in no hurry to put forward legislative proposals here, waiting a further two months before launching a Green Paper on Eurobonds (Commission 2011d).

When it came to informal agenda setting, the Commission can legitimately claim to have mobilised ideas and information in support of the proposed macroeconomic imbalance procedure. A widely cited Commission study published in November 2006 warned that 'marked and protracted divergences in growth and inflation among euro-area members, accompanied by sizeable shifts in real effective exchange rates and current account imbalances' (Commission 2006: 12). The Commission returned to this theme in a high-profile report on the first decade of the euro, which emphasised the need 'to broaden surveillance to address macroeconomic imbalances' (Commission 2008b, 8).

Ideational leadership with respect to the fiscal consequences of the crisis is more difficult to discern. The Commission's initial response to the turbulent events of mid 2007 was to defend the status quo rather than seek a supranational approach to stabilisation. In February 2008, José Manuel Barroso called not as International Monetary Fund (IMF) Managing Director Dominique Strauss Kahn had done a month earlier for 'a new fiscal policy' (Giles and Tett 2008) but for fiscal discipline and compliance with the stability and growth pact (Barber 2008). By December 2008, the Commission had come round to the idea of a modest fiscal stimulus package, putting forward a European Economic Recovery Programme that called on 'Member states and the EU to agree to an immediate budgetary impulse amounting to €200 billion (1.5 per cent of GDP; European Commission 2008c). By April 2010, Rehn (2010) was calling not only for compliance with the stability and growth pact but also a tightening of EMU's fiscal rules. The Commission was hardly ahead of the curve in doing so, EU heads of state and government having agreed in March to convene a taskforce led by European Council President Hermann Van Rompuy to explore 'all options to reinforce the legal framework' concerning crisis resolution and budgetary discipline (European Council 2010a).

Allocation

Moving from stabilisation to allocation finds the Commission more circumspect still about the need for further integration following the global financial crisis. In presenting its first round of proposals on the Multi-Annual Financial Framework for 2014–2020, the EU executive showed little appetite for budget maximisation, evoking the need for 'smart sustainable and inclusive' growth in the wake of the crisis but calling for a 6.5 per cent cut in total payment appropriations over this period (Commission 2011b, 1). This show of austerity, it is true, was balanced by the Commission's plans to devote more resources to public goods such as cohesion, although the inclusion of an additional €50 billion in funding for transport and energy infrastructure under this heading masked a €10 billion reduction in the amount allocated to the EU's structural funds (House of Lords 2011). Such cuts, it is true, were accompanied by a proposed €18 billion increase in off-budget expenditure on allocative instruments such as the Solidarity Fund and the Globalisation Adjustment Fund but this increase amounted to only around 2 per cent of total commitments over this period (House of Lords 2011). These increases can also be viewed as a concession to the European Parliament, which emerged as the 'supranational entrepreneur' par excellence here, calling for a 5 per cent increase in EU expenditure compared to 2007 levels and insisting that 'the solution to the crisis [was] more and not less Europe' (European Parliament 2011).

The EU executive was less entrepreneurial still when it came to the creation of ad-hoc instruments of allocation to provide emergency loans to euro area members in the context of the financial crisis. By the beginning of 2010 it was clear that Greece was in need of external assistance to avoid a disorderly default on its government debt but the Commission remained reluctant to be drawn on what role the EU should play in providing such support. Speaking at the European Parliament in February 2010, the outgoing Commissioner for Economic and Monetary Affairs, Joaquín Almunia, hinted only that treaty instruments were available for this purpose but refused to be drawn on what such instruments were (European Parliament 2010b). In the end, the treaty was not invoked for Greece, with member states finally agreeing in May 2010 to pledge EUR 80 billion in bilateral loans.

The Commission played a more prominent but by no means proactive role in efforts to create an ad-hoc financial firewall for euro area members, putting forward a proposal in May 2010 on the creation of a new €60 billion European Financial Stabilisation Mechanism (EFSM). In so doing, the EU sought emergency powers under Article 122 TFEU to propose the provision of loans and guarantees to a euro area member, to borrow funds for this purpose and to disburse this funding to the country in question subject to a rigorous review of its economic policy. EU finance ministers signed off on this proposal but they kept the Commission at arms length from a new EUR 440 billion fund created at the same time. Whereas the EU executive was given responsibility for raising funds for the EFSM, the larger fund was entrusted to a newly-created European Financial Stability Facility (ESFS), a public-limited company registered in Luxembourg and overseen by representatives of the member states.

The EFSM and EFSF were envisaged as ad-hoc financial instruments, with EU finance ministers agreeing in May 2010 to take forward plans for 'establishing a permanent crisis resolution framework' (Council 2010). A communication adopted by the Commission (2010a) shortly afterwards promised 'in the medium-to-long term to make a proposal for a permanent crisis resolution mechanism' but no such proposals were forthcoming by the time the European Council agreed in December 2010 to revise Article 136 TFEU with a view to the creation of a new, intergovernmental European Stability Mechanism (ESM). The resulting agreement saw member states claw back the new allocative competences ceded to the Commission in May 2010, with the heads of state and government agreeing that the EFSM would be wound down and that Article 122 TFEU would henceforth no longer be used 'to safeguard the financial stability of the euro area as a whole' (European Council 2010b).

Redistribution

Of all the legislative proposals launched by the Commission in response to the global financial crisis during the period 2007–2011, the financial transactions tax is the most clear-cut attempt to upgrade the common interest. Under a proposal presented in September 2011, financial transactions involving at least one institution located in the EU would be subject to a levy of 0.1 per cent on the exchange of shares and bonds and 0.01 per cent on the exchange of derivatives (Commission 2011c). Revenues raised from these levies, estimated to be in the region of EUR 57 billion would be divided between member states and the EU, with the latter contribution becoming a new 'own resource' for the Community offset by a reduction in national contributions.

The idea that the Commission showed ideational leadership over the EU financial transaction tax is more difficult to defend. Although José Manuel Barroso was an early supporter of plans for an international financial transactions tax, his position in September 2009 was that such a scheme would be workable only in the context of a global agreement that did not harm European competitiveness.[1] It was not until April 2010 that the Commission presented a preliminary set of ideas for a financial transactions tax at EU level (Commission 2010b). The European Parliament was, once again, more entrepreneurial on this issue, adopting a resolution on financial transactions taxes in March 2010, which called on the Commission to consider the pros and cons of such an arrangement at the EU level (European Parliament 2010a).

Explaining Commission Entrepreneurship Following the Crisis

In summary, then, the preceding section found limited evidence of Commission entrepreneurship following the global financial crisis during the period 2007–2011. The EU executive, it is true, showed itself willing to initiate new legislation on financial regulation, economic surveillance and ad-hoc crisis resolution and to propose a new financial transactions tax but only the last of these measures can be understood as a clear-cut attempt to upgrade the common interest. The Commission was, moreover, reluctant to play its hand on some reforms, with legislative proposals on a permanent crisis resolution mechanism and Eurobonds not materialising during the period in question. The Commission was shown to be less proactive still when it came to mobilising ideas and information in support of further integration, with only José Manuel Barroso's timely decision to convene a high-level group on financial supervision and the EU executive's longstanding calls to step up the surveillance of macroeconomic imbalances coming close to informal agenda setting. On wider issues of financial regulation and in debates on the need for a coordinated fiscal stimulus package and an enlarged EU budget, in contrast, the Commission's preferences prioritised the status quo over the pursuit of further integration. This section seeks to explain this lack of supranational entrepreneurship beginning with structural factors before looking to the role of agency in the Barroso administration's response to the global financial crisis.

Structure

From a structural perspective, the conditions for supranational entrepreneurship were far from favourable following the global financial crisis. Of the conditions that Pollack (1997) sees as critical for Commission influence, only the support of significant non-governmental actors for further integration comes close to being fulfilled between 2007 and 2011. Financial markets emerged as key cheerleaders for further integration during this period, with the positive reaction to Barroso's remarks on Eurobonds in November 2011 one of many such short-lived occurrences.[2] National governments, in contrast, were far from being uncertain about how to tackle the crisis, with German Finance Minister Wolfgang Schäuble's (2010) controversial but clear-sighted plans for a European Monetary Fund in March 2010 a case in point. Nor were member states in any great rush to tackle the crisis, with the long months of negotiation before EU leaders signed off in May 2010 on a financial rescue package for Greece far from being an isolated case. That the distributional consequences of decision-making in this domain were significant also made supranational entrepreneurship more difficult, according to Pollack's approach. Of significance here were member states' differing degrees of exposure to Greek debt. As of the end of 2011, claims by French banks on Greek debt were estimated at USD 39 billion, as compared with figures of USD 33 billion and USD 2 billion for German and Italian banks respectively (Bank for International Settlements 2012).

A similar conclusion emerges in relation to Moravcsik's (1999) theory of supranational entrepreneurship. The emergence of a seemingly broad coalition of support for an international financial transactions tax is the clearest candidate for the empowerment of a latent or peripheral interest group following the financial crisis. According to polls conducted on behalf of the European Parliament, support for such a tax rose from 47 per cent in 2009 to 64 per cent in 2010 (Public Opinion Monitoring Unit 2009, 2011). Pressure groups were quick to mobilise around this issue, as evidenced by the launch in March 2010 of the Robin Hood Tax Coalition, a UK based network of over 100 charities, religious organisations and civil society groups.[3] National governments moved quicker still, with UK Prime Minister Gordon Brown proposing an international financial transactions tax at a meeting of G20 finance ministers in St Andrews in November 2009. If aggregation failures were at work here they did not favour the Commission, which waited until April 2010 to present preliminary policy proposals on an EU financial transactions tax (Commission 2010b).

Although structural factors can account for the difficulties of successful supranational entrepreneurship following the crisis can they explain the Commission's reluctance to push for further integration in the first place? Moravcsik's account of supranational entrepreneurship, it should be recalled, is littered with examples of the Commission trying but failing to influence negotiations but he identifies no case in which the Commission fails to try. One explanation of this puzzle is to see the Commission as a strategic entrepreneur that supports integrationist initiatives only where they stand a chance of success. Strategy of this sort could have a number of motivations, including the Commission's need to preserve scarce bureaucratic resources and protect political credibility. Career advancement may also play a role here at the level of individuals, with members of the Commission requiring the support of national governments to secure reappointment.

Consistent with this idea of strategic entrepreneurship is the Commission's reticence over Eurobonds. Faced with a divergence of views between Nicolas Sarkozy and Angela Merkel on this issue (Hollinger *et al.* 2011) a Green Paper was arguably as far as the Commission could go without alienating one or other of the Franco–German couple. A similar story can be told about the EU financial transactions tax, with the Commission's September 2011 proposals coming after José Manuel Barroso had secured a second term and at a time when Franco–German support for such a proposal was only beginning to emerge.[4] Strategic entrepreneurship may also explain the Commission's willingness to put forward proposals on relatively uncontroversial issues such as soft law approaches to macroeconomic imbalances and financial supervision while steering clear of hard-sell issues such as a supranational permanent crisis resolution mechanism. As regards the latter, the Commission can have been in little doubt about the inevitability of an intergovernmental ESM given the limits imposed on the EFSM by member states. More problematic from this point of view is why the Commission did not chime in on those issues where political support for further integration was possible. Cases in point are Barroso's reluctance to support Sarkozy's calls for financial regulation, the Commission President's defence of fiscal discipline at a time of growing international support for a fiscal stimulus and the EU executive's reluctance to back calls by the European Parliament for a bigger budget.

Agency

From an agency perspective, these anomalies might be seen as the product of partisan preferences rather than strategy borne of structural constraints on supranational entrepreneurship. The Commission's fiscal conservatism during the early phase of the crisis provides one instance in which such agency was plausibly at play. Whereas the centrist Prodi Commission's support for the stability and growth pact was patchy—Prodi himself called for a flexible interpretation of the agreement in October 2002 (Howarth 2008)—the centre-right Barroso Commission made a concerted effort to restore compliance with EMU's fiscal rules after the controversial reforms of March 2005. In so doing, the Barroso Commission confounded expectations that it would turn a blind eye to excessive budget deficits, instead recommending corrective action against all member states (known to be) in breach of the pact. By mid 2008, this strategy appeared to have paid off with all euro area members adjudged to have budget deficits below 3 per cent of GDP for the first time since Prodi's disparaging remarks about the pact. Seen in these terms, it is hardly surprising that José Manuel Barroso's initial response was to defend the stability and growth pact rather than embrace a coordinated fiscal stimulus package, even if the latter had the potential to pave the way for the kind of ex-ante approach to EU fiscal policy coordination that economists of the centre-left had long sought (see Collignon 2003).

A similar argument can be made in relation to the Commission's planned cuts to EU expenditure over the period 2014–2020. Barroso had form here, having pushed through swinging expenditure cuts during a sharp economic slowdown during his time as centre-right Prime Minister of Portugal. Problematic from this perspective is why a Commission with centre-right preferences would also favour a new tax on financial transactions, although the Commission's September 2011 proposal, it should be recalled, proposed to offset the revenue raised from this tax with a reduction in national contributions to the EU budget (Commission 2011c).

That José Manuel Barroso was reluctant to champion the re-regulation of financial markets following the financial crisis is also consistent with the centre-right preferences of his administration. More puzzling here is how these preferences can be reconciled with the Commission's regulatory activism in this domain, especially in Barroso's second term. One explanation of this puzzle is that such activism had more to do with the preferences of the Commissioner for the Internal Market and Services than the Commission President, with the decision to give this portfolio to Michel Barnier in February 2010 paving the way for a more pro-regulation approach. Precisely how pro-regulation Barnier is is unclear but he is most certainly to the left of his predecessor, Charlie McCreevy, who came to the defence of hedge funds in the early days of the financial crisis and showed little sign of changing his views as the crisis worsened (McCreevy 2007; McCreevy 2009).

For his part, José Manuel Barroso has appeared less then comfortable with Barnier's appointment, with the Commission President threatening in November 2011 to decouple the internal market and financial services portfolio to assuage UK concerns over undue French influence in this domain (Taylor and Rankin 2009). A similar offer is said to have emerged after the European Council in December 2011, with Barroso offering to 'promote' Barnier to the post of High Representative of the Union for Foreign Affairs and Security Policy in return for UK support for the Fiscal Compact (Barker and Parker 2012). Neither threat was carried out, however, leaving Barnier to put forward legislative proposals for financial market reforms at a rate of just under one per month between February 2010 and December 2011 as compared to a rate of just over one ever four months under Charlie McCreevy between August 2007 and February 2010.

Conclusion

In conclusion, this paper has sought to evaluate and explain the degree of supranational entrepreneurship shown by the Commission following the global financial crisis. Focusing on the period between the beginning of the crisis in 2007 and the end of 2011, it found little evidence that the EU executive sought to increase its power at the expense of member states either by using its right of initiative or mobilising information and ideas in support of further integration. Structural factors partly explain this lack of entrepreneurship insofar as the Commission was reluctant to endorse integrationist initiatives that stood little immediate chance of success. The EU executive's reluctance to play its hand over Eurobonds and a more supranational ESM are illustrative in this regard. Strategic entrepreneurship of this sort cannot, however, explain the Commission's defence of the status quo against calls for a coordinated fiscal stimulus package, financial regulation and a bigger EU budget. This conservatism, it was argued, is consistent with the Barroso Commission's centre-right preferences, with fiscal discipline and light-touch financial regulation taking precedence over the pursuit of further integration.

The global financial crisis has yet to run its course at the time of writing and there is nothing to say that the Commission might not yet emerge as a supranational entrepreneur if structural conditions allow and/or political priorities are reordered. Indeed, the intensification of the euro area sovereign debt crisis in mid 2012 suggests that such a shift might already be underway, with José Manuel Barroso (2012) talking openly about the possibility of fiscal union and euro area leaders agreeing to take forward plans for a banking union (Euro Area Heads of State and Government 2012). Precisely where such ideas will lead is not yet known but the fact remains that the Commission's response to the crisis between 2007–2011 was much less integration-minded than might have been expected.

For students of the Commission, the analysis presented in this paper calls for a reconsideration of what it means for the EU executive to lead. For too long, scholars have decried the Commission as being in decline because of the failure of successive presidents to emulate the (perceived) success of Monnet or Delors in driving forward the integration process. It would be wrong to do so in relation to José Manuel Barroso, whose reluctance to embrace integrationist initiatives after the global financial crisis owed as much to political choices as political constraints. Whether these choices were right for the ailing EU economy is a discussion for another day but the fact that a leader of the EU executive had objectives other than the steady accumulation of powers at the supranational level is a mark surely of political maturity rather than powerlessness.

For students of supranational entrepreneurship, finally, this paper's findings call for further reflection on how supranational actors form their preferences. Great progress has been made over the last two decades in understanding how national governments come to a view on the desirability or otherwise of closer cooperation with EU partners. Yet scholars routinely treat the preferences of the Commission and other supranational actors as a black box. Recent research suggests that the Commission may not be alone among EU institutions in having policy priorities other than the pursuit of ever-closer union (see Hodson 2011, chapter 2; Brack and Costa 2012), with the implication being that the traditional engines of European integration run on different fuel these days than was once thought to be the case.

Notes

1. 'EU divided on German "Tobin" tax proposal', Agence France Presse, 17 September 2009.
2. 'European shares bounce back on euro bonds hopes', Reuters, 14 September 2011.
3. http://robinhoodtax.org/.
4. 'Germany says transaction tax would be EU-wide', Reuters, 17 August 2011.

References

Bank for International Settlements. 2012. *Quarterly review, June 2012*. Basle: BIS.
Barber, T. 2008. France urged to trim deficit. *Financial Times*, February 12.
Barker, A., and G. Parker. 2012. Secret deal to win UK backing for fiscal pact. *Financial Times*, March 8.
Barroso, J. 2008. Preparation European Council: speech to the European Parliament. SPEECH/08/509, Brussels, 8 October.
Barroso, J. 2010. State of the Union 2010. SPEECH/10/411, Strasbourg, 7 September.
Barroso, J. 2011. European renewal – State of the Union Address 2011. SPEECH/11/607, Strasbourg, 28 September.
Barroso, J. 2012. Speech by President Barroso at the European Parliament Plenary Debate on the European Council. Strasbourg, 3 July.
Brack, N., and O. Costa. 2012. *Diverging views of Europe: Euroscepticism within EU institutions*. London: Routledge.
Charles, P., and C. Karlsson. 2010. Climate change and the European Union's leadership moment: an inconvenient truth?. *Journal of Common Market Studies* 48, no. 4: 923–43.
Cini, M. 2005. Pragmatism prevails: Barroso's European Commission. Chatham House European Programme Briefing Paper 05/01.
Cini, M. 2008. Political leadership in the European Commission: the Santer and Prodi Commissions, 1995–2005. In *Leaderless Europe*, ed. J. Hayward, 113–30. Oxford: Oxford University Press.
Collingnon, S. 2003. Is Europe going far enough? Reflections on the stability and growth pact, the Lisbon strategy and the EU's economic governance. *European Political Economy Review* 1, no. 2: 222–47.
Commission. 2006. The EU Economy 2006 Review. European Economy No. 6. Luxembourg: Office for the Official Publications of the European Communities.
Commission. 2008a. EU G8 members meeting in London on Financial Market Turmoil: advance statement from Commission President José Manuel Barroso. ISEC/08/02, Brussels 29 January.
Commission. 2008b. EMU@10: successes and challenges after 10 years of Economic and Monetary Union. European Economy No. 2. Brussels: DG Economic and Financial Affairs.
Commission. 2008c. A European Economic Recovery Plan. COM(2008) 800 final.
Commission. 2010a. Reinforcing economic policy coordination. COM(2010) 250 final.
Commission. 2010b. Innovative financing at a global level: taxation of the financial sector. COM(2010) 0549/5.
Commission. 2011a. Single Market Act twelve levers to boost growth and strengthen confidence. COM/2011/0206 final.
Commission. 2011b. A Budget for Europe 2020. COM(2011) 500 final.
Commission. 2011c. Proposal for a Council Directive on a common system of financial transaction tax and amending Directive 2008/7/EC. COM(2011) 594 final.
Commission. 2011d. Green Paper on the feasibility of introducing Stability Bonds. COM(2011) 818 final.
Council. 2010. Extraordinary Council meeting: economic and financial affairs. Presse 9596/10, 9–10 May.
Euro Area Heads of States and Government. 2012. Euro Area Summit statement. Brussels, 29 June.
European Council. 2010a. Conclusions. EUCO 7/10, Brussels, 26 March.
European Council. 2010b. Conclusions. EUCO 30/1/10 REV, Brussels, 25 January.
European Parliament. 2009. Question Hour with the President of the Commission. Strasbourg, 15 December.
European Parliament. 2010a. European Parliament resolution of 10 March 2010 on financial transaction taxes – making them work. Ref: P7, TA(2010) 0056.

European Parliament. 2010b. Debates: difficult monetary, economic and social situation of Eurozone countries. Strasbourg, 9 February.
European Parliament. 2011. European Parliament resolution of 8 June 2011 on investing in the future: a new multiannual financial framework (MFF) for a competitive, sustainable and inclusive Europe. Ref: 2010/2211(INI).
Gauthier-Villars, D. 2007. Sarkozy letter to Merkel reflects concerns in EU. Wall Street Journal, 16 August.
Giles, C., and G. Tett. 2008. IMF head in shock fiscal warning. Financial Times, 28 January.
Haas, E. 1958. *The uniting of Europe: political, social and economic forces, 1950–1957*. Notre Dame, IN: University of Notre Dame Press.
Haas, E. 1964. Technocracy, pluralism, and the new Europe. In *New Europe?* ed. S. Graubard, 149–66. Boston: Houghton Mifflin.
Hix, S. 2008. Why the EU needs (left-right) politics? Policy reform and accountability are impossible without it. Notre Europe Policy Paper N°19.
Hodson, D. 2001. *Governing the Euro area in good times and bad*. Oxford: Oxford University Press.
Hoffmann, S. 1964. De Gaulle, Europe, and the Atlantic Alliance. *International Organization* 18, no. 1: 1–28.
Hollinger, P., C. Bryant, and P. Quentin, 2011. Germany and France rule out Eurobonds. *Financial Times*, 14 August .
House of Lords. 2011. EU Financial Framework from 2014. European Union Committee 13th Report of the Session. London: The Stationery Office.
Howarth, D. 2008. Delegation and Commission Leadership in Economic and Monetary Union. In *Leaderless Europe*, ed. J. Hayward, 28–46. Oxford: Oxford University Press.
McCreevy, C. 2007. Financial stability and the impact on the real economy: speech to the European Parliament. Strasbourg, 5 September.
McCreevy, C. 2009. Address by Commissioner Charlie McCreevy at the EP Committee on Economic and Monetary Affairs, Strasbourg, 3 February.
Moravcsik, A. 1999. A new statecraft? Supranational entrepreneurs and international cooperation. *International Organization* 53, no. 2: 267–306.
Musgrave, R. 1959. *The theory of public finance: a study of public economy*. New York: McGraw-Hill.
Parker, C.F., and C. Karlsson. 2010. Climate change and the European Union's leadership moment: an inconvenient truth? *Journal of Common Market Studies* 48, no. 4: 923–43.
Peterson, J. 2012. The College of Commissioners. In *The institutions of the European Union*, eds. J. Peterson and M. Shackleton, 96–123. Oxford: Oxford University Press.
Piper, W. 1961. *The Little Engine That Could*. New York: Platt & Munk.
Pollack, M. 1997. Delegation, agency, and agenda setting in the European Community. *International Organization* 51, no. 1: 99–134.
Public Opinion Monitoring Unit. 2010. Europeans and the Crisis II. European Parliament Eurobarometer, EB Parlemeter 74.1. Brussels: European Parliament.
Public Opinion Monitoring Unit. 2011. Europeans and the Crisis III. Eurobarometer, EB Parlemeter 75.2. Brussels: European Parliament.
Rehn. 2010. Reinforcing economic governance in Europe. SPEECH/10/160, European Policy Centre, Brussels, 15 April.
Sandholtz, W., and A. Stone Sweet. 2012. Neofunctionalism and supranational governance. In *The Oxford handbook of the European Union*, eds. E. Jones, A. Menon, and S. Weatherill, 18–33. Oxford: Oxford University Press.
Sandholtz, W., and J. Zysman. 1989. 1992: Recasting the European bargain. *World Politics* 42, no. 4: 5–128.
Schäuble, W. 2010. Why Europe's monetary union faces its biggest crisis. *Financial Times*, 12 March .
Taylor, S., and J. Rankin. 2009. Barroso poised to match names and portfolios. *European Voice*, 26 November.

Merged Into One: Keystones of European Economic Governance, 1962–2012

DAVID ANDREWS

Department of Politics and International Relations, Scripps College, USA

ABSTRACT   In this article I assess the views of the European Commission on key subjects related to Europe's economic governance. My examination is framed by a close reading of two documents, one issued in 1962 ('the Action Programme for the Second Stage') and the other in 2008 ('EMU@10: successes and challenges after ten years of Economic and Monetary Union'). The resulting comparison reveals a pattern of intellectual flexibility on certain policy issues combined with almost dogmatic commitments on others. For example, the views expressed by the Commission regarding financial liberalization have changed significantly over the past half century; at the same time the Commission has insisted tenaciously on the necessity of moving towards (or later consolidating) a European monetary union. The nature of this pattern, and especially the defense of the same policy prescription under radically different circumstances, suggests a deeply-felt commitment rather than a reasoned analysis.

With the debt crisis pushing the eurozone to the very brink of disaster, it is sometimes difficult to remember the triumphal tone that characterized official discourse about the single currency only a very short while ago. As Joaquín Almunia wrote in the foreword to a major analysis published by the European Commission in May 2008:

> ... we have good reason to be proud of our single currency. The Economic and Monetary Union are a major success. For its member

countries, EMU has anchored macroeconomic stability, and increased cross-border trade, financial integration and investment. For the EU as a whole, the euro is a keystone of further economic integration and a potent symbol of our growing unity. And for the world, the euro is a major new pillar in the international monetary system and a pole of stability for the global economy. (European Commission. 2008, III)

Almunia, who was then Commissioner for Economic and Financial Affairs, did indeed have good reason to extol the virtues of Europe's monetary union. Ten years after its introduction the euro appeared to be an unequivocal success. The infant currency had survived the bust of the dot-com boom while consolidating the market share of its predecessor currencies. The inflation-fighting reputation of the European Central Bank had become firmly established at the same time that membership in the monetary union had expanded dramatically. Certainly there was no serious talk of any participating state ever leaving the eurozone. Little wonder, then, that the underlying tone in the Commission's report—entitled 'EMU@10: successes and challenges after ten years of Economic and Monetary Union'—was so upbeat.

How distant the world described in that report now seems. After all, in the wake of the global financial crisis cross-border investment within the eurozone initially slowed down, then froze, and finally went into reverse. Rather than serving as a symbol of Europe's political unity, the eurozone has become the source of increasingly nasty disputes. And instead of regarding the euro as a pole of stability, observers from outside Europe view the EU's management of its ongoing financial crisis with fear and trepidation.

Despite these difficulties, there remains a certain logic to the analysis advanced by the Commission in EMU@10. Certainly there is a familiar ring to the view expressed therein that monetary union represents both a 'keystone of further economic integration and a potent symbol of [Europe's] growing unity'. This worldview has very deep roots; the Commission first gave voice to it in a parallel report published almost half a century earlier, in October 1962. Indeed there are several important parallels between EMU@10 and the 'Action Programme for the Second Stage' (European Commission. 1962). The Action Programme maintained that, despite Europe's many successes in the early postwar years, the entire project of regional cooperation risked collapsing unless comprehensive changes were undertaken. These changes would have to move beyond the mere liberalization of markets and instead embrace a new model of economic governance at the European level. Short-term economic policies would have to be harmonized at the same time that investment policies were introduced aiming at more balanced growth across a Europe of diverse regions. Monetary unification would serve as a necessary adjunct to these efforts, as without monetary union the harmonization and eventual merger of national economic and social policies could not be achieved.

Now fast forward to 2008. Then the Commission argued that, despite the successful revitalization of the Single Market in the 1980s and the introduction of monetary union in the 1990s, the continued success of regional cooperation depended on undertaking comprehensive reforms, including the adoption of a new model of economic governance at the European level. Short-term economic policies would have to be more effectively coordinated at the same time that longer-term reforms leading to increased investment and productivity were enacted. National economic and social policies would have to be scrutinized more closely at the European level, as without greater harmonization of these policies the monetary union could not be maintained.

The circumstances in which the two documents were produced were profoundly different. By 2008 the Cold War had ended. The membership of what used to be called the European Community had more than quadrupled. The Bretton Woods system of fixed-but-adjustable exchange rates had collapsed. At-the-border barriers to the free movement of goods, services and especially capital had been substantially reduced, not only in Europe but across most of the developed world. Yet both the underlying premises and the policy prescriptions of the two documents are remarkably similar.

What are we to make of this record of continuity amid change? In this article I use a comparison of these two texts—1962's Action Programme and 2008's EMU@10—to assess the evolution of the Commission's underlying views about the integration process.[1] The resulting organization of my analysis is straightforward. I begin by providing a brief background to the Action Programme; I then turn to its content, drawing attention to three aspects of the report that were pivotal to the Commission's analysis. First is the notion of *engrenage*, which is sometimes called the bicycle theory of integration. Second is the analytical distinction made in the report between positive and negative integration. Third is the role of monetary integration in the larger European project.

I then compare the premises of the Action Programme with counterparts to be found in EMU@10 half a century later. I begin by noting that the Commission's analysis of the dangers faced by the eurozone ten years after its founding was essentially correct: although neither the pace nor scale of the ensuing debt crisis was foreseen, the report's analysis of the essential problems was spot on. I then turn to the report's prescriptions, and again assess the role of *engrenage* and the positive/negative dichotomy in the Commission's thinking.

I conclude by identifying elements of change as well as continuity in the Commission's deeply held intellectual commitments. The Commission has shifted its views very considerably on the relative merits of positive and negative integration—which is another way of saying it has become far more enthusiastic about economic liberalization. By contrast, the Commission's views about *engrenage*, specifically with respect to monetary integration, have changed very little over the years. I find that the Brussels executive has held fast to a set of principled commitments about integration generally, and monetary integration in particular, while adapting its intellectual defenses of the same as circumstances require. Commission officials have exhibited heightened willingness to embrace market and decentralized solutions for a host of issues... always excluding the monetary question.

Background to the Action Programme

The monetary provisions in the Treaty of Rome were quite weak.[2] This was a cause of sincere regret for European federalists, many of whom felt betrayed by the project. Given these sentiments, all that was required was a spark—an event that could serve as a pretext for revisiting these issues and taking a stronger line on monetary union.

That spark was the unilateral revaluation of the D-mark as announced by German authorities in March 1961. In the European Parliamentary Assembly, a hotbed of federalism, the mark's realignment provoked a series of hearings, the publication of a report calling for monetary union (the 'van Campen Report'), and a resolution in early October 1962. The Commission took careful measure of these developments and arranged for its own recommendations to be published exactly one week after the Parliamentary Assembly's October resolution. Those recommendations took the form of 'The Action Programme for the Second Stage'.[3]

The document's awkward title refers to the multistage framework called for in the Treaty of Rome for the introduction of the Common Market. The first stage had commenced on 1 January 1959; and the commencement of the second stage had been delayed in order to allow for the successful completion of the Common Agricultural Policy (or CAP) negotiations. These had at last been completed, and the second stage–now scheduled to begin in January 1963—was to oversee implementation of the resulting agreement. But further 'action' would be required, the Commission argued, in preparation for the launch of the Community's third and final stage, scheduled for January 1967, during which supranational decision-making procedures (including a majority voting scheme in the Council of Ministers) were to be introduced. It was to prepare for this later transition that the Action Programme was produced.

The introduction to the Commission's report, in which the guiding philosophy of its recommendations was spelled out, was written primarily by the Commission's first president, Walter Hallstein. Hallstein's commitment to European federalism was shaped by personal experience, and deeply felt.[4] Hallstein began the document as follows:

> What we call the economic integration of Europe is in essence a political phenomenon. Together with the European Coal and Steel Community and Euratom, the European Economic Community forms a European political union embracing the economic and social spheres. (European Commission 1962, 5)

The balance of Hallstein's introduction was equally bold, laying out an expansive agenda. The accompanying memorandum included separate chapters on free movement within the single market, competition policy, and social and economic policies; the establishment of common policies in agriculture, transport and energy; the Community's external relations and aid to developing countries; and the administration and finance of Community policies. The chapter on monetary policy was of particular note: there the Commission's recommendations culminated in a call for European monetary unification. The linkage between these different components relied upon a theory of social action known as *engrenage*.

The Theory of *Engrenage*

The economic context of the Action Programme was auspicious: tariffs between the member states had been cut by half since the foundation of the EEC, trade between members was booming, and establishment of the Common External Tariff was proceeding ahead of schedule. Acknowledging this, the 1962 memorandum argued that:

> ... the customs union has proved to be the right take-off point for a vigorous advance towards a unified economy. At the same time as it has provided a foundation for the Community's economic power, it has acted as a unifying factor among the member states.

Nevertheless, the Commission argued:

> ... this swift demolition of trade barriers has also confirmed that the Treaty was rightly heedful of economic requirements in prescribing that the establishment of economic union proper should proceed in parallel with the customs union, and not lag behind. (European Commission 1962, 5–6)

This distinction between 'economic union proper'—sometimes called 'broader economic union'—and economic union in a narrower sense appeared throughout the document. The narrower usage simply meant the adoption of common policies across a very wide range of issues, which was conceived as a necessary but insufficient step towards the establishment of 'economic union proper'. The Commission was emphatic on this point, and on the insufficiency of narrow measures (European Commission 1962, 7).

This analytical distinction rested upon the theory of *engrenage* that so animated the thought of Hallstein (and before him Jean Monnet) and that would later inspire a generation of neofunctionalist theorists.[5] According to this school of thought, successful integration in one sector of society or the economy initiated pressures for a chain reaction of integrative efforts in functionally adjacent spheres.[6] It was by no means predetermined that such pressures would result in integration elsewhere[7]—or in other words, that such pressures would result in functional 'spillover'. On the other hand, failure to achieve functional spillovers would ultimately call into question even the apparently successful initial integrative step. Hence failure to make progress towards 'broader economic union' would put at risk the integrative accomplishments of the five years since the adoption of the Treaty of Rome—including the foundation of the customs union and, more recently, the Common Agricultural Policy.

The integration process, then, was like riding a bicycle: absent forward movement, the whole project was likely to fall down. Hence there was a certain 'logic of integration', as Hallstein put it in memoirs, which 'may be described as the final factor in the unification of Europe'. Though 'anonymous'—indeed, 'it might be called material logic'—it nevertheless 'only works through human will' (Hallstein 1972, 24). Hallstein and at least some other members of his Commission saw themselves as agents of this will, and proposed the agenda laid out in the Action Programme for the Second Stage in order to fulfill their resulting mandate.

It would therefore be necessary to pursue both 'the customs union and the economic union (in the narrower sense of the term)' as 'complementary and interdependent' parts of the larger task of establishing 'economic union proper' (European Commission 1962, 5). This ambitious policy program would preserve the remarkable success of the Community project to date while at the same time preparing the ground for the eventual realization of the deeper goals of European integration as outlined in the Treaty of Rome.[8] The theory of engrenage linked these two efforts, and indeed suggested that they were part and parcel of the same enterprise.

Positive and Negative Integration

Engrenage was not the only idea animating the Commission memorandum; the Action Programme also reflected a particular understanding of the European political economy. That understanding was colored in equal parts by the premises of the German social market economy and the alternative French tradition of *dirigisme*, especially as practiced by Jean Monnet while head of the Fourth Republic's economic planning efforts. While too much can be made of this distinction—there were, after all, liberal elements to French planning efforts, and the German economic model was always modified by the adjective 'social'—the fact remains that these national models were distinctive and at least potentially in conflict.[9]

It was hardly clear how these two national systems could be made compatible with one another, as further economic integration seemed to require; but the Commission took it upon itself to suggest a solution to this conundrum. Accordingly, the Action Programme made the following striking argument: that 'an economic order based on freedom can only exist in the world of today at the price of constant State intervention in economic life'. In other words, a liberal economic order—one 'based on freedom'—could only be maintained in the context of an expansive economic policy role for the state.

The tension so evident in this formulation might have been resolved by arguing that 'constant State intervention' would be limited to specific spheres of the economy; but this was not the case. Instead the Commission argued as follows:

> Such intervention takes a two-fold form: in the first place, the State sets up a framework of controls covering every branch of the economy as well as every adjacent field; secondly, it is constantly altering the factors called into play, through the innumerable adjustments involved in its day-to-day economic activity: in short, by pursuing a 'policy' in the proper sense of the term. (European Commission 1962, 6)

This was a tall order. How would the Community, with its complex system of policy instruments at both the national and European levels, undertake such a comprehensive approach to state intervention? The Action Programme argued that the answer lay in developing a powerful centralized steering capacity located in the Commission itself. For the Brussels executive, henceforward:

> ... the main emphasis will no longer be, as with the customs union, on the negative purpose of abolishing systems and regulation impeding progress, but on a positive goal, public responsibility in economic affairs. (European Commission 1962, 7)[10]

This distinction between the negative agenda of removing barriers to economic freedom and the positive agenda of coordinating national social and economic policies influenced a generation of integration theorists and continues to shape debate about the appropriate scope of Community action today.[11] For the Hallstein Commission, however, the conclusion was clear: 'we are constrained to press onwards from a pooling of markets to the sharing of public responsibility for economic affairs within a Community system' (European Commission 1962, 7).

There was of course a linkage between this analysis and the Commission's views about the forward-leaning nature of European integration. Without taking the positive step forward of introducing a coordinated framework for state intervention, including the introduction of a set of common policies at the Community level, the existing project risked collapse. That was, after all, the implication of *engrenage*. But what did this commitment to positive integration imply, in concrete policy terms? To begin with, comprehensive state intervention across all facets of the economy would be required, coordinated at the Community level. Chapter VI of the Action Programme therefore called for an early version of regional policy (including structural funds) as a feature of long-term development policy;[12] it also called for an active incomes policy as a feature of the Community's social policy.[13] The latter policies in particular, the Commission memorandum emphasized, 'will be the indispensable complement of economic and monetary policy' (Economic Commission 1962, 48–9).

Chapter VII of the Action Programme, devoted to the general subject of economic policy, likewise outlined the Commission's aim 'gradually to create a Community short-term economic policy, into which the national policies will merge'. The instruments to be employed towards this end consisted of an array of annual forecasts, quarterly surveys, and studies of short-term economic policies in each of the six member states. All of this effort was intended to inform discussions to be undertaken 'every autumn, with the Commission taking part, by the authorities responsible for economic and financial policy in the Six countries'. During these discussions, 'the scope and context of national policies will be examined and consideration given to their expected results and the advisability of adjustments' (European Commission 1962, 52–3)—a process foreshadowing the use of Broad Economic Policy Goals some 40 years later, and more recently the heightened mutual surveillance of economic policy promised as part of Europe's new fiscal pact.

Monetary Policy: 'Merged Into One'

Thus far the Action Programme had left unanswered what a Community-level economic and monetary policy would look like. Where would decision-making authority lie—the authority, for example, to determine 'how to bring about the fastest possible expansion while maintaining stable prices' (European Commission 1962, 57)? This was, as the Commission saw it, the very nub of the matter. After all, the success of its planning efforts—which constituted the essence of positive integration—would be called into question 'if economic activity for some substantive period gets too far out of line with the programme'. In such an event—'if economic activity... [were] going ahead too fast or too slowly while the bases of the initial forecast remain unchanged'—then 'it would be for the economic and financial authorities to take general measures to stimulate or put a brake on activity as the case may be' (European Commission 1962, 53–4).[14] The memorandum did not specify, at least at this point, whether those authorities would be at the national or the Community level.

These questions were instead saved for chapter VIII of the Action Programme—the culminating chapter dedicated to the Community's internal policies. 'The preceding two chapters', referring to the chapters on social and economic policy:

> ... have shown how the Community must move towards the establishment of one single centre for economic policy. Nevertheless such a co-ordination of national policies, leading to their being eventually merged into one, would be incomplete, and therefore possibly ineffective, if no comparable action were taken in the field of monetary policy. (European Commission 1962, 63)

Three specific arguments were then marshaled in support of this claim.

First, a merger of national monetary policies was essential because of the likely effects of further exchange-rate changes on economic relations within the Community. As the Commission saw it, both the CAP and 'the Common Market itself could be imperiled'. Second, a monetary merger was necessary because of stresses within the broader international monetary system. 'This is not the place to discuss the merits of [that] system', read the memorandum—although it was clear enough that the Commission took a critical view of the subject.[15] Finally, the report argued, there was an unavoidable connection between these first two points—that is, between the Community's internal monetary situation and its external monetary circumstances. As a result, 'what is at stake here is not only the stability of the world monetary system but also the cohesion of the Common Market'. The latter 'would inevitably be deeply affected by serious monetary difficulties even if these primarily concerned countries outside the Community' (European Commission 1962, 63–4).

Given these concerns, the Commission argued, the way forward was clear. 'From the end of the transition period' of the Common Market—that is to say, beginning in 1970, 'if not even sooner'—the progressive establishment of 'economic union will involve fixed rates of exchange with very narrow limits on the variations allowed' (European Commission 1962, 64). In 1962, this meant narrower variations than those permitted within the Bretton Woods system. In other words, the member states of the Community were being called upon to bind their monetary policies more closely to one another in the context of an international monetary system already premised on limited exchange-rate movements.[16]

Once established, the Commission argued, 'these fixed rates of exchange are the very essence of a monetary union'. Why? Because 'when they are firmly guaranteed by appropriate institutions and methods, it is a matter of indifference to the citizens of any member state whether they hold assets in one particular Community currency or another'. Once this was the case—once 'appropriate institutions and methods' were in place—the distinction between the national currencies of the member states would be no more important than the variation among the different notes and coins of any given currency (European Commission 1962, 63).

How would this de facto monetary union come about? Developments elsewhere in the Community, and especially 'the progressive merging of the short-term and long-term economic policies' within the nascent economic union, 'will certainly help considerably in achieving' the desired outcome. Still, such efforts 'would not be sufficient' if they remained 'unsupported by specific action in the monetary field' (European Commission 1962, 63). Those specific actions were spelled out in an additional communication of the Commission transmitted in June 1963. The details of that proposal need not concern us here; suffice it to say that they were intended to put into place 'appropriate institutions and methods' leading first to a de facto and then to a de jure monetary union.[17]

Those proposals were put forward at a time when the world looked very different—with Europe divided asunder by the Cold War, exchange rate movements strictly limited under the terms of the Bretton Woods system, capital movements subject to stringent regulation, significant at-the-border restrictions on trade still widespread, and the European Community limited to six members. Half a century later none of those conditions would obtain. What aspects of the Commission's thinking had changed? What remained the same?

Background to EMU@10

Unlike its 1962 counterpart, 'EMU@10: Successes and challenges after 10 years of Economic and Monetary Union' lacks a sense of urgency: the document resembles an inventory more than it does a call to action. Notwithstanding these differences, it addresses much the same subject matter as the Action Programme, albeit nearly 50 years later, and hence comparison of the two documents can help provide insights into both the stability and the trajectory of key ideas.

EMU@10 consists of three parts: a one-page foreword by Commissioner Almunia; a 13-page Communication from the Commission, officially adopted (at Almunia's initiative) on 7 May 2008; and a 300-page analytical report prepared by the Commission's Directorate-General for Economic and Financial Affairs. In essence the Commission Communication summarizes the analytical report, and the foreword by Almunia summarizes the Communication. Here I focus primarily on the Commission Communication—a document of approximately the same length as the introduction to the 1962 Action Programme—with some attention to the accompanying report as well.

For present purposes, there are three striking features of the Commission Communication. First, it demonstrated a clearheaded understanding of the problems—primarily in the periphery of the eurozone—that would soon haunt European markets and governments. Second, and more to the point of this article's central focus, there are deep continuities between the Commission's 2008 analysis and its 1962 predecessor. Much as the Action Program had done earlier, EMU@10 explicitly connected the political and economic dimensions of European integration, focused on the role played by monetary integration in linking the two, and argued that forward movement in the integration process was essential to maintaining even existing levels of regional cooperation. Third, and in sharp contrast to the Commission's evident commitment to the theory of *engrenage*, its earlier reticence about market liberalization (especially with regard to financial liberalization) had been almost entirely erased during the years between the two reports.

Foreshadowing the European Debt Crisis

While the global financial crisis was already unfolding at the time of the adoption of the Commission Communication (in May 2008), it was still at a fairly early stage in its development. Financial markets had not yet frozen; Lehman Brothers had not yet collapsed; and the debt crisis that would dominate EU politics for the next several years was as of yet nowhere in sight. Thus while the Communication made repeated reference to 'turbulence in financial markets' and 'the highly turbulent period of the last few months', that turbulence was only one of several broad concerns highlighted in the Communication's conclusions (European Commission 2008, 4–5).[18] In other words, it was far from clear when the Commission Communication was published that such turbulence localized in the EU would soon become a leading global problem.

It is all the more noteworthy, then, the extent to which the Communication (and especially the accompanying report) identified the chief problems that would characterize that later crisis. As the Commission saw it, certain economic challenges—such as low rates of potential growth and an ageing population—affected the eurozone and indeed the EU as a whole. But other problems were clearly concentrated in the eurozone's periphery; and these had to do chiefly with competitiveness. For example, 'there have been substantial and lasting differences across countries in terms of inflation and unit labor costs'. Prices and wages 'have not adjusted smoothly across products, sectors and regions'. As a result, there have been 'accumulated competitiveness losses and large [national] external imbalances, which in EMU require long periods of adjustment'. Thus while 'EMU has brought significant benefits to its member countries engaged in a catching-up process'—that is to say, in the countries of the eurozone's periphery—significant problems remained (European Commission 2008, 5–6).

Why were these particular problems so pronounced? 'Essentially, this protracted adjustment reflects the fact that structural reforms have been less ambitious [since EMU's formation] than in the run-up to the euro'.[19] As a result, we have witnessed 'developments within [particular] member states such as the growth of current account deficits, persistent inflation divergences or trends of unbalanced growth'. Such developments:

> ... need to be monitored given that the occurrence of spillover effects and the growing interdependence of euro-area economies mean these developments represent a concern not just for the country in question but for the euro area as a whole. (European Commission 2008, 6–8)[20]

Indeed, the report found that:

> ... the evidence of the first ten years of EMU indicates that while market integration, particularly in financial services, is beneficial overall for EMU... it can also, if not accompanied by appropriate policies, amplify divergences among the participating countries.

This was a particular point of concern. 'While some of these divergences can be benign—reflecting the catching-up process or even normal adjustment—they may also be harmful and the result of inefficient adjustment'. As a result, the Commission memorandum maintained, 'the euro area has a special interest in the success of structural reform'. For whereas 'stepping up reforms' was 'of course welcome in the EU as a whole', it constituted 'an absolute must for the euro area' (European Commission 2008, 8–9).[21]

This was a cogent summary of the situation then prevailing in Greece, Portugal and elsewhere in the eurozone's periphery. Of course the Commission failed to anticipate either the scale or timing of the resulting debt crisis, but in this regard it was hardly alone. What is remarkable is the degree to which the underlying features of the impending crisis were accurately identified and assessed.

Engrenage Redux

If the Commission's analysis of pending problems in the eurozone demonstrated great professionalism, the policy prescriptions on offer tended to be doctrinaire. Highly-indebted governments needed to get their fiscal houses in order. Structural reforms needed to be undertaken in order to lower employment costs and increase international competitiveness. Surveillance of national budgets needed to be both stepped up and broadened, ultimately taking in matters that went well beyond fiscal policy—an expanded enterprise in which the Commission envisioned a key role for itself (European Commission 2008, 8–10).

At a deeper level, the assumptions underlying the Commission's analysis clearly echoed the premises behind the 1962 Action Programme. Although the 2008 Communication avoided some of the explicitly theoretical linkages between economic and political action outlined in that earlier report, the connections drawn between the two were practically ubiquitous. Thus:

> ... the move to the last phase of EMU—Economic and Monetary Union—on 1 January 1999, marked a watershed in European integration. Although economic in substance, it sent a very powerful political signal to European citizens and to the rest of the world that Europe was capable of taking far-ranging decisions to cement a common and prosperous future.

Nor was that signal limited to the moment of the euro's conception. Instead, 'ten years into its existence, the euro is a resounding success. The euro has become a symbol of Europe'. This symbolism was anticipated and deliberate; after all, 'from the outset EMU was conceived as a crucial step in the process of European integration'. This did not mean simply market integration; for 'although its objectives and achievements are predominantly economic, EMU has never been solely an economic project'. Instead, it meant the broader purpose of binding the EU's member states together. For this reason, EMU represented 'a milestone of EU integration' (European Commission 2008, 3, 13).

Hence although *engrenage* was not specifically invoked, there was a continuing supposition that political support for existing integration projects depended on further progress in other domains.[22] Other suppositions were possible—for example, the democratic premises on which the principle of subsidiarity rests. The idea that decisions should be taken at the lowest possible level of government had formed part of EU treaty law since 1992; but unlike *engrenage*, subsidiarity had never developed into a principle of action. There are no units of the Commission actively formulating proposals to return existing Community competences to the member states (or for that matter assessing which elements of national and state law might better be assigned to regions or localities). Certainly subsidiarity was not the animating force behind the work of the Directorate-General for Economic and Financial Affairs in preparing EMU@10. Instead the prevailing view of integration was as a one-way street—a ratcheting process—in which there was either successful forward progress or there was failure.

This insistence on the dynamic and forward-leaning character of European integration has become such an article of faith among integration's advocates that some might argue it hardly bears mentioning. But it is precisely because this understanding remains so widely shared that it ought to be noted and identified as a key characteristic of the shared intellectual assumptions underpinning the project. One does not have to look far for evidence of this shared understanding. For the authors of EMU@10, 'a well-functioning EMU is a major asset for the EU as a whole', as 'a thriving euro-area economy will contribute to the wealth and dynamism of the whole EU, reinforcing public support for EU integration both within and outside the euro area' (European Commission 2008, 13).[23] The alternative possibility—that establishing a monetary union with such a diverse membership was always a stretch, and that the problems in the eurozone's periphery identified elsewhere in the Commission's report might not simply tarnish but eviscerate public support for integrative developments in other domains—does not seem to have been seriously considered.

Where does that leave us? As the 2008 report proudly trumpeted, 'one in two people in the euro area asserts that for them, the EU means the single currency' (European Commission 2008, 8). This identification would soon prove a double-edged sword, however, as failure to manage the eurozone's financial crisis risked sapping faith in the European project more generally.

Embracing Liberalization

While EMU@10 reflects a fairly uncritical acceptance of *engregage*, another of the central premises of the 1962 Action Programme had practically disappeared by the time the Commission authored its 2008 report. This was the assertion that negative and positive modes of integration needed to be distinguished, and that progress in the former needed to be counterbalanced by parallel developments in the latter.

As a practical matter, the distinction between negative and positive modes of integration reflected a left-wing critique of the tendency of the Community (and later the EU) to liberalize national economic systems. That battle has recently been reengaged, in the wake of the global financial crisis; but in 2008, when the Commission produced its analysis, the left had largely thrown in the towel on this issue. There are passing references to social solidarity in the document, but these are mostly framed in terms of the necessity to adopt further structural (e.g., labor market) reforms in order to boost economic productivity and—in the long-term—wages.[24] The wisdom of these reforms was taken to be self-evident, requiring no serious defense. This represented a sea change from the

Commission's earlier assertion that a liberal economic order could only exist 'at the price of constant State intervention in economic life'. While a complete genealogy of that transformation cannot be offered here, a few words are in order about one of its most important aspects: the Commission's attitudes towards capital controls.[25]

During the 1960s, when the regulation of international capital movements was a central feature of the international monetary system generally and the western European political economy in particular, the Commission had been an early advocate of financial liberalization. But influenced first by the French crisis of 1968 and later by the first oil shock the Brussels executive eventually abandoned this position, maintaining instead that strict regulation of international capital movements was a prerequisite for the reductions in exchange-rate movements that were to lead to monetary unification. By the mid 1980s, yet another policy reversal was in the offing; a key development was the 1987 publication of the report by a study group commissioned by Jacques Delors, then the Commission president, and chaired by Tomasso Padoa-Schioppa, a former head of the Directorate-General for Economic and Financial Affairs. The resulting report argued that the pursuit of independent national monetary policies was incompatible with the attainment of full capital mobility, an open trading regime and exchange-rate stability (Padoa-Schioppa 1987).[26] Since the latter two goals were regarded as unassailable, the implication was that capital market liberalization should be accompanied by efforts to establish a centralized European monetary authority. This argument carried the day and two years later was reflected in the conclusions of the Delors Report, on which Padoa-Schioppa served as a rapporteur.

The Padoa-Schioppa report made it intellectually fashionable for pro-Europeans to embrace (or re-embrace) financial liberalization, since capital account liberalization was once again viewed as an adjunct rather than a rival to monetary unification. But while the views of the Commission on the desirability of capital mobility changed completely (and more than once), its stance on the desirability of monetary union remained consistent throughout.

Conclusions

In this article I have briefly surveyed the evolution of several important premises about the nature of European integration, especially in the thinking and proposals of the European Commission. Rather than trying to sketch out a history of European monetary integration efforts I have instead provided a close analysis of two texts, widely separated in time, in a search for clues about what has changed and what has remained constant in the Commission's thinking about these matters.

My conclusions are quite simple: most of the central premises (or 'keystones') of Europe's economic governance model have proved remarkably resilient. Above all else, what has remained constant across the two periods is the Commission's view about the nature and direction of European integration itself. This principled commitment to the *engrenage* model has influenced not only the Commission's analysis but its recommendations as well. Whatever the nature of the problems at hand, the Commission's answer is always the same: more Europe.

Why does this matter? It matters because Europe now finds itself in an incredibly complicated fix. As a result, changes in the fundamental architecture of European integration—not just at its margins but in its core construction—may very well prove necessary in order to save the eurozone from itself. Undertaking such a fundamental redesign will require fresh and original thinking—thinking that is well outside the box. It is not clear where this fresh thinking will come from. But if the past is any guide to the future, we should not expect it from the European Commission.

Acknowledgements

I would like to thank the participants in the Bruges workshop as well as one anonymous reviewer for their comments and suggestions. The remaining errors are my own.

Notes

1. A much more important document, co-authored by the Commission and entitled *Towards a Genuine Economic and Monetary Union* (attributed to Herman Van Rompuy in close collaboration with José Manuel Barroso, Jean-Claude Juncker and Mario Draghi) was published on 5 December 2012, well after the time that this article was written and accepted for publication. However, the same fundamental observations made here about EMU@10 could likewise be applied to it.
2. The Spaak Report, by contrast, had called for more robust provisions; but its recommendations were strongly criticized by Europe's central banking community, and the resulting treaty text reflected those concerns.
3. The resolution in the Parliamentary Assembly was passed on October 17; the Action Programme was published on October 24.
4. Among other aspects of his background, Hallstein had served as an officer in the German military, was captured by Allied forces, and had spent time in the United States as a prisoner of war... and later as a professor of international law at Georgetown University.
5. From Haas (1958) through Moravcsik (1998) and Stone-Sweet et al. (2001).
6. 'The psychological chain reaction set off by integration does not stop at the frontiers of social policy. Even such matters as foreign and defence policy, which are not covered by any Community treaty, more and more demand a common European discipline. Politics is indivisible; and necessity is the spur' (Hallstein 1972, 28).
7. 'Common interests were to be resolutely served by joint efforts to create a balanced, stable structure. That, in a nutshell, was the "European" idea. [But] it was not automatic. It was a conscious choice by those responsible' (Hallstein 1972, 20–1).
8. These lofty objectives (cited in the preamble to the Treaty) included ensuring economic and social progress while making constant improvement to living and working conditions, guaranteeing steady economic expansion and harmonious development, and reducing regional economic disparities.
9. Shonfield (1966) provides a classic as well as more or less contemporaneous analysis of those distinctions while making the case that modern capitalism should be viewed as a vast planning exercise.
10. As the Commission saw it, 'without such programming, it would become extremely difficult to implement the common policies for agriculture, energy and transport' outlined elsewhere in the Action Programme (European Commission 1962, 54).
11. Among academics, Tinbergen (1954) employed this terminology but Pinder (1968) was the first to define the framework in the fashion now most familiar to EU analysts. Today its most famous practitioner is Fritz Scharpf (e.g., Scharpf 1996).

12. The Commission memorandum described a 'community policy on structures' as 'a necessary adjunct to development policy'. There was thus to be understood 'a distinction between economic development policy and structural policy, the first taking structures as they stand and the second seeking, by their constant improvement, to raise steadily the maximum yield of the economic system' (European Commission 1962, 51).
13. Thus the Commission argued that the 'broad outline' of wage policies 'should be clarified by discussions between both sides of industry [i.e., labor and management] and Governments' — in other words, in classic corporatist fashion (European Commission 1962, 49).
14. Note that policy would be altered in order to keep economic activity consistent with the plan, rather than adapting the plan to reflect changes in the behavior of the market.
15. Thus prevailing international monetary arrangements were seen as making for 'a certain fragility calling for constant action if undue strains are to be avoided' (European Commission 1962, 64).
16. The international implications of establishing closer monetary ties within the Community figured prominently in the Commission's analysis. Thus in the future 'the Community will be able to act more effectively' in the international monetary arena 'as it will function as a single unit'. This development would increase Europe's collective clout and thereby influence the course of future worldwide developments in a positive direction, as 'the emergence of a European reserve currency would considerably facilitate international monetary co-operation and a reform of the present system' (European Commission 1962, 64).
17. The only significant recommendation of the June 1963 Commission memorandum to survive Council scrutiny was the establishment of the Committee of Central Bank Governors.
18. Those conclusions included attention not only to 'high energy, food and commodity prices, financial turbulence and global exchange rate adjustment', but also globalization, the scarcity of natural resources within the EU, climate change and the effects of an ageing population. These problems were introduced on p. 3 of the Communication from the Commission, discussed at some length throughout the document, and then reiterated on p. 13.
19. This was in contradistinction to the expectations of so-called endogenous optimum currency area theorists; see, e.g., Frankel and Rose (1998).
20. Communication from the Commission, p. 8. Thus Commission officials were well aware that the eurozone's problem 'isn't just fiscal', a conclusion that academic economists were reaching at about the same time; see, e.g., Wihlborg et al. (2010).
21. As part of its analysis, the Commission noted empirical evidence suggesting that 'structural reforms in countries sharing the single currency have higher "multipliers" than elsewhere'. In other words, 'countries undertaking structural reforms can accrue more benefit while those falling behind may pay a higher price for their inaction' (European Commission 2008, 9).
22. Thus 'a well-functioning euro area lays the foundations for EMU to play a strong role externally'. That 'strong role' was not limited to leadership 'in the macroeconomic sphere and in the area of global financial supervision and responsibility'. Rather, 'a strong EMU will also foster the EU's leadership in the global economy more generally', including key policy areas 'where the EU aspires to global leadership, e.g., sustainable development, development aid, trade policy, competition [policy] and human rights' (European Commission 2008, 13).
23. Indeed EMU@10 maintains that 'this role [of binding Europe together] has become even stronger' and an even more important function of the monetary union as a result of the EU's enlargement from 15 to 27 member states. After all, 'all newly acceded EU member countries are preparing for the euro adoption'; in fact the prospect of euro adoption 'has been one of the main drivers of these countries' convergence with the EU's standard of living' (European Commission 2008, 13).
24. For example, 'reforms of social expenditure programmes and active labour market policies should aim to offer better income protection while strengthening incentives to work' (European Commission 2008, 10).
25. For a comprehensive examination of changes in the policies and attitudes of European governments from the 1960s to the early 1990s on this subject, see Bakker (1996).
26. The 1987 report built on previous work by the contributors, especially Padoa-Schioppa (1982).

References

Bakker, A. 1996. *The liberalization of capital movements in Europe: The Monetary Committee and financial integration, 1958–1994*. Dordrecht: Kluwer Academic Publishers.

European Commission. 1962. Memorandum of the Commission on the action programme of the Community for the second stage. COM (62) 300, Brussels: European Commission.

European Commission. 2008. EMU@10: Successes and challenges after ten years of Economic and Monetary Union. European Economy 2, published by the Directorate-General for Economic and Financial Affairs.

Frankel, J., and A. Rose. 1998. The endogeneity of the optimum currency area criteria. *Economic Journal* 108: 1009–24.

Haas, E. 1958. *The uniting of Europe: political, social, and economic forces, 1950–1957.* Stanford, CA: Stanford University Press.

Hallstein, W. 1972. *Europe in the making.* New York: Norton.

Moravcsik, A. 1998. *The choice for Europe: social purpose and state power from Messina to Maastricht.* Ithaca, NY: Cornell.

Padoa-Schioppa, T. 1982. Capital mobility: why is the Treaty not implemented? In *The road to monetary union in Europe,* ed. T. Padoa-Schioppa. Oxford: Clarendon Press.

Padoa-Schioppa, T. 1987. *Efficiency, stability, equity: a strategy for the evolution of the economic system of the European Community.* New York: Oxford.

Pinder, J. 1968. Positive and negative integration: some problems of economic union in the EEC. *The World Today* 24, no. 3: 88–110.

Scharpf, F. 1996. Negative and positive integration in the political economy of European welfare states. In *Governance in the European Union,* ed. G. Marks et.al., 15–39. London: Sage.

Shonfield, A. 1966. *Modern capitalism: the changing balance of public and private power.* New York: Oxford.

Stone-Sweet, A., W. Sandholtz, and N. Fligstein. 2001. *The institutionalization of Europe.* New York: Oxford.

Tinbergen, J. 1954. *International economic integration.* Amsterdam: Elsevier.

Wihlborg, C., T. Willett, and N. Zhang. 2010. The Euro crisis: it isn't just fiscal and it doesn't just involve Greece, Claremont McKenna College Robert Day School of Economics and Finance Research Paper No. 2011-03. Available at SSRN: http://ssrn.com/abstract=1776133, last accessed March 18, 2013.

Banking on Stability: The Political Economy of New Capital Requirements in the European Union

DAVID HOWARTH* & LUCIA QUAGLIA**

*Faculté des Lettres, des Sciences, Humaines, Laboratoire des Sciences Politiques,
University of Luxembourg,
Luxembourg
**Department of Politics, University of York, UK*

ABSTRACT The Basel III Accord on a 'Global regulatory framework for more resilient banks and banking systems' was issued in late 2010 as the cornerstone of the international regulatory response to the global financial crisis. Its adoption into European Union (EU) legislation has, however, been met with considerable member state reticence and intra-EU negotiations are ongoing. This paper investigates the political economy of new capital requirements in the EU, arguing that the institutional features of national banking sectors convincingly account for the divergence in EU member state preferences on capital rules.

Introduction

Since the global financial crisis delivered a major blow to the financial stability of much of the European Union (EU), financial regulation has moved to the centre stage of debates about the future of EU economic governance. Capital requirements for banks have traditionally been regarded as one of the main instruments to ensure the stability of the banking sector and hence financial stability *tout court*. Capital requirements are regulations limiting the amount of leverage that financial firms can take on.[1] As the US treasury minister Timothy Geithner put it in the wake of the financial crisis, 'The top three things to get done are capital,

capital and capital' (Leonhardt 2010). At the peak of the crisis the interbank markets froze, highlighting the importance of banks' holding of liquid assets[2] in order to meet short-term obligations. Hence, in addition to capital requirements, liquidity rules also made it into the *zeitgeist* of banking regulation.

In 1988, the Basel Committee on Banking Supervision (BCBS) issued the Basel I Accord on 'International convergence of capital measurement and capital standards', which was updated by the Basel II Accord in 2004 (revised in 2005). Over time, these 'soft' international rules have been incorporated into (legally binding) national legislation. In the EU this was done through the Capital Requirements Directives (CRD) (see Underhill 1997; Christopoulos and Quaglia 2009; Quaglia 2010). The Basel III accord (hereafter Basel III) was issued in late 2010 as the cornerstone of the international regulatory response to the global financial crisis (BCBS 2010a). Its adoption into EU law has, however, met with considerable member state and EU institutional reticence. The EU directive and regulation to be adopted (referred to collectively as CRDIV) will likely qualify the application of the Basel III capital requirements in the EU.

The EU is one of the largest financial jurisdictions worldwide and some scholars have indeed pointed out its 'market power' (Damro 2012; see also Dür 2011). In terms of total banking assets and liabilities, the EU's internal market is larger than that of the US. Hence, the implementation of Basel III into EU legislation will be consequential not only for its large internal market and the 6000 European banks therein, but also for the stability of the international financial system. Third jurisdictions, first and foremost the US, which is the main counterpart of the EU in international financial fora (Posner 2009; Posner and Véron 2010), are also concerned about potential regulatory arbitrage and competitive advantages accruing to European banks as a result of the 'distinctive' implementation of Basel rules in the EU.

In the making of the Basel III accord first and in the negotiations of the CRD IV later, the core of the controversy concerned the distributive implications of the regulatory changes proposed. The definition of capital (in particular the list of financial instruments that count as capital); the level of capital requirements; the definition of liquid assets and the amount of liquid assets affect different banks and national banking systems in different ways, imposing costs as well as benefits that are not equally distributed. Different banks have different sources of capital; some banks have capital instruments or liquid assets that other banks do not have; some banks are better positioned than others to meet higher capital requirements or liquidity coverage. Hence, banks and national banking systems face different adjustment costs to the proposed rules: it very much depends on the features of the national banking system and the domestic regulatory framework. It also depends on the link between the financial system and the real economy, in particular in terms of the major sources of funding for non-financial companies and the relative importance of bank credit. If companies mainly rely on credit from banks, rather than raising funds on the stock market or issuing securities, higher capital and liquidity requirements are more likely to result in a credit crunch for the real economy.

In order to explain the politics of the CRD IV, that is member states and industry preferences in the negotiations on the new capital and liquidity rules, this article builds on and develops further the literature that examines the specific features of national banking systems (Allen and Gale 2000; Deeg 2010; Hardie and Howarth 2013) and links these features to member states and industry preferences concerning EU financial regulation (Busch 2004; Fioretos 2001, 2010; Macartney 2010; Zimmerman 2010; for a somewhat different version of this argument see Mügge 2010). Adopting a comparative political economy analysis, this article sees member state and industry preferences determined by a combination of political economy factors and, notably, the institutional features of the national banking sector. This analysis involves digging into the balance sheets of banks in the main EU countries, their assets and liabilities (i.e., how banks are funded). The impact of state intervention during the recent financial crisis on banks' capital position is also considered.

The paper proceeds as follows. The second section provides an overview of the negotiations and the content of the new capital rules in the EU. The third section investigates the political economy of these rules in the main European countries. It is argued that the divergence in EU member state preferences on Basel III / CRDIV—rooted in differences in national banking systems—explains the incomplete nature of European economic governance in the area of financial regulation and accounts for the intergovernmental character of many EU negotiations in this policy field.

The Content and Negotiations of the New EU Capital Legislation

The Basel III accord was signed by the BCBS in December 2010 (BCBS 2010a). The new rules: provide a more restrictive definition of what counts as bank capital; increase the risk weight of several assets in the banking book and introduce capital buffers; set up a recommended and potentially obligatory leverage ratio; and outline international rules on liquidity management. All in all, the new rules increase the proportion of capital that must be of proven loss absorbing capacity (going concern)—i.e., core tier one (equity) capital—over Basel II requirements, and will be phased in gradually from January 2013 until 2019. The Basel III accord is an agreement between national regulators gathered in the BCBS; hence it has to be implemented into national (and/or EU) legislation in order to become legally binding.

In July 2011, after extensive consultations conducted in parallel with the work of the BCBS, the EU Commission adopted the CRDIV legislative package designed to replace the CRDII with a directive that governs the access to deposit-taking activities (Commission 2011a) and a regulation that establishes prudential requirements for credit institutions (Commission 2011b). After its approval, the proposed directive (Commission 2011a) will have to be transposed by the member states in a way suitable to their own national environment. It contains rules concerning the taking up and pursuit of the business of banks, the conditions for the freedom of establishment and the freedom to provide services, the supervisory review process and the definition of competent authorities. The directive also incorporates two elements of the Basel III accord, namely the introduction of two capital buffers in addition to the minimum capital requirements: the capital conservation buffer identical for all banks in the EU and the countercyclical capital buffer to be determined at national level. The proposed EU regulation (Commission 2011b) contains prudential requirements for credit institutions and investment firms. The proposed regulation covers the definition of capital, increasing the amount of own funds that banks need to hold as well as the quality of those funds; it introduces the Liquidity Coverage Ratio (LCR)—the exact composition and calibration of which will be determined after an observation and review period in 2015; and the need to consider a leverage ratio, subject to supervisory review.

The Commission's CRDIV draft, which would implement Basel III into EU law, is the most substantial of all the post-financial crisis regulatory measures entertained to date at the EU-level but its draft also involved watering down or modifying the Basel III guidelines in ways to meet EU member state demands (IMF 2011a). Indeed, the CRDIV draft was criticised by many regulators and by the IMF for significantly watering down key Basel III elements. Speaking at a meeting of EU Economic and Finance ministers held to discuss the CRD IV, the British Treasury minister complained that: 'We are not implementing the Basel agreement, as anyone who will look at this text will be able to tell you' (Barker and Masters 2012).

The Commission 'softened' its definition of core tier 1 capital relative to the Basel III recommendations in some areas. Notably, the Commission draft allows 'silent participations', that is, state loans that make up a significant part of the capital of many EU banks, including the publicly owned German Landesbanken. The Commission's draft also limits the role of the leverage ratio designed to limit risk-taking at banks. The almost unique reliance on Basel III's risk-weighted core tier 1 ratio in the Commission's draft CRDIV was criticised for inadequately representing the health of the European banking sector (Lanoo 2010).[3] On liquidity, the Commission adopts the less prescriptive definition of liquid assets: for the LCR to include 'transferable assets that are of extremely high liquidity and credit quality' and 'transferable assets that are of high liquidity and credit quality'. The Commission's draft lacks a firm commitment to implement the Net Stable Funding Ratio by 2018 called for in Basel III. The Commission's proposed regulation also sets higher capital requirements for Over the Counter derivatives that are not cleared though Central Counterparties.

The use of a regulation, which once approved is directly applicable without the need for national transposition, is designed to ensure the creation of a single rulebook in the EU. The regulation will eliminate a key source of national divergence. In the CRD III, more than one hundred national discretions (differences in national legislation transposing the EU directive) remained. Yet, the Commission's draft regulation also proposes a maximum capital ratio which was opposed by many who argued in favour of EU standards that exceed the Basel minimum because of prevailing balance sheet uncertainties in the EU, the lack of EU-wide resolution arrangements and a fully unified fiscal backstop. The analysis below will demonstrate that most of these modifications to Basel III in CRDIV owe to French and German government demands.

Following the agreement on Basel III and during the intra-EU negotiations on CRDIV, some of the compromises reached in the BCBS unravelled. Several EU member states, the European Parliament (EP) and even the Commission itself called for the taking into account of 'European specificities' in incorporating the Basel III rules into the CRD IV, reopening some of the issues that had caused friction within the BCBS. Basel III applied to internationally active banks, whereas EU legislation was to apply to all banks, making some Basel III provisions—notably the calculation of tier 1—impossible to apply in EU member states without a massive shift in the structure of a large range of banks and banking systems. The Commission has justified its decision to apply Basel III rules, as with Basel I and Basel II, to all EU banks on both stability grounds and reasons linked to the application of EU Competition Policy (Paulis 2012). Both the Commission and the EP have also expressed concern as to the international competitiveness of European banks and the need to ensure an 'international level playing field.' Of particular concern has been the fact that in the US, the Basel III accord would be applied only to financial institutions with over US$50bn in assets (EP 2010, 2011).

The Political Economy of New EU Capital Rules

This section engages in a political economy analysis of national preferences on EU capital requirements. These preferences reflect three factors: the capital, and thus competitive, position of national banks; national banking and financial system structure; and related macro-economic considerations, that is the impact of Basel III on the wider economy.

Capital Position

The first explanation focuses specifically on the capital position of banks and relates to the likely impact of recapitalization upon their market share and competitiveness. Basel III/CRDIV will force banks to hold 6 per cent tier 1 and 8 per cent tier 1 and tier 2 capital by 2015 and four years later—with the capital conservation buffer of 2.5 per cent to be phased in by 2019—8.5 per cent and 10.5 per cent respectively. The obligation to raise a bank's tier 1 capital ratio can have one or both of two effects. To meet those requirements the banks either need to reduce their assets (including lending) (i.e., decrease the Risk Weighted Assets (RWA) denominator) or retain earnings (i.e., increase the capital base numerator). If the former is undertaken then profits will be lower; if the latter then discretionary payments such as dividends on equity will decrease. *Ceteris paribus*, both developments make the bank less attractive to investors. However — it should also be noted — that many investors are also focused upon the long-term stability of banks, especially in the difficult market conditions of the early 2010s, which provides an incentive to banks to recapitalise.

While the capital position of different banks within a national economy varies considerably, systemic patterns can be detected. The studies and impact assessment of the BCBS of new Basel III rules were conducted at the aggregate level. Nonetheless, even the BCBS warned about differentiated effects across countries, without identifying those with banking systems most affected (BCBS 2010). A perusal of the equity and tier 1 capital for systemically important British, French and German banks shows why the German government in particular had good reasons to oppose the rigid tightening of capital requirements. The German government also favoured a maximum harmonization rule in order to prevent better capitalized banks from gaining competitive advantage and expanding market share at the expense of undercapitalized (German) banks (see Table 1 and 2). Faced with adverse capital conditions, the two large German commercial banks would only narrowly respect the Basel III target for 2015. The data also show that most of the main British banks would have limited difficulties in meeting the Basel III standards. The data help to explain why the British government was most in favour of tighter capital rules and most opposed to a maximum harmonization rule. The data on French banks suggest their strong position but the double counting of insurance subsidiaries — which Basel III recommends banning — inflates the tier 1 capital ratio significantly in most cases.

Table 1. Bank equity as percentage of total assets (core tier 1) and leverage ratio in parentheses

Recall: core tier 1 ratio of 4.5%/or 7% with the 'capital conservation buffer' from 2019	UK	France	Germany
2008	3.7 (27)	3.8 (26.3)	2.93 (34.1)
2009	4.87 (20.5)	4.91 (20.4)	3.76 (26.6)
2010	5.37 (18.6)	5.07 (19.7)	3.88 (25.8)

Source: ECB statistical data warehouse. Domestic banking group and stand alone banks only.

Table 2. Tier 1 capital (as a percentage of total assets) main British, German and French systematically important banks (non-weighted average)*

Recall: Basel III target of 6% / or 8.5% with the 'capital conservation buffer' from 2019.	2012 baseline scenario	2012 adverse	2011 baseline scenario	2011 adverse
UK	10.4	7.45	9.75	7.95
France	9	7.4	8.5	7.7
Germany	8.8	6.4	7.85	6.75

Source: EBA *results of the stress test based on the full static balance sheet assumption without any mitigating actions, mandatory restructuring or capital raisings post 31 December 2010/11 (all government support measures fully paid in before 31 December 2010/11 are included). Figures cover the largest four banks in UK and France and largest two in Germany.

The implications of the new capital rules were potentially greatest for the many non-listed public sector and mutual banks (a much more significant element of the German and French banking systems than in the UK) which did not use equity, relying on other capital to meet capital requirements in the past including hybrids — that is, capital which has some features of both debt and equity and notably 'silent participations' (government loans) (Bowles 2010). Basel III menaced a significant overhaul of the capital structure and legal status of internationally active publicly-owned banks and mutuals — although exceptions could have been allowed which did not apply to commercial banks with listed equity. Proportionately, the ban on hybrids would hit the German banking system the most and in particular the Landesbanken which explains the Commission's CRDIV draft provision to continue to allow only the one form of hybrid on which they rely to meet the core tier 1 ratio: 'silent participations'. The ban on all other hybrids was incorporated into the European Banking Authority's late 2011 stress-tests of systemically important banks, resulting in the withdrawal of one German LB, Helaba (the Hessen-Thüringen LB) in order to avoid public failure (Wilson 2011). The Basel III ban on hybrids has also already hit the two large German commercial banks despite the qualification of the ban in the CRDIV draft. In early 2012, Commerzbank moved to boost investor confidence by replacing its hybrid capital ('silent participations') with equity in order to improve its core tier 1 position (Wilson 2012).

The IMF estimated that a ban on double counting of capital in banks' insurance subsidiaries would result in French banks losing a total of 28.9 per cent of their tier 1 capital, preventing several from meeting the 6 per cent threshold and all from meeting the 8.5 per cent threshold (with the capital conservation buffer to be in place from 2019) (IMF. 2011b). It is not surprising then that the French government (and to a less extent the German) lobbied to lift the restrictions in Basel III on double counting. A ban would hit the three large French commercial banks particularly hard because of the longstanding feature the French banking system of *bancassurance*, in which insurance companies (often subsidiaries of banks) make use of banks to market their products. The system predominates in certain other EU member states, including Spain and Austria. However, the lifting of the Basel III restriction also benefited the part-state owned Lloyds–TSB, which is one of Britain's largest insurance providers.

Basel II guidelines and CRDII rules on bank capital allow banks to amass assets with high credit ratings without setting capital aside to cover potential losses. This allowed many banks in Europe to become highly leveraged despite meeting international rules on capital cushions. European Central Bank (ECB) and several other central bank officials pushed for a leverage ratio as a simple mechanism to curb excessive risk-taking (Masters 2012). The French, German and a range of other EU member states governments opposed the adoption of a leverage ratio to determine the quantity of capital to be held by banks, which explains why the specific Basel III provision (3 per cent or an assets to tier 1 capital ratio of approximately 33) was made more flexible in the Commission's CRDIV draft.

French and German opposition reflected the much higher leverage ratios of most large banks in France and Germany (compared to the UK), the difficult situation facing German Landesbanken and French mutual banks having to respect a new leverage ratio and the fear of the need to force through a rapid de-leveraging of banks. While the leverage ratio of British banks increased dramatically in the two years prior to the outbreak of the financial crisis, this had been historically amongst the lowest in the EU and it dropped quickly in 2009 and 2010. The figures for French banks appear similarly low. However, the Basel III ban on double counting the capital of insurance subsidiaries — if adopted in EU legislation — would hit the leverage ratios for the three biggest French commercial banks considerably.

The British government has been the most in favour of the big three for closely aligning CRDIV and Basel III (IMF 2011a). The British Conservative–Liberal Democrat government (joined by several other member state governments including the Swedish) criticised the Commission's CRDIV draft on the grounds that it did not go far enough (see for example, Djankov 2011). In particular, the British opposed the move under CRDIV to embrace a leverage ratio for guidance purposes only and sought to keep open the possibility of imposing capital requirements higher than those eventually set by EU legislation, which the Commission's CRDIV draft explicitly blocked by imposing a cap. Many British policy-makers, including the Governor of the Bank of England, were critical of the Commission's position on a maximum capital ratio, arguing that the new level of required capital should have been many times higher than the levels set out in Basel III (Robinson, 2010). The British Independent Commission on Banking recommended that large retail banks be required to have a minimum core tier 1 ratio of 10 per cent of risk-weighted assets which would significantly exceed the Basel III minimum of 7 per cent (core tier 1 at 4.5 per cent plus the 2.5 per cent capital conservation buffer and the proposed surcharge for global systemically important banks — possibly up to 2.5 per cent). Other (mainly continental) policy-makers, such as the former Governor of the Bank of France, Jacques de Larosière, argued that 'Basel rules risk punishing the wrong banks', that is the 'diversified' and 'safer' continental European banks, rather the Anglo-Saxon banks which, he claimed, engaged in riskier investment banking activities (de Larosière 2010).

The Structure of Banking and Financial Systems

The second political economy explanation focuses on the structure of banking and financial systems and how these structures shape the activities of banks (Allen and Gale 2000; Hardie and Howarth 2009, 2013). This explanation reminds us that British and French commercial banks are better capitalised because, on average, they rely more on equity finance in relative terms than banks in most continental European countries (see Table 1 above). As noted above, many banks on the continent, such as the publicly owned German Landesbanken, cooperative and savings banks and most French mutuals, do not have equity finance. Indeed, this aspect proved problematic in the incorporation of the Basel III accord into EU legislation, which contains specific provisions for the cooperative and mutual banks. Basel III was written having in mind banks funded by equity finance (hence the emphasis on common equities in core tier 1 capital), whereas many banks in the EU rely upon on other sources of funding.

The overall equity position of banks in all three countries improved following the financial crisis (with increases of 45 per cent in the UK; 45 per cent in France; and most in Germany at 67 per cent although from a lower position). This improvement was due in part to significant government interventions in the banking system which involved share purchases. For the UK, government intervention came far more, in comparative terms, in the form of share purchase (6.3 per cent of GDP versus only 1.2 per cent in Germany, where the government opted more to purchase toxic assets, and 1.1 per cent of GDP in France — at end 2009) (National Central Bank figures). No other national share purchase programme came close to reaching the British level, in either real terms or in terms relative to GDP.

There are other, less obvious, features of national banking systems which explain positioning on CRDIV. French and German bank and government opposition to the use of a simple leverage rule, as opposed to risk-weighted assets, owes in large part to the relative importance of trade financing in their operations. Trade financing is high in terms of overall assets but low in terms of risk-weighted assets. Similarly, different levels of bank and banking system exposure to short-term funding on wholesale markets directed national preferences on CRDIV liquidity rules.

Basel III liquidity rules effectively discourage reliance on short term funding (less than a year) on wholesale markets. Clearly British bank reliance on short-term funding was the highest of the three countries in 2007, and much of this was short term funding of less than three months. The boom in British bank lending over the decade preceding the crisis owed in part to this short-term funding. But by 2010 this reliance had dropped dramatically, moving from above 60 per cent of GDP to 30 per cent (own calculations on the basis of central bank data), contributing to the credit crunch in the British economy (see below). UK banks have gone the furthest, and by a significant margin, to reduce their reliance on short-term funding and increase the resilience of their funding positions and thus they and the British authorities are most comfortable with the liquidity rules and ambitious phase-in dates. This improved position owed in large part to the early introduction in 2009 of restrictive liquidity rules in the UK, on which the Basel III and CRDIV rules were largely modelled. British banks thus had a head start on liquidity.

The German government was less preoccupied about Basel III liquidity rules given that German bank debt was issued principally in the form of longer maturity covered bonds — *pfandbrief* — itself a reflection of the 'patient capital' that characterises the German financial system. For German banks, reliance on short term funding was low, dropping from slightly above 10 per cent in 2007 to slightly below 10 per cent of GDP in

2010. However, in the case of French banks, reliance on short term funding was far greater and dropped only marginally from a high of 45 per cent of GDP in 2007 to 40 per cent by 2010. The comparatively high reliance of French banks — and bank lending — on short-term debt largely explains the French government's push to make CRDIV liquidity rules less prescriptive (Masters 2012). Basel III includes a prolonged phase-in period for the Liquidity Coverage Ratio (2015) and the Net Stable Funding Ratio (2018), while the Commission's CRDIV draft waters down the first ratio and fails to impose the second. This preference for gradualism and flexibility can be explained by concerns about the potential impact of these liquidity measures on bank lending.

Differences in national financial systems — and notably, differences in the funding of non-financial companies — also shaped government policy. Small and medium-sized companies in the three countries were most exposed to potential de-leveraging given their limited access to other funding sources. However, overall non-financial company reliance on bank credit, as opposed to equity and securities, varied markedly. Reliance was particularly high in Germany, where bank credit comprised about 50 per cent of non-financial company external funding in 2011. In France, bank credit amounted to only 30 per cent of non-financial company external funding in 2011, while in the UK, the figure reached only 27 per cent (ECB statistics data warehouse, national central bank data). The comparison with non-financial company external funding in the United States — only 13 per cent from bank credit — indicates even more clearly the comparatively heavy reliance in Germany and its underdeveloped equity markets (Federal Reserve Flow of Funds, December 2011 release).

Differing Macro-economic Concerns

The heavy reliance of non-financial companies in most European countries on bank credit finance, the comparatively limited role of equity and corporate debt markets in many countries and the strong bank–industry link (*hausbank*/relational banking in Germany) further explains the preoccupation of many European governments as to the impact of Basel III on bank lending and the real economy. This leads us to the third, macroeconomic, factor that explains differing national positions on Basel III/CRDIV. The BCBS accepted the negative implications of pushing too hard and too fast with capital rules — especially in the aftermath of a deep post-crisis recession in many European countries (see BCBS a,b 2010).

These concerns were particularly acute in some countries. The United Kingdom was not one of them. From the outbreak of the financial crisis, bank lending in the UK shrunk dramatically (Table 3). This is part of a more general story about the early deleveraging of British banks and the collapse of lending, which had previously relied on securitisation and short term bank funding on wholesale markets (Hardie and Howarth 2013). The British Treasury Minister George Osborne spoke repeatedly of the 'British dilemma' — namely the desire to retain Britain's world leading position in financial services but to avoid placing the British government

Table 3. Monetary financial institution lending to non-financial companies (national currencies)

	UK to NFCs (domestic only)	France to NFCs (euro area)	Germany to NFCs (euro area)
2007	691.3	764.7	859.4
2008	606.1	845.6	947.5
2009	588.7	827.6	901.7
2010	561.5	838.8	893.8
2011	536.2	877.5	906.8

Source: National central bank data.

(and tax payer) in a position in which it was forced bail the banks out again. Despite, the raft of measures adopted to encourage and facilitate bank lending (e.g., Project Merlin), the British government has effectively accepted the lending and economic growth implications of restricting bank activities and specifically decreasing the bank lending that relied directly on shorter-term unstable funding.

Euro area lending by German and French banks remained comparatively strong in the five years following the outbreak of the financial crisis, and was limited principally by growth in the broader economy rather than the deleveraging efforts of banks. Forcing French and, more significantly, German banks to deleverage during a recessionary period could result in a credit crunch if banks reduced their lending (cut their risk-weighted assets denominator) instead of boosting their capital (lifting their equity numerator). One IMF study from 2011 on the differential impact of Basel III rules on national banking systems echoes the findings in a range of other studies: to demonstrate a particularly significant impact upon bank lending in Germany (with a decline of upwards of 7.73 per cent) and a smaller but still significant drop in the UK, with France somewhere in between (Cosimano and Hakura 2011).

The two largest German commercial banks engaged in a significant de-leveraging from 2008 and shrunk their loan book, while Landesbanken lending was largely stagnant. Stable bank lending levels in Germany since the outbreak of the financial crisis thus owed to a rise in lending from smaller Cooperative and Savings Banks, the backbone of German small and medium-sized companies (the *Mittelstand*) (Bundesbank figures). Thus, imposing significantly higher capital requirements on these smaller banks would have a devastating impact upon the German economy. It is the largest French commercial banks — comparatively more engaged in retail banking than their large German competitors — and the French economy as a result that were most exposed to deleveraging because of higher capital requirements. Indeed, this fact explains why the French led the charge for the addition of a maximum harmonisation rule in CRDIV — also supported by the Germans — fearing that the British and Swedish push to move beyond Basel requirements would force French banks to be just as capitalised because of investor expectations (Peston 2011). The French government thus sought to use EU rules to try and limit the fall-out from market pressures for greater capital: it did not matter if the markets wanted banks to increase their capital, EU rules would not allow it.

Conclusion: The 'Battle of the Systems' in EU Economic Governance

More than fifteen years ago, Story and Walter (1997) argued that 'the battle of the systems' impinged upon financial integration and regulation in the EU. Despite the progress made following the introduction of the single currency and the re-launch of financial market integration in the early 2000s (Mügge 2010), the financial systems of EU member states retain distinctive features. These features largely explain national positions on CRDIV and the intergovernmental character of the negotiations in this field. Despite the 'new era in financial regulation' (Helleiner and Pagliari 2010) heralded by some authors in the wake of the crisis, the 'new' politics of EU financial regulation is rather similar to the 'old' one (Quaglia 2012), at least in certain respects, and notably with the core issue of banking regulation.

In countries, such as Germany, with less developed equity markets and greater non-financial company reliance on bank credit, governments were more opposed to high capital requirements that would restrict lending. Clearly, British banks were concerned about the implications of higher capital requirements and struggled to raise capital. However, they were in a better position — on average — than most of their French and German competitors and the British government was less preoccupied with the impact of Basel III rules upon the British economy because of earlier deleveraging.

The implementation of the Basel III rules on capital requirements is politically controversial in the EU and the negotiations on the new EU legislation are — as of mid-February 2013 2012 — ongoing. The intergovernmental politics of the CRDIV provides a useful case study of the importance of political economy explanations that undermine EU-level efforts to construct financial regulation that effectively stabilises the EU banking system. A conclusion of this article of relevance to this special issue is that the construction of EU economic governance is bound to be less effective than sought because of the diverging implications of EU-level rules for national economies. This core economic fact casts doubt on the ability of the EU to satisfy both markets, by facilitating cross border financial integration, and politics, through the provision of the public good of financial stability.

Notes

1. Capital represents the portion of a bank's assets which have no associated contractual commitment for repayment. It is, therefore, available as a cushion in case the value of the bank's assets declines or its liabilities rise.
2. Liquid assets are cash or any other negotiable assets that can be quickly converted into cash.
3. There are wider questions being asked about the whole foundation on which the Basel agreement is built — i.e., risk weighted assets — hence the desire for the leverage ratio which looks at overall assets.

References

Allen, F., and D. Gale. 2000. *Comparing financial systems*. Cambridge: MIT press.
Barker and Masters 2012. The reference in the bibliography should be: Barker, A. and B. Masters. 2012. Britain stands alone on EU financial reform. *Financial Times*. 3 May.
BCBS. 2010a. *Group of Governors and heads of supervision announces higher global minimum capital standards*, 12 September.
BCBS. 2010b. *Assessing the macroeconomic impact of the transition to stronger capital and liquidity requirements: final report*, 17 December.
Bowles, S. 2010. Basel III faces repeat of old problems. *Financial Times*. 11 September.
Busch, A. 2004. National filters: Europeanisation, institutions, and discourse in the case of banking regulation. *West European Politics* 27, no. 2: 310–33.
Christopoulos, D., and L. Quaglia. 2009. Network constraints in EU banking regulation: the case of the capital requirements directive. *Journal of Public Policy* 29, no. 2: 1–22.
Commission of the European Communities (CEC). 2011a. Proposal for a Directive on the access to the activity of credit institutions and the prudential supervision of credit institutions and investment firms. 2011/453/EC, 20 July.
Commission of the European Communities (CEC). 2011a. *Proposal for a Directive on the access to the activity of credit institutions and the prudential supervision of credit institutions and investment firms 2011/452/EC*, 20 July.
Commission of the European Communities (CEC). 2011b. *Proposal for a regulation on prudential requirements for credit institutions and investment firms 2011/452/EC*, 20 July.
Cosimano, T.F. and Hakura, D.S. 2011. Bank behavior in response to Basel III: a cross-country analysis. *IMF Working Paper*, WP/11/119, Washington: IMF.
Damro, C. 2012. Market power Europe. *Journal of European Public Policy* 19, no. 5: 1–18.
Deeg, R. 2010. Institutional change in financial systems. In *The Oxford handbook of comparative institutional analysis*, eds. M. Glenn, J.L. Campbell, C. Crouch, O.K. Pedersen, and R. Whitley, 312–51. Oxford: Oxford University Press. accessed on 10 September 2011.
Dür, A. 2011. Fortress Europe or open door Europe? The external impact of the EU's single market in financial services. *Journal of European Public Policy* 18, no. 5: 619–35.
Djankov, S. 2011. Letter to Commissioners Michel Barnier and Ollie Rehn, May, http://www.secure-finance.com/analyses/1110.pdf.
Parliament (EP). 2010. *Resolution on Basel II and revision of the Capital Requirements Directives (CRD 4)*. Committee of Economic and Monetary Affairs, Brussels, 21 September.
European Parliament (EP). 2011. *Draft report on the proposal for a regulation of the European Parliament and of the Council on prudential requirements for credit institutions and investment firms*. Committee on Economic and Monetary Affairs, Rapporteur: Othmar Karas.
Fioretos, K.O. 2001. The domestic sources of multilateral preferences: varieties of capitalism in the European Community. In *Varieties of capitalism*, eds. P. Hall and D. Soskice, 213–44. Oxford: Oxford University Press.
Fioretos, K.O. 2010. Capitalist diversity and the international regulation of hedge funds. *Review of International Political Economy* 17, no. 4: 696–723.
Hardie, I., and D. Howarth. 2009. Die Krise but not La Crise? The financial crisis and the transformation of German and French banking systems. *Journal of Common Market Studies* 47, no. 5: 1017–39.
Hardie, I., and D. Howarth. 2013. *Market-based banking and the international financial crisis*. Oxford: Oxford University Press.
Helleiner, E., and S. Pagliari. 2011. The end of an era in international financial regulation? A postcrisis research agenda. *International Organization* 65, no. 1: 169–200.
IMF. 2011a. United Kingdom: staff report for the 2011, Article IV consultation—supplementary information, July. *IMF Country Report*, No. 11/220, supplementary report.
IMF. 2011b. France: selected issues paper. *IMF Country Report* No. 11/212, July.
de Larosière, J. 2010. Basel rules risk punishing the wrong banks. Financial, Times, 26 October, p. 11.
Leonhardt, D. 2010. Heading Off the Next Financial Crisis. New York Times. 25 March. Accessible at http://www.nytimes.com/2010/03/28/magazine/28Reform-t.html?_r=0.
Macartney, H. 2010. *Variegated neoliberalism: EU varieties of capitalism and international political economy*. London: Routledge.
Masters, B. 2012. Strasbourg hears call for tougher rules for banks. *Financial Times*. 2 February.

Mügge, D. 2010. *Widen the market, narrow the competition: banker interests and the making of a European capital market*. Colchester: ECPR.
Paulis, E. 2012. Deputy Director General, DGMARKT. Presentation and after dinner discussion at the University of Edinburgh, 14 March.
Peston, R. 2011. EU block on making banks safer, 16 June, http://www.bbc.co.uk/news/business-13789813.
Posner, E. 2009. Making rules for global finance: transatlantic regulatory cooperation at the turn of the millennium. *International Organization* 63, no. 4: 665–99.
Posner, E., and N. Véron. 2010. The EU and financial regulation: power without purpose? *Journal of European Public Policy* 17, no. 3: 400–15.
Quaglia, L. 2010. *Governing financial services in the European Union*. London: Routledge.
Quaglia, L. 2012. The 'old' and 'new' politics of financial services regulation in the European Union. *New Political Economy* 17, no. 4: 515–35.
Robinson, G. 2010. King and Pandit clash on Basel III. *Financial Times*. 26 October.
Story, J., and I. Walter. 1997. *Political economy of financial integration in Europe: the battle of the systems*. Manchester, NH: Manchester University Press.
Underhill, G.R.D. 1997. The making of the European financial area: global market integration and the EU single market for financial service. In *The new world order in international finance*, ed. G.R.D. Underhill, 101–23. London: Macmillan.
Wilson, J. 2011. Helaba pulls out of European stress tests. *Financial Times*. 13 July.
Wilson, J. 2012. Commerzbank debt swap to boost capital. *Financial Times*. 23 February.
Zimmermann, H. 2010. Varieties of global financial governance? British and German approaches to financial market regulation In *Global finance in crisis*, eds. E. Helleiner, S. Pagliari, and H. Zimmerman, 121–38. London: Routledge.

Keeping the Agents Leashed: The EU's External Economic Governance in the G20

CHARLOTTE ROMMERSKIRCHEN

Politics and International Relations, University of Edinburgh, Edinburgh, UK

ABSTRACT The functioning of the external economic governance of the European Union (EU) hinges on the functioning of the internal economic governance structure to ensure cohesion between the EU's external voice and its internal actions. Consequently the debate has focused almost in its entirety on the internal aspect of economic governance reform. This article, swimming against this current of economic governance analyses, examines the EU's external economic governance in the G20 during the Great Recession using a principal–agent framework. More specifically, it argues that although the terms of delegation in the G20 are incomplete and open to the agents' interpretation, two important sources of agency control limit the discretion of the EU delegation. The system of multiple agents with its inherent inter-institutional rivalry and the presence of the G20/EU members ultimately increase the control of the collective principal at the cost of presenting a unified EU position. At the same time the current design of the EU's external economic governance has fuelled tensions between the EU and underrepresented developing countries. Along similar lines, looking at the possibilities of interest representation, the terms of delegation, with an unequal collective principal, are biased towards large and powerful EU/G20 member states. On the basis of probit analyses it is argued that these states are likely to oppose the increased delegation that would enable the establishment of an external economic governance.

Introduction

In sharp contrast to the Great Depression, the Great Recession of 2008–2010 saw an unprecedented number of attempts to coordinate macroeconomic policies internationally, notably at the freshly re-organised G20.[1] Underpinning these global efforts of economic diplomacy was the harsh realisation of heightened policy interdependence in the face of the transnational integration of capital, finance and trade. Despite the elaborate nexus of cooperation and joint competences within the European Union (EU), the Great Recession and particularly the sovereign debt crisis have revealed and exacerbated the inaptitude of the EU's economic governance framework. This is true both for the internal and the external aspect of economic governance.

The functioning of the external economic governance of the EU is to a large extent determined by the internal economic governance structure. Consequently, the debate has focused on internal aspects of economic governance reform. Without denying its centrality to the EU's current woes, this article focuses on the neglected external dimension. The EU's feeble external economic governance poses a paradox: in spite of clear advances over the past decade, possible gains of efficiency and high public support for increased cooperation (see *Eurobarometer* 2010, 74.2), the EU has failed to create a consistent system of external representation that might enable it to play a more prominent role on the global stage, considering its overall economic might and the competences that supranational bodies have acquired in the European policy process. To scrutinise the current set-up of the EU's external economic governance in the G20, principal–agent (PA) theory is employed as framework of analysis. This explanatory device suggests itself as the issue of (imperfect) delegation is at the heart of the EU's external governance. PA analysis has established itself as a prominent theoretical lens through which to look at international organisations (see Hawkins, Lake, Nielson, & Tierney 2006; Howarth & Sadeh 2011) and supranational governance within the European Union (see Franchino 2001; Mügge 2011). Yet, Dür and Elsig (2012) argue that there has been little research using a PA framework in the context of the EU's external economic relations. This article contributes to this underdeveloped aspect in the PA literature applying a by now standard approach to European integration studies to the new case of the EU's external economic governance in the G20 during the Great Recession. So doing this article seeks more than to follow events.

Although this article examines the EU in a specific situation and context, its wider themes and findings are applicable in the realm of global policy coordination more broadly. Notably, the distinct PA structure of the EU's external economic governance is representative of the EU's overarching system of delegation; first, the presence of multiple agents competing with one another, second, the 'hydra factor' (Adams 1996), that is the presence of a collective principal, where a collection of principals disagrees over the modes and content of delegation. Analyzing the EU's system of external economic governance this article is informed by systematic interviews with key officials (both principals and agents), working on the G20 in the International Monetary Fund (IMF), the European Commission, the European Council and Member States' Permanent Representations, conducted in the spring of 2011 in Washington, DC and Brussels.

The remainder of this article proceeds as follows. The next section discusses delegation in the context of the EU's external economic governance before shedding light onto the realities of delegation regarding the two key features of the EU's external representation in the G20; multiple agency and collective principals. It is argued that the rivalry between the two agents, the Commission and the Council, ultimately increases the control of the collective principal. Over-representation of the EU and the ongoing sovereign debt crisis further weakened the EU delegation as an agent at the G20. Secondly, the EU's current delegation set-up is skewed towards the larger and more powerful member states with greater possibilities of interest representation. To empirically test whether the current system is benefiting those member states, which in turn are likely to oppose increased delegation towards external economic governance, probit analyses are employed in the penultimate section.

The EU's External Economic Governance

One of the key assumptions in the PA literature is that agents pursue policy outputs that correspond to their own preferences instead of the principal's preferences. This behaviour is known as *agency slack*, defined as 'independent action by an agent that is undesired by the principal' (Hawkins *et al.* 2006, p. 8). Given this concern why would sovereign states choose to delegate competence of external economic governance to a supranational body, such as the Commission, or an intergovernmental body, such as the Council?[2]

One argument frequently advanced in the literature is that delegation ensures expertise (see Demski & Sappington 1987).[3] Delegation is further said to ensure 'speedy and efficient decision-making' (Pollack 2003, 381) especially where a centralised authority has to 'overcome coordination problems of national mistrust' (Moravcsik 1998, 71). In the case of the EU's external economic governance delegation can lock in commitments by the member states and effectively tie their hands in matters of international cooperation. This motive is relevant in liberal intergovernmentalist analyses which claim that delegation 'occurs primarily where governments seek credible commitment under conditions of uncertainty, particularly where they seek to establish linkages and compromises among issues where non-compliance is tempting' (Moravcsik 1995, 612). Accordingly, delegation is a mechanism to constrain time-inconsistent behaviour and to exert self-constraint (cf. Elster 2000).

And yet despite these theoretical arguments favouring delegation, the EU's current system of global economic diplomacy is still essential state-centric and a far cry from the 'foreign economic governance' Commissioner Almunia (2009) called for. Although the international legal personality of the EU is universally recognised, in matters of international cooperation, its position is muddled at best (see Hervé 2012). Within the EU's multi-level governance framework, competences concerning most domains of macro-economic management reside within member states,[4] albeit subject to EU processes of internal macro-economic policy coordination. While Stage 3 of EMU saw an increase in internal coordination in the field of monetary policy and a growing role for the European Central Bank (ECB) in representing the eurozone's interests in international fora, the creation of external economic governance, with the notable exception of trade and competition policy, is still wanting. This remains true for most institutions of international cooperation; for instance in the Organisation for Economic Co-operation and Development (OECD), the EU has mere observer status, while in the IMF and the World Bank the Union is represented by its member states.

Compared to the G8/7 the participation of the EU in the G20 suggests a step towards external economic governance. The decision to let the Commission and Council Presidency join the G7 negotiations in 1977 was controversial and not formalised by providing a mandate or other formal powers (Niemann & Huigens 2011, 421). In contrast the creation of the G20 in 1999, albeit without charter or official treaty base, made away with these ambiguities. In all G20 documents, the EU is referred as one of its members and the EU holds its own seat. Prior to the re-launch of the G20 at the head of state/government level in 2008, the EU was represented at G20 meetings by the ministers of finance and central bankers from its four European G8/7 members, the ECOFIN presidency and the ECB whereas the Commission participated only at a technical level in the delegation. With the Lisbon Treaty in effect, EU representation in the G20 underwent an important change; the rotating Presidency gave up its seat for the newly created President of the Council who now jointly with the Commission represents the Community. According to the Treaties, the Commission holds a privileged role concerning the international representation of the EU. Article 17, paragraph 1 TEU, explicitly foresees that 'with the exception of the common foreign and security policy, and other cases provided for in the Treaties, [the Commission] shall ensure the Union's external representation'. Member states argued successfully in favour of a joint representation by the Council and Commission pointing to the fact that, although in the context of the post-crisis G20 marginal, foreign policies were also discussed.[5] Hence a system of multi-headed agency was preserved with respect to the new G20 (CEPS, Egmont, & and EPC. 2010, 79).

Multiple Agents

For the new G20 a flexible division of labour was constructed according to which only one of the Commission and Council would attend meetings and participate in the discussions, depending on the policy issue at stake as indicated by the legal framework of the EU. Most issues of macroeconomic policy, notably discussions concerning external imbalances and fiscal stimulus programmes, were delegated to the Commission. Officially, the EU delegation arrangement for the G20 was presented as ensuring 'full coherence, complementarity and clarity... in reaching [the] objective that the EU should speak with one voice' (*EUobserver* 19 March 2010 EUobserver, 19 March 2010, *Van Rompuy and Barroso to both represent EU at G20*, Valentina Pop, available at http://euobserver.com/news/29713 (accessed 15.03.2013)). But behind the scenes this decision remained contested. Barroso's cabinet, without much success, 'used all the tricks in the book'[6] to achieve single representation of the Community interest at the G20 by the Commission. Yet, already in 2009 campaigning unilaterally to convince the South Korean summit organizers, it had failed to persuade other G20 non-EU members that it alone represented the EU and to shun the Council in the preparation process of the G20 meeting in Seoul.[7]

This attempt in agency slack can be explained by timing and self-perception. First, the Commission considers itself to be the only genuine defender of the 'community interest' and argues that an increase in its scope to represent the member states in matters of external economic governance should be in the interest of its principals. Given the Commission's mandate, many of its officials were frustrated by the limited delegation to represent the 'Community interest' at the G20 level.[8] This vexation is more than a reflection of the legal self-understanding of the Brussels institution. Benson-Rae and Shore (2011) highlight that the majority of Commission staff sees their employer as the *only* EU institution that is independent and thus capable of 'serving only the European ideal' (*ibid.*). Secondly, prior to the upgrade of the G20 any attempts from the Commission's side to obtain a single seat seemed unlikely due to its limited status in the international forum at that time. It is only since the emergence of the leaders' G20 in 2008 that the Commission gained entry to the G20 at a political level instead of a mere technical level. What is more, the European Council President Van Rompuy took office in 2010. Therefore the Council representation was in flux as the Lisbon Treaty heralded changes for the EU's external representation. Besides establishing his sphere of influence on a personal level, the European Council President had to mark the territory of this role without institutional precedence. Any efforts from the Commission to cast the Council as a dispensable understudy were more likely to succeed while the agency was in its infancy.

Due to the strong position of the Council, the Commission was constrained as an agent of the member states. It was subject to inter-agency oversight. Specifically, its delegation had to coordinate closely with the Cabinet of Van Rompuy led by Franciskus van Daele to reach a joint position for all policy issues. Both agents of the member states watched one another Argus-eyed, providing the principals with a form of agency based police-patrol (cf. McCubbins & Schwartz 1984, 1666) as a control mechanism to prevent agency slack. Delegation theory predicts that the competitive interaction created by a system of multiple agency, would encourage the agents to take greater account of the principals' preferences (Ferejohn 1999). This opportunity to instigate competition between multiple agents and, hence, increased responsiveness of the Commission or the Council to member state preferences promised therefore an additional benefit to the collective principals in addition to restricting the agent(s) themselves.

A second source of *ad locum* control (Delreux & Kerremans 2010) are the five[9] G20/EU members. In this particular scenario one of the main assumption of PA models, namely imperfect observability of the agent's actions (see Bendor *et al.* 2001), applies consequently less strongly, despite a still existing modicum of secrecy associated with international diplomacy. That is not to suggest that the G20/EU member states did not perceive the need to monitor the EU delegation's activities; instead since the Commission was only bound by an informal 'gentlemen's agreement' on how to represent EU interest, the five G20/EU states vigorously monitored the EU delegation.[10] In addition to the joint EU position papers prepared in advance of the various summits in agreement with member states, the EU delegation also sought to consolidate the different positions of the Union's five G20 members by setting up regular meetings a few hours before the actual meetings of all G20 states in a 'vain attempt to chart the course'.[11] But 'at the end of the day these internal coordination efforts just added another layer of paper to put on old cracks'.[12] Debeare (2009, 144) suggests that the imprecision of these intra-EU agreements assured a comfortable negotiation margin for the European representatives in the G20.[13] The position papers are an example of what is called 'incomplete contracts' (Williamson 1985) in delegation theory, which are said to arise in situations where the content of an agreement is contested and the negotiation process difficult. This incomplete nature of agreements meant that the other five EU/G20 members did not see their diplomatic margin of manoeuvre curtailed either. Moreover, EU/G20 member states felt only partially bound by the internal agreement since the Commission was there to represent the Community interest.[14] During the negotiations these features weakened the EU delegation in comparison to its participating member states. In a similar line, according to Marsh and Mackenstein (2005, 56) the EU/G20 member states are traditionally in a stronger position as 'the *sui generis* nature of the EU means that international organizations and fora vary in their willingness to recognize it as an actor in its own right as opposed to its constituent member states'. Given that the international system is still by and large dominated by state-centric norms (Rosamond 2005) the voices of the EU/G20 member states are able to benefit from an amplifier not available to the EU delegation (see also Peterson 2010).

The Voices of Multiple Agency

The challenges of presenting a united EU are arguably at odds with one of the underlying reasons for delegation identified in the PA literature; credibility (Majone 2001). As Dür and Elsig (2011, 329) suggest 'the need for strategic behaviour in international negotiations and the advantages of speaking with a single voice may also be reasons for delegation in the case of the EU'. Examinations of the EU's vocal cords in international relations have emerged ever since it entered multilateral fora (see Taylor 1982). Again, the Great Recession has been met with an unprecedented level of attempts to coordinate policy responses and has brought the need of global policy cooperation into bolder relief. Unsurprisingly, especially in light of the unresolved problems of the Union's external economic governance, renewed calls to an end of the 'cacophony of European voices' in international relations have emerged (see Gstöhl 2011).

Conversely to Hodson's (2011) claim that 'when member states agree on international economic priorities, there is little point in establishing a more unified system of external representation', there is a case to be made for increased 'unification'. The many voices of the EU may be harmful to the EU's standing in international relations *regardless* of the strength of intra-EU agreements. Despite a shift towards the inclusion of emerging market countries, the new G20 is still biased in favour of EU representation failing to reflect global economic power constellations. The issue of EU overrepresentation flared up from the very beginning of the new G20. During the inaugural meeting in Washington, six EU countries were represented at the roundtable.[15] Not only do EU leaders currently take up more than 1/3rd of the summit chairs, most of the key international civil servants (from the IMF, the World Trade Organization, and the Financial Stability Board) present at the international gatherings are also Europeans.

Moreover, the relationship between the EU and other non-EU/G20 member states is strained by the sovereign debt crisis. The Council of Ministers, the Commission and the ECB faced criticism for failing to provide a timely and effective response to the crisis (e.g., Featherstone 2011, 193). Consequently, 'the EU can no longer dictate to less [wealthy] countries what to do, whilst being unable to get its own act together'.[16] The credibility of the Commission in advocating, for example, economic policy coordination more generally and austerity measures more specifically, is weakened by the perceived lack of the former within the member states' economies and the ongoing discussion in the eurozone about the pace of fiscal consolidation (e.g., *Financial Times*, 23 April 2012 *Financial Times*, 23 April 2012, Backlash against eurozone austerity, Ralph Atkins and Robin Wigglesworth, available at http://www.ft.com/cms/s/0/3872fd76-8d39-11e1-8b49-00144feab49a.html#axzz2NcCjcSdw (accessed 15.03.2013)). Moreover, the deliberate involvement of the IMF in managing the sovereign debt crisis fuelled discontent on the part of many developing nations (*Financial Times*, 6 November 2011 *Financial Times*, 6 November 2011, The Eurozone decouples from the world, Gavyn Davies, available at http://blogs.ft.com/gavyndavies/2011/11/06/the-eurozone-decouples-from-the-world/ (accessed 15.03.2013).).[17] This was in part due to the moderation of the Fund's infamous position on fiscal consolidation for eurozone member states which resulted in fierce discussions within the G20 about the appropriate policy mix for IMF programme countries, and the previously standard fiscal austerity prescriptions by the Fund (Rommerskirchen 2011, 12). In addition to a problem of communication regarding IMF programmes,[18] which made other G20 countries feel ignored, the crisis also put the agreement to treat the eurozone as a single bloc into question when discussing issues such as external imbalances: 'If we cannot maintain stability within our own monetary bloc, but need money from China and other IMF contributors, what does this mean for our line of argument?'.[19] The challenges of internal reform for the E(M)U's economic government have therefore had a negative effect on the EU's external representation in the G20 and threaten the credibility of the EU's multiple agents. As the crisis continues to reveal the weaknesses of the EU's existing system of macroeconomic management, the success of economic policy coordination and by implication the strength of the collective principal's union are put into question. It is here that the intrinsic relationship between external and internal economic governance becomes apparent.[20]

Collective Principal

Gstöhl (2009, 17) posits that the more 'uneven the underlying power distribution in an international institution and the more diverse the member states' preferences, the less likely the EU is speaking with one voice'. The case of the EU in the G20 is marked by a complex web of interest representation, with the EU being a 'variable and multidimensional presence' (Allen & Smith 1990), in addition to the underlying diversity of preferences between the member states on matters of economic and financial management. The collective principal renders the problem of alignment between agent and principal preferences even more complex given that this set of principals may themselves not all agree on the most-desired outcome. Although the hydra structure of the EU's external economic governance renders agency slack unlikely, this comes at the cost of an inconsistent EU position. Like in other international fora, only a small sub-set of EU member states hold their own seat, whereas the others rely formally on the EU delegation to represent the Community interest and their own national interests by proxy. Arguably powerful EU member states are already placed in a more favourable position within the Council, where the delegation prior to every G20 summit takes place in the penumbra of galvanised intergovernmentalism with the national governments at the centre of political gravity (Puetter 2012, 161). EU member states' attitudes towards further delegation is likely marked by whether or not they are simultaneously also members of the G20; states lacking international influence will favour some form of delegation to an agent representing their interest at the international level. Collective action problems predict that, where a potential policy change promises marginal advantages to a larger group, but threatens concentrated losses on a smaller group, the preferences of the latter group are likely to prevail because it has a greater incentive to organise (Olson 1965). Applied to the external economic governance of the G20, greater delegation would immediately entail large perceived losses of reputation and influence for those member states currently holding their own seat, whereas the gain for the rest of the Union's members might be more diffuse and delayed.

The 2010 *Eurobarometer* (74.2) survey can help to test the hypothesis that the populations of large/powerful member states are likely to be against comprehensive reform of the current system of delegation. Indeed, respondents from the 'Big Three' and the 5 EU/G20 countries are less convinced that the EU is well placed to deal with the economic and financial crisis than respondents from non G-20 member states. To further test the apparent division of opinion between large/powerful and small/weak member states probit analyses[21] are used. The dependent dummy variables of the five models are, (1) EUACTOR ('1' if EU is thought to be best able to take effective actions against the effects of the crisis); (2) GOVACTOR ('1' if national government is thought to be best able to take effective actions against the effects of the crisis); (3) TOGETHER ('1' if EU member states should work together more in tackling the crisis); (4) ROLE ('1' if the EU should take a less strong role in the economy); and (5) VOICE ('1' if EU's voice in the world is thought to count). Independent variables

Table 1. Variables, definitions, summary statistics

Variables	Definition	Mean	SD
Dependent variables			
TOGETHER	EU member states should work together more in tackling the financial and economic crisis'; 1 if 'totally agree' or 'tend to agree', 0 otherwise.	0.94	0.24
ROLE	The EU should take a stronger role in the economy'; 1 if 'totally agree' or 'tend to agree', 0 otherwise.	0.40	0.49
EUVOICE	'The EU's voice counts in the world'; 1 if 'tend to agree', 0 otherwise.	0.74	0.44
EUACTOR	In your opinion, which of the following is best able to take effective action against the effects of the financial and economic crisis'; 1 if 'the EU', 0 otherwise.	0.33	0.47
GOVACTOR	'In your opinion, which of the following is best able to take effective action against the effects of the financial and economic crisis'; 1 if 'the national government', 0 otherwise.	0.37	0.48
Independent variables			
BIG3	1 if respondent lives in Germany, France or the UK, 0 otherwise	0.15	0.35
G20	1 if respondent lives in a G20 member state, 0 otherwise	0.22	0.42
NEWMS	1 if respondent lives in a new EU member state, 0 otherwise	0.41	0.49
AGE	Age of respondent	48.28	18.12
MALE	1 if male, 0 if female	0.47	0.50
RIGHT	1 if placed right on the left-right self-placement, 0 otherwise	0.28	0.45
EDUCATION	Years of schooling	18.75	4.92
BILLS	1 if respondent had difficulties to pay his/her bills at the end of the month during the last twelve months 'most of the time' or 'from time to time', 0 otherwise	0.41	0.49
GDP	Gross domestic product at current market prices, in Mrd €	539.11	734.43

Note: Data from Eurobarometer 74.2: November–December 2010 and AMECO database.

are standard characteristics on the individual-level controlling for the specific socio-economic background as well as the variable GDP controlling for the size and state of the economy (see Table 1). The dummies BIG3 ('1' if respondent lives in Germany, France or the UK), EUG20 ('1' if respondent lives in G20 member state), NEWMS ('1' if respondent lives in new EU member state) control for the political/economic clout.

The results of the probit models, presented in Table 2, suggest that size and representation at the G20 matters. Citizens of the 'Big Three' and the EU/G20 are more likely to favour national governments as crisis actors, to think that the EU's voice does not count, to support less involvement of the EU in economic matters, to be against closer cooperation and to have a negative view of the EU in dealing with the effects of the Great Recession. This gives some credence to the presumption that the most resistance

Table 2. Probit regression and correlation results

Variables	1 EUACTOR	2 GOVACTOR	3 TOGETHER	4 ROLE	5 VOICE
BIG3	−0.26 * 0.16	0.52 *** 0.11	−0.31 0.35	0.23 0.3	−0.28 0.33
G20	−0.16 0.18	1.12 *** 0.16	−0.01 0.34	0.71 ** 0.32	−0.11 0.32
NEWMS	0.06 0.06	0.27 ** 0.12	0.26 ** 0.11	0.05 0.11	0.25 ** 0.11
AGE	−0.004 *** 0.001	0.01 *** 0.002	0.000 0.001	0.002 0.002	−0.002 * 0.001
MALE	−0.01 0.02	−0.1 *** 0.03	0.03 0.03	−0.03 0.03	0.01 0.03
EDUCATION	−0.001 0.004	−0.03 *** 0.01	0.01 0.01	−0.02 *** 0.004	0.02 *** 0.004
BILLS	−0.24 *** 0.04	0.86 *** 0.06	−0.21 *** 0.05	0.12 *** 0.05	−0.27 *** 0.05
RIGHT	0.001 0.03	−0.14 *** 0.04	−0.05 0.05	0.06 *** 0.03	0.06 0.04
GDP	0.0001 0.0001	−0.001 *** 0.0001	0.0002 0.0003	−0.0006 *** 0.0002	0.0002 0.0002
Constant	−0.11 0.09	−0.4 *** 0.2	1.34 *** 0.19	0.001 0.17	0.38 ** 0.19
Observations	19,686	19,686	19,160	8,669	18,407
Pseudo R2	0.01	0.14	0.01	0.02	0.02
Correlation between (1) and	1.00	−0.52 ***	0.01	0.02	0.05 ***
Correlation between (2) and	−0.52 ***	1.00	−0.03 **	0.07 ***	−0.13 **
Correlation between (3) and	0.01	−0.03 *	1.00	−0.08 ***	0.16 ***
Correlation between (4) and	0.02 **	0.07 ***	−0.08 ***	1.00	−0.13 ***

Note: Clustered by member state. In all models, except Model 1, BIG3, G20 and NEWMS are jointly significant at the .5 or .1 level. *** = significant at the .01 level, ** = significant at the .5 level, * = significant at the .1 level. For a description of all variables see Table 1.

towards further delegation of powers to Union bodies is likely to emerge from the big and powerful member states. The situation is reminiscent of the 1970s when smaller member states asked for independent Community representation at the G7 to safeguard their adequate representation, instead of (rather than *in addition to*) that of the European summit members (Hainsworth 1990, 14). According to Puetter (2012, 172) the support for more delegation does not only entail increased delegation to the Commission as an agent; besides favouring strong involvement of the Commission, small and new member states tend to perceive the Council as a further intermediate against big member states bias. Indeed, improved coordination of external representation has become a key topic for discussion during the informal parts of the ECOFIN meetings due to concerns that the Community is not adequately represented in the G20 context (*ibid.*)

But does the reserved public esteem of the EU as a crisis manager really suggest that the tides in those member states holding a seat at the G20 are against a reform of the EU's external economic governance? Put differently, do respondents prefer their government to deal with the Great Recession because they are against increased integration, or because they consider the current capacity of the Union's institutions as insufficient? Unfortunately, corresponding survey data is lacking. What is more, due to the nature of virtually all of the key variables and the hence arising endogeneity problem[22] it is not feasible to include them in a regression model and shed light on their causal relationship. This leaves the route of correlation analysis. Table 2 displays the results of the dependent variables correlated with each other to clarify the alleged reputation–delegation linkage; there is a strong positive relationship between the wish for further integration and the evaluation of the EU's political clout. Likewise viewing the EU as the most capable crisis actor is positively linked to an endorsement of stronger economic policy coordination. Conversely, viewing the national government as the most capable crisis actor is negatively linked to support for further integration. Interestingly, these correlation coefficients are markedly larger if only the subset of the 'Big Three' (n = 2940) are taken, suggesting that among the respondents of these member states opposition to further economic policy coordination is even more strongly linked to a preference of the national government as crisis actor and a negative view of the EU's voice in the world.[23]

Conclusion

This article has analysed the EU's external economic governance in the G20 and the P-A relationship between the EU member states, the collective principal, on the one hand and the Commission and Council, the multi-headed agency, on the other hand. Although the terms of delegation in the G20 are incomplete and open to the agents' interpretation, two important sources of agency control exist which render agency slack unlikely. First, the system of multiple agency has created institutional rivalry between the Commission and the Council which effectively functions as an inter-agency based policy patrol. Second, the fact that five of its principals participate in the negotiations, means that agents can less easily diverge from the implicit or explicit mandate. At the same time, the design of the EU's external economic governance has fuelled tensions between the EU and underrepresented developing countries and emerging markets. In a similar line, looking at the possibilities of interest representation, the current terms of delegation, with an unequal collective principal, are biased towards large and powerful EU/G20 member states. As the empirical section of this analysis suggests, these states in turn are likely to oppose increased delegation (a single EU seat) towards the establishment of an external economic governance which could unleash the EU agents.

Acknowledgements

I gratefully acknowledge financial support by the German National Merit Foundation as well as the MERCURY Project through the EU's Framework VII programme. Thanks are due to all interviewees who generously gave me their time, allowing me to benefit from their insight and first-hand experience. I am grateful to Mark Aspinwall, David Howarth, and John Peterson for their perceptive comments on an earlier draft of this article. I also wish to thank all participants of the College of Europe Conference on economic governance in Bruges on 1 March 2011 for their helpful comments, in particular Michelle Chang. The usual disclaimer applies.

Notes

1. The G20 consists of 19 countries — Argentina, Australia, Brazil, Canada, China, France, Germany, India, Indonesia, Italy, Japan, the Republic of Korea, Mexico, the Russian Federation, Saudi Arabia, South Africa, Turkey, the United Kingdom, the United States — and the EU.
2. Although the Council is usually qualified as being closer to the preferences of the member states and easier to control by its principals, an EU representation by the President of the Council still entails considerable delegation of a previously national prerogative.
3. While this might hold true in the context of numerous policy fields, it is difficult to see how any of the EU's organs has more expertise in economic governance than many of its member states. One Commission official echoed this caveat suggesting that 'as things are currently, the entire Commission is stretched to its utmost limits. If we have two guys working on any given issue you can be sure that bigger member states, such as Germany, have 20' (author interview, 3 March 2011). The same is arguably true for the Council. However whereas delegation in the context of the G20 and fiscal policy coordination may not be propelled by the wish to benefit from the policy content expertise of the supranational agent, the considerable summitry expertise of EU officials was perceived to have advanced the G20 considerably (Rommerskirchen 2011).
4. The most striking exception is monetary policy for EMU member states.
5. Author interview 24 March 2011, see also Chaffin (2009).
6. Ibid.
7. Author interview, 22 May 2011.
8. Author interview 23 May 2011.
9. Spain has secured a standing invitation to G20 summits giving it a de facto permanent EU seat.
10. Author interview, 24 March 2011.
11. Author interview, 24 May 2011.
12. Ibid.
13. Nielson and Tierney (2003) discuss how diverging preferences among the principals may lead to a less strict mandate for the agent.
14. Author interview, 25 May 2011, see also Giovannini *et al.* (2012, 54).
15. Spain and the Netherlands (the latter was to hold the rotating EU Council presidency) had argued that it should be invited due to the size of its economy and participated as part of the French and the EU delegation respectively.
16. Author interview, 24 May 2011, see also Angeloni and Pisani-Ferry (2012).
17. Author interview, 12 April 2011.
18. One interviewee described the reaction of the Chinese delegation to the decision to loan money to Portugal 'the Chinese were furious. No one had told them in advance and they were under the

impression that the Europeans considered the IMF to be *their* institution which they could use in any way they wanted' (25 May 2011).
19. Author interview, 24 May 2011, see also El-Erian (2012).
20. For an evaluation of the performance of the G20 in facilitating macroeconomic policy coordination see for example Angeloni and Pisani-Ferry (2012).
21. Probit models are non-linear regression models designed to estimate relationships involving dependent variables that are binary in nature.
22. The presence of an endogenous explanatory variable which is determined by the equations in the system.
23. Correlation coefficients not reported to conserve space, but can be obtained from the author upon request.

References

Adams, J. 1996. Principals and agents, colonialists and company men: the decay of colonial control in the Dutch East Indies. *American Sociological Review* 61, no. 1: 12–28.
Almunia, M. 2009. Commissioner Almunia calls for a stronger EU foreign economic policy. Brussels.
Allen, D., and M. Smith. 1990. Western Europe's presence in the contemporary international arena. *Review of International Studies* 16, no. 1: 19–37.
Angeloni, I., and J. Pisani-Ferry. 2012. The G20: characters in search of an author. *Bruegel Working Paper*, 2012/04.
Bendor, J., A. Glazer, and T. Hammond. 2001. Theories of delegation. *Annual Review of Political Science* 4, no. 1: 235–69.
Benson-Rea, M., and C. Shore. 2011. Representing Europe: the emerging 'culture' of EU diplomacy. *Public Administration* 90, no. 2: 480–96.
CEPS, EGMONT, and EPC. 2010. *The treaty of Lisbon: a second look at the institutional innovations*. Brussels: CEPS, Egmont and EPC.
Chaffin, J. 2009. Barroso still seen as 'number one' in Brussels. *Financial Times* 20, no. 11: 2009.
Debaere, P. 2009. The output and input dimension of the European representation in the G20. *Studia Diplomatica* LXIII: 2.
Delreux, T.A., and B. Kerremans. 2010. How agents weaken their principals' incentives to control. *Journal of European Integration* 32, no. 4: 357–74.
Demski, J., and D. Sappington. 1987. Delegated expertise. *Journal of Accounting Research* 25, no. 1: 68–89.
Dür, A., and M. Elsig. 2012. Principals, agents, and the European Union's foreign economic policies. *Journal of European Public Policy* 18, no. 3: 323–38.
EUobserver, 19 March 2010, Van Rompuy and Barroso to both represent EU at G20, Valentina Pop, available at http://euobserver.com/news/29713 (accessed 15.03.2013).
El-Erian, M. 2012. G20 must protect the IMF from Europe. *Financial Times*, 24 February, available at http://blogs.ft.com/the-a-list/2012/02/24/g20-must-protect-the-imf-from-europe/#axzz2NcAyZqPn (accessed 15.03.2013).
Elster, J. 2000. *Ulysses unbound*. Cambridge: Cambridge University Press.
Financial Times, 6 November 2011, The Eurozone decouples from the world, Gavyn Davies, available at http://blogs.ft.com/gavyndavies/2011/11/06/the-eurozone-decouples-from-the-world/ (accessed 15.03.2013).
Financial Times, 23 April 2012, Backlash against eurozone austerity, Ralph Atkins and Robin Wigglesworth, available at http://www.ft.com/cms/s/0/3872fd76-8d39-11e1-8b49-00144feab49a.html#axzz2NcCjcSdw (accessed 15.03.2013).
Featherstone, K. 2011. The Greek sovereign debt crisis and EMU: a failing state in a skewed regime. *Journal of Common Market Studies* 49, no. 2: 193–217.
Ferejohn, J. 1999. It's not just talk. *Virginia Law Review* 85, no. 8: 1725–43.
Franchino, F. 2001. Delegation and constraints in the national execution of the EC policies: a longitudinal and qualitative analysis. *West European Politics* 24, no. 4: 169–92.
Giovannini, A., D. Gros, P. Ivan, P. Kaczynski, and D. Valiante. 2012. External representation of the Euro area, study for the Directorate General for Internal Policies, Economic and Scientific, Policy, 2012/05.
Gstöhl, S. 2009. Patchwork power Europe: the EU's representation in international institutions. *European Foreign Affairs Review* 14, no. 3: 385–403.

Hainsworth, S. 1990. Coming of Age: The European Community and the economic summit, *Country Study Centre for International Studies, University of Toronto, Toronto* available at http://www.g7.utoronto.ca/scholar/hainsworth1990/biscen.htm (accessed 15.03.2013).

Hawkins, D.G., D.A. Lake, D. Nielson, and M.J. Tierney. 2006. *Delegation and agency in international organisations.* Cambridge: Cambridge University Press.

Herve, A. 2012. The participation of the European Union in global economic governance. *European Law Journal* 18, no. 1: 143–61.

Hodson, D. 2011. The paradox of EMU's external representation: the case of the G20 and the IMF. Paper presented at the EUSA Twelfth Biennial International Conference, in Boston, Massachusetts.

Howarth, D., and T. Sadeh. 2011. In the vanguard of globalization: the OECD and international capital liberalization. *Review of International Political Economy* 18, no. 15: 1–24.

Majone, G. 2001. Two logics of delegation: agency and fiduciary relations in EU governance. *European Union Politics* 2, no. 1: 103–22.

Marsh, S., and H. Mackenstein. 2005. *The international relations of the European Union.* New York: Pearson/Longman.

McCubbins, M.D., and T. Schwartz. 1984. Congressional oversight overlooked. *American Journal of Political Science* 28, no. 1: 165–79.

Moravcsik, A. 1995. Liberal intergovernmentalism and integration: a rejoinder. *Journal of Common Market Studies* 33, no. 4: 611–28.

Moravcsik, A. 1998. *The choice for Europe: social purpose and state power from Messina to Maastricht.* Ithaca, NY: Cornell University Press.

Mügge, D. 2011. The European presence in global financial governance: a principal–agent perspective. *Journal of European Public Policy* 18, no. 3: 383–402.

Niemann, A., and J. Huigens. 2011. The European Union's role in the G8: a principal–agent perspective. *Journal of European Public Policy* 18, no. 3: 420–42.

Nielson, D., and M. Tierney. 2003. Delegation to international organizations: agency theory and World Bank environmental reform. *International organization* 57, no. 2: 241–65.

Olson, M. 1965. *The logic of collective action.* Cambridge, MA: Harvard University Press.

Peterson, J. 2010. Multilateralism and the EU: a 'cheap date'? *The International Spectator* 45, no. 4: 43–8.

Pollack, M. 2003. *The engines of European integration. Delegation, agency and agenda setting in the European Union.* Oxford: Oxford University Press.

Puetter, U. 2012. Europe's deliberative intergovernmentalism: the role of the Council and European Council in EU economic governance. *Journal of European Public Policy* 19, no. 2: 161–78.

Rommerskirchen, C. 2011. Fiscal multilateralism in times of the great recession, *MERCURY E-paper*, available at http://mercury.uni-koeln.de/index.php?id=10076 (15.03.2013).

Rosamond, B. 2005. Conceptualizing the EU mode of governance in world politics. *European Foreign Affairs Review* 10, no. 4: 463–78.

Taylor, P. 1982. The European communities as an actor in international society. *Journal of European Integration* 6, no. 1: 7–41.

Williamson, O.E. 1985. *Economic institutions of capitalism.* New York: Free Press.

Eurozone Crisis and European Integration: Functional Spillover, Political Spillback?

RAMŪNAS VILPIŠAUSKAS

Institute of International Relations and Political Science, Vilnius University, Vokiečių 10Vilnius, Lithuania

ABSTRACT This paper analyzes the decisions taken since the start of the financial and economic crisis in the European Union and assesses them in the light of the traditional debates of integration theories. It discusses the key characteristics of the process of responding to the crisis since 2008–2009 when the problems of Greece have been increasingly publicized, the main actors involved, and provides an interpretation of the key decisions dealing with the crisis and their implications in terms of further European integration. First assessing these events in the light of the neo-functionalist and liberal intergovernmentalist debate, it then presents a framework linking the accounts of the integration process with a domestic politics approach. In this respect it contributes to the literature on European integration as well as the changing nature of EU polity, policy-specific effects of politics and how politics in member states constrains decisions on the further deepening of the Economic and Monetary Union and efforts to move towards transfer union. The incremental process of centralizing redistributive policies accompanied by the debates about financial transfers from some EMU countries to the others have altered popular 'permissive consensus' about the process of European integration and exposed territorial cleavages which became a key constraint in responding to the crisis and pressures for further integration.

Introduction

Recent years have seen a significant change in the European Union (EU) agenda and its politics compared to the widespread euphoria a decade ago when the single currency has been introduced, EU has been preparing for enlargement into Central and Eastern Europe and economic growth in most its countries fuelled optimism over the implementation of the Lisbon Strategy goals. This optimism has given away to a growing pessimism since the start of financial crisis in 2007–2008, which soon turned into a crisis of sovereign debt and competitiveness, exposing serious problems of public finances, lack of structural reforms and excessive borrowing during the first decade of the EMU in many eurozone countries. It revealed persistent divergences among members of the eurozone against the hope of the 'founding fathers' of the EMU that monetary integration and fiscal and economic policy coordination would lead towards convergence of these economies. It also prompted talks about the deficiencies of EMU institutions which have been left since the adoption of the Maastricht Treaty. This was expressed by calls to complete the institutional architecture of the EMU, to create 'a genuine' EMU with the adoption of fiscal or transfer union also referred to as 'its own fiscal capacity' or 'shock absorption function' (European Commission (2012), Van Rompuy (2012b)).

Most of the debates about the substance and direction of reforming the EU's economic governance are characterized by a strong normative element, often reflecting the underlying preferences of analysts and other actors, their ideas about the desired division of functions between the EU and its member states, and desired limits to these interventions, on the one hand, and the functioning of markets, on the other. Many recommendations about how to solve the eurozone crisis and what the EU should do are informed by ideas regarding the prospect of the federal EU as well as the degree of interventionism of the federal and national institutions into the markets. Much less has been written about the actual direction that EU integration has been taking since the start of the crisis, its defining characteristics and limits to different scenarios proposed by economists and policy-makers on both EU and national levels.

This contribution analyzes from a positive perspective the decisions that the EU has taken in recent years, the vectors of reforms and constraints to further deepening of integration. It draws on the insights of the main integration theories to describe the characteristics of the response of the EU and its member states to the crisis. In doing so it links the traditional debate about the causes, motives and process of European integration with the more recent discussions of EU's polity, its policies and politics which have drawn on the insights of comparative politics. It assumes that the current state of the EU and EMU in particular requires a combination of insights from both integration theory and domestic politics approaches to understand better the reforms that EU has been implementing, the dominant actors and the constraints which are posed by these interconnections between international, EU and domestic levels.

It is argued that the changing nature of politics in Europe, with new types of policies being gradually transferred to the EU level, has altered the 'permissive consensus' about the process of European integration. Traditionally regulatory policy has been the main instrument used by the EU in advancing the objectives set in its treaties and creating legal obligations for member states and their citizens. Redistributive policy has been relatively limited and restricted to specific policy areas like agriculture. However, since the start of the crisis most debates have focused on significant transfer of competences, which involved important elements of redistribution between different member states. To be sure, many popular debates simplify those centralized mechanisms—such as the European Financial Stability Facility (EFSF) or the European Stability Mechanism (ESM)—portraying them as outright transfers rather than lending and guarantee. However, the issue of redistribution between member states goes to the essence of politics, compared to mostly very technical issues of regulatory policies. The public disapproval of financial transfers from their countries to other EMU members or public protests in recipient countries against conditionality which links bail-out support to a set of domestic reforms has become a new and increasingly important constraint on further processes of European integration. The widely criticized response of EU member states, especially Germany, in dealing with the crisis—expressed by the phrase 'too little too late'—can be understood better if we take into account the importance of domestic politics for any new step in the direction of central pooling of resources. Moreover, every decision on financial assistance from ESF and ESM as well as ECB interventions into bond market should be seen in the context of the debate about how to advance reforms in the recipient eurozone countries. Every decision regarding financial assistance to countries in trouble is linked directly to taking politically unpopular and difficult measures aimed at regaining competitiveness and reducing fiscal imbalances. The main contribution of this analysis is in highlighting the importance of domestic politics as a constraint to the creation of joint supranational transfer mechanisms, due to the much higher politicization of redistributive policy compared to regulatory policy.

The article first presents the main characteristics of the EU's response to the eurozone crisis in the light of the debate between neofunctionalism and liberal intergovernmentalism, discussing the differences of these accounts and pointing out the issues which are left unaddressed by these approaches. It then proposes how to link the analysis of European integration during the crisis with the concepts of comparative politics, in particular, the differentiation of policies and their salience to the public. Finally, it concludes with observations and the implications of this analysis to further processes of crisis resolution and reforms of European economic governance as well as their conceptualization.

Revenge of Neofunctionalism?

The proliferation of the debates about the need for EU- or EMU-wide fiscal, banking, transfer or some other type of union which could constitute an important step towards political union provides a good background for employing the concepts of the traditional integration theories to describe what has been taking place in the EU during the last several years. Here, the response of the EU to the crisis is discussed by assessing the process, key actors and the outcomes of EU decision-making at the time of crisis using the propositions of neofunctionalist and liberal intergovernmentalist accounts of European integration.

The neofunctionalist account, especially its original version, which has been most widely referred to in scholarly work on European integration, places emphasis on several elements which describe the process of integration: integration is an incremental process which is driven by the demands of interest groups for market integration and supranational institutions responding to these demands following the functional logic which characterizes highly interdependent economies and linkages between different policy areas (Haas 1968b; Rosamond 2005). The process is characterized by a gradual transfer of competences from member states to the EU, the process which itself is likely to lead in the future to further demands from economic interest groups to integrate functionally linked policy areas. Incrementalism, dominance of interest groups and supranational institutions, and the transfer of competences to the EU in functionally linked policy areas are the key characteristics of a neofunctionalist account.

How could the process of responding to the crisis by the EU be described in terms of its nature, the key actors and outcomes achieved so far? First, it should be noted that the language of many EU leaders and analysts has an implicit reference to the 'spill-over' process. The talk about 'incomplete', 'unfinished' projects of the EMU implies that single monetary policy established by the Maastricht Treaty and the introduction of the single currency in 1999 has gradually exposed the need to move ahead with other functionally linked policy areas, which due to political reasons were left under the competences of member states when the eurozone was created. Fiscal union and banking union as well as central transfer mechanism to deal with the instances of divergent economic cycles in eurozone members are the most often cited policy areas where centralization would stabilize financial markets and strengthen the monetary union, equipping it with better tools to react to the future crisis. Thus, it is not surprising that some scholars have been quick to announce the 'vindication of the first grand theory of European integration' and the 'revenge of neofunctionalism' (Copper 2011). It took almost 20 years after the Maastricht Treaty and about a decade after the introduction of the euro, until, according to this view, the functional pressures for spill-over worked at full force. According to this account, the EFSF and the ESM are just the first steps towards the central pooling of resources that in the future is likely to become a federal transfer mechanism. Paralleled by the adoption of centralized regulation of financial institutions and the move towards a harmonization of corporate tax rules, regularly discussed in such documents such as *Pact for Competitiveness* and European Commission proposals, this would represent a spill-over process from the monetary policy to the fiscal policy of the EMU.

There is another resemblance of the process of decision-making at the time of the crisis to the incrementalism so prominent in the neofunctionalist account. It is this muddling through the decision-making in the EU from one 'historic' summit to another implementing gradual reforms of the economic governance rules, for example, strengthening the coordination and monitoring procedures in the form of European semester, aligning two processes of national convergence programs and national reform programs, introducing stricter financial sanctions by the secondary legal acts such as the 'six pack' or introducing limited treaty change. Since the start of the crisis until mid 2012, there have been around 20 EU summits dealing with reforms of economic governance and discussing measures of further integration. Although there have been many declarations about 'historic' decisions, they seemed mostly aimed at calming down financial markets, while the real work has focus on incremental procedural change. Besides, many of these procedural changes are rather technical and are actually 'tying the hands' of national governments without major popular debates. An introduction of the rules of the fiscal discipline into the national law to restrict excessive spending during good times and over the political cycles is expected to further constrain the governments of member states which signed up to the Treaty on Stability, Coordination and Governance in the Economic and Monetary Union (TSCG).

Furthermore, in terms of the key actors pushing for the process of further integration international financial markets as well as supranational institutions such as the European Commission and the ECB merit attention. Financial markets, investors into the bonds of the eurozone countries are probably the most visible actors that have constantly been fuelling political debate about the measures required to maintain confidence in the project of European integration and preserve the eurozone. The introduction of the euro and resulting drop of risk premium on less productive eurozone members' bonds fostered investments into those periphery economies and contributed to growing financial integration. However, when the crisis started and doubts over the ability of those countries to service their obligations grew, financial markets started pressing for centralized solutions in order to minimize possible losses if countries like Greece left the eurozone or/and defaulted. The financial markets have been motivated by a maximization of profits, or rather insuring against possible losses, rather than ideological support for a federal EU.

Compared to the lobbying of the European business associations and other interests groups, the pressure exerted by financial markets is different. Instead of, or in addition to, directly interacting with policy-makers and demanding for centralized solutions, they are indirectly pushing EU institutions and member states to look for measures on how to bring down the costs of borrowing for eurozone members in trouble. But the actual effect of this pressure is arguably the same as that described by neofunctionalists: to pressure the EU and its member states to look for centralized solutions to the problems of particular member states which belong to the common currency area because, due to economic and financial interdependencies, the default of one of them would cause serious problems for the others.

In addition to this indirect pressure exercised by the markets, centralized solutions are elaborated by commercial bank analysts who provide regular commentary on EU's response to the crisis. They are often presented in the form of possible scenarios for the eurozone, which predicts a gloomy future in the case of the default of some countries, and a possible disintegration of the eurozone. For example, some studies have discussed the breaking up of the eurozone forced by financial markets unconvinced by EU decisions and the lack of progress towards fiscal union; this is described as a worst case scenario, possibly even leading to civil unrest and military conflict (Deo *et al.* 2011a, b). Similarly, integration scenarios have been advocated by prominent investors (Soros 2011). The underlying idea of the need for centralized solutions to the eurozone crisis in order to avoid possible disintegration has also been taken up by some leaders in the European Parliament and EU member states calling for political union.

Supranational institutions have also been active in proposing solutions to the eurozone crisis, which would delegate more competences to the EU level, set stricter common rules of monitoring and control, and centralize financial resources. Leaders of EU institutions—for example, the President of the European Commission M. Barroso and the President of the EU Council H. Van Rompuy—have been calling to draw lessons from the past and to improve the economic governance of the EU (EMU) by integrating further economic policies of the member states (Barroso 2011, 2012; Van Rompuy 2011, 2012a, 2012b). In terms of concrete legislative proposals, the European Commission has drafted the 'six pack' and the 'two pack'. The European Commission also publicly circulated proposals for the introduction of euro bonds and creation of a banking union. Some of the initiatives have been coordinated among several EU institutions, for example, between the European Commission and the President of the European Council as in 2010 which led to the adoption of the 'six pack'. Among more recent joint initiatives is the so-called 'report of four', officially presented by the President of the European Council H. Van Rompuy but prepared in 'close cooperation' with the President of the European Commission, the Eurogroup and the European Central Bank (Van Rompuy 2012a). The latter is expected to serve as a basis for further debates about the creation of a banking union, the integration of fiscal policies and reforms of EU institutions; it was followed in the second half of 2012 by the 'blueprint for a deep and genuine EMU', presented by the European Commission (2012) and another 'report of four' (Van Rompuy 2012b).

The ECB is another supranational institution which has been at the center of efforts to deal with the eurozone crisis. Despite resistance from some eurozone members—in particular, Germany—the ECB has gradually become active in intervening in financial markets with the aim of reducing the costs of borrowing and stabilizing the financial system. It intervened in financial markets several times throughout 2010–2011. At the end of 2011 and again in the winter of 2012, the ECB started its three-year long-term refinancing operations to provide liquidity to the banking system, totaling around one trillion euro; this was credited with driving down the costs of borrowing and servicing the obligations of such countries as Spain and Italy (Chancellor 2012). The most forceful and widely commented pronouncement came from the ECB governor M. Draghi in July 2012 when he declared that ECB will do 'whatever it takes' to save the euro, followed in September 2012 by the publicly announced intention to start a program of purchasing eurozone member state's short-term bonds in the secondary market (Steen *et al.* 2012). These measures imply a redistribution of financial obligations from eurozone member level to the ECB.

Finally, the ideas of epistemic communities also merit attention as they can play an important role as supporters of supranational solutions. Indeed, the advocates of further integration and centralized solutions to the eurozone crisis included many leading commentators and European economists. It can be maintained that it is the supporters of centralized solutions who dominate the debates most vocally criticizing EU policymakers—in particular, Germany's Chancellor A. Merkel for 'doing too little too late' (The Economist 2011). The key lesson to be drawn from the experience of the EMU exposed by the crisis, according to those analysts, is that the fiscal (transfer) union should complement the monetary union because uniform interest rates can lead to divergence of economic cycles in different euro area members and the financial transfers are required to stabilize the economies negatively affected by a single monetary policy and asymmetric shocks (see, for example, the report of the T. Padoa-Schioppa Group 2012).

It should be noted that the concept of a fiscal union can refer to quite different institutional and redistributive arrangements. For example, some economists proposed a 'limited fiscal union' which would include 'a euro area finance ministry' able to veto 'national budgets that could threaten euro-area sustainability' and 'provide support to illiquid but solvent governments' relying 'on federal tax resources' (Marzinotto *et al.* 2011). This arrangement would also imply setting up a euro-area deposit insurance corporation with banking supervision and resolution authority as well as the ECB becoming a lender of last resort. Other analysts have discussed the creation of a fiscal union, characterizing it by the introduction of the euro bonds, harmonization of taxes and the key feature of a possibility to transfer resources from a country in a boom state to a country experiencing recession (Morelli *et al.* 2011).

Establishing fiscal union would require a new EU treaty with new provisions delegating powers to supranational institutions with authority on the fiscal, structural and banking policies of its members, even though the fiscal union might be created only among euro area members (or euro plus pact members). In particular, a more active role of the ECB in addressing what are perceived to be the short-term pressures of the financial markets on some eurozone members, spreading the contagion to increasingly more countries and endangering the existence of the EMU itself, has been advocated by a number of economists (see De Grauwe 2011; Wolf 2011). All these recommendations have been summarized before the EU Council meeting of December 2011 into three categories of, first, the ECB providing unlimited guarantee of a maximum bond spread and increasing short-term liquidity for the banking sector; second, a firm time table for a eurozone bond; and, third, a fiscal union with a treasury (Munchau 2011).

However, when the EU's response to the crisis in terms of the actual outcomes rather than recommendations and initiatives publicly suggested by supranational institutions, investors and analysts is assessed, the decisions made and adopted by the EU member states so far seem to focus mostly on strengthening the implementation of already existing norms governing fiscal policy coordination and structural reforms. Besides, so far no country has been sanctioned because of the excessive imbalances. Hungary has been warned by the European Commission threatening to suspend almost 500 million euro of structural funds in 2013 if it does not follow its deficit reduction schedule, but it remains to be seen if such warnings and possibility of sanctions are really effective. Therefore, it is difficult to find any evidence of both functional and political spill-over in terms of the delegation of new competences to the EU or the eurozone. Even the proposals on the banking union which have been given most urgency were still being debated by the end of 2012, and some basic elements such as its supervisory structure and its mandate were contested by member states such as Germany. Agreement on euro bonds or a deposit guarantee scheme seems still further away.

Still Divergent National Preferences?

Liberal intergovernmentalism maintains that European integration is driven by EU member states, especially those which are relatively less dependent on other EU economies and therefore have stronger bargaining power. Governments of EU member states responding to the demands of domestic economic interests are the key actors, using the EU and its institutions to better manage growing flows of economic activities across borders and in such a way enhancing their capacities to manage these interdependencies (Moravcsik 1991, 1998). The current eurozone crisis has also been explained by the divergences of eurozone economies rather than by the lack of a central transfer mechanism (Moravcsik 2012).

Thus, despite the fact that the incrementalism of dealing with the crisis resembles closely the process described by neofunctionalists, it is because the member states, first of all, Germany set the pace and the tone for the search of the joint solutions acting strategically with a view to their economic interests and domestic politics. Yet again, as at the time when the Maastricht Treaty was adopted, the terms of the debate and the mechanisms adopted reflect the preferences of Germany. Decisions on a stricter enforcement of the rules governing fiscal discipline and structural reforms as well as the adoption of the TSCG are examples of the German influence (Kreilinger 2012). It can be maintained that the muddling through the eurozone crisis can be interpreted as a sequence of strategic decisions coordinated by Germany and ECB aiming at preventing full scale market panic, on the one hand, and keeping the pressure and incentives to undertake structural reforms for the eurozone countries and bring their finances into order, on the other. At the same time, reports of eurozone banks pulling out from troubled economies indicate that actual interdependency has been decreasing as a result of the crisis, decreasing exposure and reducing the costs of disintegration. According to some accounts, consolidated BIS bank exposure to Greece went down to $72bn in mid 2012 from a peak of just above $300bn in 2009 (Nordvig 2012). Thus, Berlin rather than Brussels has been the center of the crisis resolution, although Frankfurt has taken important short-term measures. The resistance of the member states to the idea of completely automatic sanctions in cases of breeching budgetary discipline and excessive imbalance rules also shows the limits of supranational entrepreneurship.

The divergence of national preferences has also manifested itself in the growing differentiation of EU membership. The initial division into eurozone members and non-members was further supplemented in March 2011 by the newly formed group of euro-plus countries, comprising 23 members who joined the initiative for closer cooperation on economic reform measures and the reviewing of each other's progress. Furthermore, the negotiations of the TSCG resulted in 25 EU members signing to the Treaty, with the United Kingdom and Czech Republic deciding to stay out of this process. Although after the negotiations of the TSCG the supranational institutions of the EU such as the European Commission and the European Court of Justice were assigned important roles, the proliferation of different groups of EU members complicates the application of the Community method and exposes the limits to the supranational delegation of powers in the fields of fiscal and economic policies. Some eurozone members have signaled their readiness to move ahead with the adoption of a financial transaction tax, but not all of them. Moreover, non-members of the eurozone also have divergent preferences regarding the centralization of competences. Some, which have permanent opt-outs like UK, are increasingly distancing themselves from further efforts of integration, provided that the single market is not affected by this process. Others like Sweden are supporting the measures of fiscal discipline and structural reforms but have postponed the introduction of the euro indefinitely and regard initiatives aimed at harmonizing taxation with caution. Still others like Poland urge the EU to forge ahead with fiscal integration, but react quite sensitively to any new measure which is likely to exclude non-eurozone members, adopting a 'wait and see' approach with regards to euro introduction before the eurozone sorts out its difficulties. The latter approach seems to be shared by most other non-eurozone members as well.

Although differentiated integration has been practiced since the adoption of the Maastricht Treaty, it has not been used so often to manage differences of national preferences as it has been during the recent years. The divergence of preferences regarding the new initiatives aimed at further integration of fiscal and economic policies among eurozone members and non-members alike is not so much an outcome of their diverging economic structures, patterns of mutual interdependence and lobbying of interest groups—factors stressed by liberal intergovernmentalism—but seem to be explained better by domestic politics. In other words, growing public interest in what takes place in the EU and eurozone and the negative sentiment towards centralized solutions of the eurozone crisis is becoming increasingly important as a constraint of European integration and supranational solutions to the eurozone crisis.

Popular Resistance to EMU Wide Redistribution

Although neofunctionalism and liberal intergovenmentalism differ on the causes, processes and driving forces of European integration, both approaches have one common feature—they prioritize elites (supranational or national) and economic interest groups over the population. In other words, it is elites who formulate and negotiate decisions in the EU, with an input from the transnational society and supranational institutions. However, in order to account properly for recent developments in the EU, this is not sufficient. It is argued here that popular opinion is becoming as important as it has never been before in the political debates on European integration. To be sure, the importance of domestic politics for the process of European integration was recognized at least 30 years ago when it was stressed that 'electioneering may play an important part in a member state's behavior in the EC' (Bulmer 1983, 351). It has also been used recently by analysts explaining the creation of the Stability and Growth Pact (Heipertz and Verdun 2010). However, this contribution develops further the use of domestic politics in explaining the state of European integration by connecting the decisions of member state leaders with the popular resistance to the efforts to centralize redistributive policy. The changing nature of public policies being centralized can explain to a large extent this shift and the growing importance of public opinion as a constraining factor.

For most of the history of European integration the EC/EU has dealt with regulatory policies that have been linked to the removal of non-tariff barriers to the functioning of the single market or justified by the arguments of the need to correct 'market failures'. Most of the EU policies have been about regulations which have been complex and too technical for the wider population to become interested in, becoming important only for those companies that have been subjected to those norms (usually businesses involved in cross-border activities) and regulators overseeing their enforcement. The process of integration has been taking place under 'vague but permissive public opinion' (Haas 1968, xii). Although the regulatory policies usually involve a redistributive element, as Central and Eastern European countries discovered during the process of adopting sometimes rather expensive EU norms, their redistributive effects have been indirect and hardly visible to the wider public. Also, though some redistribution has been established on the EU level it involved a relatively very small share of financial resources (around 1 per cent of EU's GDP) compared to what has been redistributed in the member states, and covered only specific areas like agriculture. Even this highly limited redistributive policy has been criticized strongly by analysts who maintain that the EU is 'a regulatory polity' and does not possess required characteristics for the effective and democratic redistribution of resources through its budget (Majone 1993).

The debate about EU- or EMU-wide solutions to the eurozone crisis from the start revolved around the centralized pooling of financial resources to help countries in trouble now and to create an insurance mechanism in the situations of asymmetric shocks in the future. The dominant view among commentators and economists is that the crisis necessitates the creation of a fiscal or transfer union—something which had to be done at the outset when the EMU was established. In other words, this implies a significant redistribution of budgetary resources from member states to the EU (EMU) or between member states, as it is more often perceived by the public. Redistribution of budgetary resources or 'who gets what when and how' is considered to be the essence of politics, and therefore the debates about the centralization of redistributive policies have been causing growing public interest with regards to the eurozone crisis and exposing territorial cleavages, often described as North versus South. The permissive consensus has been gradually replaced by public discontent, fuelled by the economic crisis, and growing uncertainty about the sustainability of the postwar welfare system.

Although the debates in the popular press about EU member states probably overstate the popular resistance to centralization and transfer of financial resources among EU member states, the rise of eurosceptical parties in a number of eurozone countries, changes in the ruling coalitions which took place in more than 10 EU countries during recent years, and growing popular protests in some countries provide indications which could be pointing to the changing political dynamics in Europe and new constraints to EU reform. The 'rift between north and south', which is not 'merely a matter of scathing articles in German or Greek newspapers', has been recognized by such figures in European politics as Delors (2012, 3). It is not just during the ratification of EU treaty changes in national referendums when policy-makers have to take popular opinion seriously. The growing public interest in the eurozone crisis and the potential solutions with their effects on the rest of the EU is becoming an important constraint in the day-to-day politics of the EU, with national leaders obliged to take popular opinion seriously when they gather in the EU summits for yet another attempt at calming down the financial markets with promises of centralized solutions. Popular debates in countries like Germany, Netherlands, Finland and Slovakia problematize the issue of transfers to Southern Europe when austerity continues to be enforced in the former. On the other hand, a significant share of the population in countries like Greece resist structural reforms and austerity measures, which are seen as imposed by the EU and IMF, with the Northern countries and their banks behind them.

These popular debates expose the absence of solidarity among EU member states, which in turn shows the absence of EU-wide polity comparable to the polities of its member states. While this observation is by no means new, the debate about the completion of the 'incomplete' EMU adds an additional element. It explains the incrementalism of the EU's response to the crisis and shows the limits of a possible centralization of powers and the transfer of resources. Although these limits could become especially constraining if new amendments to the treaty are required, they are also important in the current gradual movement of the EU in directions of both strengthening the enforcement of earlier agreed norms, implementing structural reforms, harmonizing some policies on the EU level without treaty changes and growing differentiation.

Conclusions

The analysis presented here shows that the EU's response to the crisis of the eurozone cannot be understood by using dominant theories of

European integration without adding the dimension of domestic politics, previously often ignored due to the absence of public interest in the EU. Although at first glance the EU's economic governance reforms present a case of financial markets and supranational institutions gradually pushing the transfer of competences and resources to the federal level, closer examination of decisions taken so far reveal the dominant role of Germany and the diverging national preferences of both EMU and non-eurozone members.

The particularly striking feature of recent debates and attempts to reform the EU has to do with a disappearance of popular permissive consensus for the process of European integration that characterized most of its history. As calls for a fiscal or transfer union to supplement monetary union and save the euro imply that regulatory policies of the EU have to be supplemented by a much stronger redistributive element, the public becomes increasingly interested and concerned about the potential implications of these measures on their welfare. The growing importance of domestic politics creates new constraints for EU and national policy-makers, which have to be taken into account, and so far the ideas circulated by EU leaders on addressing the accountability and legitimacy issues do not seem to respond adequately to this. The need to watch for popular opinion at home, financial markets on the European and global scale as well as incentives for reforms in the recipient countries makes the process of reacting to the crisis slow and incremental.

This dynamic has resulted in diverging trajectories of EU reform, with measures taken to enforce already adopted norms coordinating fiscal and economic policies of member states, some procedural amendments to define more explicitly certain norms such as the 'golden rule' limiting structural annual deficit to 0.5 per cent of GDP or voting by reversed qualified majority voting, to more significant changes in introducing the EFSF to become a permanent ESM and short-term measures taken by the ECB. Besides this, different groups of countries have been taking part in different initiatives, further complicating the process and the application of centralized solutions. So far the resolution of the eurozone crisis presents a gradual move in several directions, all aiming at preserving the euro with instruments other than a big leap towards a federal transfer union to supplement the monetary union of the EU.

References

Barber, T. 2010. EU keeps economic targets firmly in its sight. *Financial Times* blog, June 16, http://blogs.ft.com/brusselsblog/2010/06/eu-keeps-economic-targets-firmly-in-its-sights/ (accessed 20 June 2010).

Barroso, J.M. 2012. State of the Union Address, European Parliament, Strasbourg, 12 September Speech/12/596.

Bulmer, S. 1983. Domestic politics and European Community policy-making. *Journal of Common Market Studies* XXI, no. 4: 349–363.

Chancellor, E. 2012. ECB 'saves' banks as economies sink. *Financial Times*, February 5, http://www.ft.com/cms/s/0/af0f74ba-4d82-11e1-b96c-00144feabdc0.html#ixzz1li4yYU5r (accessed 6 February 2012).

Cooper, I. 2011. The euro crisis as the revenge of neo-functionalism, http://euobserver.com/7/113682 (accessed 25 August 2012).

De Grauwe, P. 2011. Only a more active ECB can solve the euro crisis, CEPS Policy Brief No. 250, August 4.

Delors, J. 2012. Consolidating the EMU, a vital task, Notre Europe, 7 December.

Deo, S., P. Donovan, and L. Hatheway. 2011a. Euro break-up—the consequences, UBS Investment Research, Global Economic Perspectives, September 6.

Deo, S., P. Donovan, and L. Hatheway. 2011b. A brief history of breakups, UBS Investment Research, Global Economic Perspectives, October 11.

European Commission. 2010. Enhancing economic policy coordination for stability, growth and jobs—tools for stronger EU economic governance, COM (2010) 367 final, Brussels.

European Commission. 2012. A blueprint for a deep and genuine economic and monetary union. Launching a European debate, communication from the Commission, COM (2012) 777 final, Brussels, 28 November 2012.

Haas, E.B. 1968. *The uniting of Europe*. Stanford: Stanford University Press.

Heipertz, M., and A. Verdun. 2010. *Ruling Europe, The politics of the stability and growth pact*. Cambridge: Cambridge University Press.

Kreilinger, V. 2012. The making of a new treaty: six rounds of political bargaining, Notre Europe, Policy Brief No. 32, February.

Majone, G. 1993. The European Community between social policy and social regulation. *Journal of Common Market Studies* 31, no. 2: 153–70.

Marzinotto, B., A. Sapir, and G.B. Wolff. 2011. What kind of fiscal union? Bruegel Policy Brief, Issue 2011/06, November.

Moravcsik, A. 1991. Negotiating the Single European Act: national interests and conventional statecraft in the European Community. *International Organization* 45, no. 1: 19–56.

Moravcsik, A. 1998. *The choice for Europe*. Ithaca, NY: Cornell University Press.

Moravcsik, A. 2012. Europe after the crisis. How to Sustain a common currency. *Foreign Affairs* 91, no. 3: 54–68.

Morelli, M., J. Luque, and J. Tavares. 2011. The case for a fiscal union beyond a Eurobond, October 21, http://www.eurointelligence.com/eurointelligence-news/home/singleview/article/the-case-for-a-fiscal-union-beyond-a-eurobond.html (accessed 22 October 2011).

Munchau, W. 2011. The eurozone really has only days to avoid collapse. *Financial Times*, November 27, http://www.ft.com/intl/cms/s/0/d9a299a8-1760-11e1-b00e-00144feabdc0.html#axzz1ezKTXPSD (accessed 28 November 2011).

Nordvig, J. 2012. The Eurozone break up debate: uncertainty still reigns, http://www.voxeu.org/article/eurozone-breakup-debate-uncertainty-still-reigns#fn (accessed 20 November 2012).

Rosamond, B. 2005. The uniting of Europe and the foundation of EU studies: revisiting the neofunctionalism of Ernst B. Haas. *Journal of European Public Policy* 12, no. 2: 237–54.

Soros, G. 2011. A route map through the eurozone minefield. *Financial Times*, October 13, reproduced at http://www.georgesoros.com/articles-essays/entry/a_routemap_through_the_eurozone_minefield/ (accessed 15 October 2011).

Steen, M. et al. 2012. ECB signals resolve to sve euro. *Financial Times*, September 6, http://www.ft.com/cms/s/0/b70ff9a8-f84c-11e1-b0e1-00144feabdc0.html#ixzz25nFKmVkv (accessed 7 September 2012).

The Economist. 2011. The new iron chancellor. As the euro totters, the world waits for the German chancellor to act. Will she?, November 26, http://www.economist.com/node/21540283 (accessed 28 November 2011).

T. Padoa-Schioppa Group. 2012. Completing the Euro. A roadmap towards fiscal union in Europe, Report of the Tomasso Padoa-Schioppa Group, Notre-Europe.

Van Rompuy, H. 2011. Beyond the crisis: lessons for the future of the eurozone. Speech at the LSE, 7 September. http://www.european-council.europa.eu/the-president/speeches?lang=en (accessed 20 September 2011).

Van Rompuy, H. 2012a. Towards a genuine economic and monetary union. Report by President of the European Council. Brussels, 26 June. http://www.consilium.europa.eu/ (accessed 27 June 2012).

Van Rompuy, H. 2012b. Towards a genuine economic and monetary union. 5 December. http://www.consilium.europa.eu/ (accessed 6 December 2012).

Wolf, M.2011. Be bold, Mario, put out that fire. *Financial Times*, October 25, http://www.ft.com/intl/cms/s/0/bd60ab78-fe6e-11e0-bac4-00144feabdc0.html#axzz1bgUaJlsx (accessed 26 October 2011).

Index

Note:
Page numbers in **bold** type refer to tables
Page numbers in *italic* type refer to figures
Page numbers followed by 'n' refer to notes

accountability: and European Central Bank 95–7; vs responsiveness 95, 98–9
accounting standards 85, 110
'Action Programme for the Second Stage' (European Commission, 1962): background 6, 124–5; comparison with 'EMU@10' 122–3; *engrenage* theory 125–6, 127; 'merged into one' monetary policy 128–30; negative vs positive integration 126–8
agency: agency slack 155, 157, 160, 163; and European Commission entrepreneurship 116–17; G20 and multiple agency 156–9; *see also* principal-agent theory
Allen, D. 160
allocation, European Commission entrepreneurship and financial crisis (2007-) 112–13
Almunia, Joaquim 77, 121–2, 130, 155
American federalism 80
Andrews, David 6, 7
Anglo-American jurisprudence, 'open texture' of primary rules 17, 19
Asmussen, Jörg 68
austerity policies 2, 4, 10, 88, 89
automaticity 38, 68, 69, 70, 71

bail-outs: and banks 80, 89–90; and EFSF creation 50; and EMU 85; Greece 47–8, 85–8; 'no-bail-out' clause (Maastricht Treaty) 14, 33, *33*, 34, 35, 48; and private bond holders 9; *see also* redistribution
bancassurance 145
Bank for International Settlements (BIS) 115, 174
banks: and bail-outs 80, 89–90; bank debts and sovereign debts 22, 23; banking regulation, Europeanization of 11; banking union 22, 99, 118, 170, 172, 174; bank-sovereign feedback loop 35, 39; British banks 146–7, 148 (Lloyds–TSB 145); central banks and principal-agent theory 95; consolidated BIS bank exposure to Greek debt crisis 174; 'constructive ambiguity' skills 23; decreasing interdependency of 174; European Banking Authority (EBA) 38, 145; European Investment Bank (EIB) 52, 55; financial market integration and banking crises 16; French banks (diversion of public funds to 1; and Greek debt crisis 47, 115; mutual banks 146); German banks (Commerzbank 145; diversion of public funds to 1; and Greek debt crisis 47, 115; *hausbank* 148; Helaba (Hessen-Thüringen LB) 145; Landesbanken 142, 145, 146, 149; structure of banking and financial systems 146–8; *see also* Bundesbank); 'lender of last resort' function 21; lending and financial crisis (2007–) 148–9, **149**; Liquidity Coverage Ratio (LCR) 142, 148; liquidity provision (Dec. 2011) 21–2, 23; liquidity rules 140, 141, 142, 147–8; recapitalisation 22, 23, 39, 53; TARGET2 payment system balances 21, 37; and 'two-pack' of legislation 38; *see also* 'Action Programme for the Second Stage' (European Commission, 1962); Basel Committee on Banking Supervision (BCBS); capital requirements; Capital Requirements Directives (CRD); European Central Bank (ECB)
Barber, T. 56
Barnier, Michel 117
Barroso, José Manuel: and Barnier, Michel 117; centre-right orientations 5, 7, 108, 109, 116, 117, 118; and EFSF 53; and EU integration 172; and EU representation in G20 156–7; and Eurobonds 111, 115; and financial transactions tax 114, 116, 117; and fiscal union 118; pragmatism 108; and regulation/supervision 110–11; and re-regulation of financial markets 117; and Stability and Growth Pact (SGP) 112, 116–17; *Towards a Genuine Economic and Monetary Union* (Rompuy,

INDEX

Barroso, Juncker and Draghi) 135n1; and Van Rompuy Task Force (VRTF) 65; *see also* supranational entrepreneurship and the Barroso Commission
Bartolini, S. 98
Basel Committee on Banking Supervision (BCBS): Basel I Accord 140, 143; Basel II Accord 140, 141, 143, 145; Basel III Accord 16, 140, 141–6, **144**, 147–8, 149, 150; and EU law 7
Benson-Rea, M. 157
Bentham, Jeremy 17, 18–19, 27
'bicycle theory' of integration 7, 123, 126
bilateral loans 47, 48, 50, 86, 113
Bini Smaghi, Lorenzo 34
BIS (Bank for International Settlements) 115, 174
'blueprint for a deep and genuine EMU' (European Commission, 2012) 172
Blyth, M. 89
Böfinger, Peter 89–90
Bowles, Sharon 69
Bretton Woods system 123, 129
Broad Economic Policy Goals 128
Brown, Gordon 115
Buiter, W. 96, 99
Bulmer, S. 176
Bundesbank: and ECB 8, 19, 21–2, 24; and fiscal/monetary union 22; and Ordo-liberalism 21; and Securities Markets Programme (SMP) 23; and supreme emergency 25; and TARGET2 payment system balances 21
'buying time' strategy, and euro crisis 14

Cameron, David 35
capital requirements: abstract and main issues 139–41; new EU capital legislation 141–3; political economy analysis (capital position 143–6, **144**; differing macro-economic concerns 148–50; structure of banking and financial systems 146–8, 150)
Capital Requirements Directives (CRD): CRD II 141, 145; CRD III 142; CRD IV 140–6, 147–8, 149, 150
Capoccia, G. 37–8, 49
Cavaco Silva, Aníbal 35
CDO (Collateralized Debt Obligation) 57
central Europe: budgetary problems 10; eltes' support for eurozone membership 11
Chang, Michele 6
Co-Investment Funds 54
Collateralized Debt Obligation (CDO) 57
collective principal 160–3
Commerzbank 145
Common Agricultural Policy (CAP) 124, 126, 128

Common External Tariff 125
Common Market 6, 124, 128–9
Community method: definition and characteristics 62–3; and delegation within EMU 62–4; and proliferation of different EU groups 175; shift away from 2, 3–4; and 'six-pack proposals' 68, 72; and TSCG 72; vs Union method 8, 22, 61–2, 73; *see also* fiscal policy coordination and Community method; intergovernmentalism; Union method
Competition Policy, and Basel III Accord 143
consequentialism 17
'constructive ambiguity' skills 23
contingent commitments 14, 19–21, 22, 23, 26, 27
Cooper, I. 170
counterfactual analysis 32, 57
credibility: and EMU 95, 96, 97; and EU representation in G20 158, 159
credit rating 55, 86, 145; credit rating agencies 110
Czech Republic, and TSCG 72, 175

Daele, Franciskus van 157
Dallara, Charles 88
Deauville agreement (Oct. 2010) 9, 67–8, 70
Debaere, P. 158
debt *see* European Debt Agency proposal; sovereign debts
delegation: and Community method 63; and EU external economic governance 154–5; as a governance tool 9; and legitimacy 96, 104n2; and principal-agent theory 63–4, 96; and probit analyses of EU system 160–1, **161**, **162**, 163; and Union method 73
delegation theory: 'incomplete contracts' 158; and multiple agency 157
Delors, Jacques 32, 107–8, 118, 134, 177
democracy: democratic deficit 14, 26; and EU economic governance 88; *see also* popular opinion
deposit insurance 39, 110
derivatives: and financial transactions tax 114; over-the-counter derivatives 110, 142
developing countries, and EU external economic governance 159, 164
DG ECFIN (Directorate General for Economic and Financial Affairs) 65
dirigisme 126
DMO (German Debt Management Office) 52, 55
Doyle, Sir Arthur Conan, Sherlock Holmes quote 30
Drachenberg, R. 63

INDEX

Draghi, Mario: and ECB's strategic role 100, 103, 104n11, 104n13; and OMT Programme 23, 24, 26; and purchase of bonds in secondary markets 172; and Securities Markets Programme (SMP) 23; *Towards a Genuine Economic and Monetary Union* (Rompuy, Barroso, Juncker and Draghi) 135n1; and TSCG 72
Drazen, A. 96
Dür, A. 154, 158
Dyson, Kenneth 3, 63, 95, 104n12

EAMS (Euro Area Member States) *see* Euro Area Member States (EAMS)
ECB *see* European Central Bank (ECB)
ECOFIN *see* Economics and Finance Council (ECOFIN)
Economic and Monetary Union (EMU): background and weaknesses 1, 2, 14, 15; and bail-outs 85; 'blueprint for a deep and genuine EMU' 172; and Community method 62–4; and ECB as guardian of 100–1, 103; and external economic governance 155–6; legitimacy issues 93–5, 96, 97, **98**; and Maastricht Treaty 32, 164; pre-crisis success 121–2; and redistribution 8, 113–14, 168–9, 175–7, 178; and risk management 78–81, 89; and 'six-pack' of economic reforms 62; and supreme emergency 19, 24, 25, 27; *Towards a Genuine Economic and Monetary Union* (Rompuy, Barroso, Juncker and Draghi) 135n1; *see also* Economic and Monetary Union (EMU) and sovereign debt crisis; 'EMU@10' (European Commission, 2008)
Economic and Monetary Union (EMU) and sovereign debt crisis: abstract and main issues 29–31, 40–1; EMU design 32–3, **33**; gaps (EMU in practice) 33–5; options to fill gaps (EMU in crisis) 36–8; redesigning EMU governance 38–40; theoretical approach 31–2
economic governance: evolution and redefinition 2–4, 11; *see also* economic governance and European Commission; G20 and EU external economic governance; supreme emergency
economic governance and European Commission: abstract and main issues 121–4; 'Action Programme for the Second Stage' (background 6, 124–5; comparison with 'EMU@10' 122–3; *engrenage* theory 125–6, 127; 'merged into one' monetary policy 128–30; negative vs positive integration 126–8); 'EMU@10' (background 130; comparison with 'Action Programme' 122–3; *engrenage redux* 132–3; foreshadowing debt crisis 130–2; monetary union and liberalization 133–4); summary and conclusion 134–5; *see also* G20 and EU external economic governance; supreme emergency
Economics and Finance Council (ECOFIN): and EFSF 5, 50–1; and EU representation in G20 156, 163; and fiscal policy coordination 64; and Greek debt crisis 85–6; and redefined economic governance 2; and shift away from Community method 4; and Stability and Growth Pact (SGP) 34–5; and supreme emergency exemption 21; and Van Rompuy Task Force (VRTF) 65, 66, 67
Economist, The: on the EFSF 52; on the ESM 56
EFSF *see* European Financial Stability Facility (EFSF)
EFSM (European Financial Stabilisation Mechanism) 50, 51, 54, 113
EIB (European Investment Bank) 52, 55
elite consensus 10–11
Elsig, M. 154, 158
EMF (European Monetary Fund) 48, 56, 115
EMU *see* Economic and Monetary Union (EMU); Economic and Monetary Union (EMU) and sovereign debt crisis; 'EMU@10' (European Commission, 2008)
'EMU@10' (European Commission, 2008): background 130; comparison with 'Action Programme' 122–3; *engrenage redux* 132–3; foreshadowing debt crisis 130–2; monetary union and liberalization 133–4
engrenage theory 6, 123, 125–6, 127, 130, 134–5; *engrenage redux* 132–3
entrepreneurship *see* supranational entrepreneurship and the Barroso Commission
ESM *see* European Stability Mechanism (ESM)
ESRB (European Systemic Risk Board) 110
EU Competition Policy, and Basel III Accord 143
Euro Area Member States (EAMS): and creation of EFSF 51; and Greek bail-out funding 47, 49
Eurobarometer (2010): and external economic governance 154, 160, **161**, **162**; *see also* popular opinion
Eurobonds 9, 111, 114, 115, 116, 118
euro crisis: and 'buying time' strategy 14; characteristics and official response 1–2; crisis resolution and ECB 2, 3, 4, 5, 6, 8, 9; crisis resolution and European

INDEX

Commission 2, 3–4, 5–7, 8, 9; estimated economic costs of Eurozone exit 36; and fiscal federalism 4–5; French and German initial responses 4, 9; future of euro and elite consensus 10–11; IMF involvement and developing countries 159; national economic divergence 7–8; political upheaval 9–10; potential for further instability 11; *see also* Economic and Monetary Union (EMU) and sovereign debt crisis; Eurozone crisis and European integration; sovereign debts

Eurogroup 21, 39, 65, 70, 172

European Banking Authority (EBA) 38, 145

European Central Bank (ECB): and austerity programmes 4; and Basel regulations 145; and Bundesbank 8, 19, 21–2, 24; and crisis resolution 2, 3, 4, 5, 6, 8, 9; and EFSF 51, 52, 53, 55; and EMU's weak democratic foundations 37; and ESM 39; and ESRB 110; and EU representation in G20 156; and European Council 97; and European Parliament 101–3; and financial markets, interventions in 172; and fiscal union proposals 173; and Germany 100, 172; and Greek debt crisis 47, 86; growing role of 2, 4, 6, 156; independence of 15; inflation-fighting reputation of 122; and intergovernmentalism 63; 'lender of last resort' function of 21; and liberal intergovernmentalism 174; and liquidity provision (Dec. 2011) 21–2, 23; and OMT Programme 23, 24, 25, 26, 40, 99; and principal-agent theory 95, 96, 97, 102–3; and professional socialization and consensus 10; 'report of four' 172; and Securities Markets Programme 23, 36; and short-term measures vs transfer union 178; and 'six-pack' of economic reforms 69; and sovereign bonds (purchase of on primary market) 14, 23; and sovereign bonds (purchase of on secondary market) 19, 23, 40; and sovereign debt markets 35, 36, 37; and supreme emergency 21, 24, 26, 27; and TARGET2 payment system balances 21, 37; and TFEU (monetary financing prohibition) 30, 31, 32, 36; and TSCG 72; and Van Rompuy Task Force 65; *see also* European Central Bank (ECB) and legitimacy

European Central Bank (ECB) and legitimacy: abstract and main issues 93–5; independence and accountability 95–7; rationale to act strategically 97–101; strategic collaboration with European Parliament 101–3

European Commission: and automaticity principle 71; and Basel III/CDR IV 143; 'blueprint for a deep and genuine EMU' (2012) 172; and crisis resolution 2, 3–4, 5–7, 8, 9; and EFSF 51, 52, 53, 55, 113; and EU representation in G20 155, 156–8, 159, 163; and Eurobonds 116, 118; and European Monetary Fund (EMF) proposal 48; and European Stability Mechanism (ESM) 116, 118; and European Systemic Risk Board (ESRB) 110; and financial transactions tax 114, 115, 116, 117; functions of 63; and Greek debt crisis 47, 81, 84, 85, 86, 113; and integration 7, 108, 115–16, 118, 172; and Macroeconomic Imbalances Procedure 38; and market discipline 79; and neoliberalism 8; 'report of four' 172; and 'six-pack' of economic reforms 3–4, 9, 38, 62, 64–9, 67, 88; and Stability and Growth Pact (SGP) 34–5, 38–9; and stabilization fund proposal (alternative to EFSF) 5, 49, 56; and TSCG 64, 71, 175; and 'two-pack' of legislation 38; waning entrepreneurship of 6, 7; *see also* 'Action Programme for the Second Stage' (European Commission, 1962); Barroso, José Manuel; Community method; economic governance and European Commission; 'EMU@10' (European Commission, 2008); supranational entrepreneurship and the Barroso Commission

European Council: and automaticity principle 71; and ECB 97; and EU representation in G20 155, 156, 157, 160, 163; and European Stability Mechanism (ESM) 113; and fiscal policy coordination 64; and integration 172; and market discipline 79; and principal-agent theory 69; and redefined economic governance 2, 4; 'report of four' 172; and 'six-pack' of economic reforms 64–5, 70; and supreme emergency 21, 24; and Van Rompuy Task Force 62, 65, 66, 67, 68; *see also* Community method; Eurozone Summits; Union method

European Court of Justice (ECJ) 62, 63, 175

European Debt Agency proposal 48–9

European Economic Recovery Programme 112

European Financial Stabilisation Mechanism (EFSM) 50, 51, 54, 113

European Financial Stability Facility (EFSF): creation and implementation 3 (ECOFIN meeting and creation 5, 50–1; Greek debt crisis and options 46–50; implementation 51–3; initial investment 45–6, 52; move to ESM 53–6); and Deauville deal 68; and European Commission 51, 52, 53,

INDEX

55, 113; and European integration 169, 170, 178; and historical institutionalism 46, 56–7; and OMT Programme 23; and supreme emergency 22; *see also* European Stability Mechanism (ESM)
European integration: 'bicycle theory' 7, 123, 126; differentiated integration 175; and EFSF 169, 170, 178; and euro 2; and European Commission 7, 108, 115–16, 118, 172; and European Council 172; and European Parliament 172; and European Stability Mechanism 169, 170, 178; and financial markets 115, 171–2; and Franco–German alliance 9; vs intergovernmentalism 57; and monetary financing prohibition (Article 123 TFEU) 31, 40–1; negative vs positive integration 7, 123, 126–8, 133; thriving on difficulty 3; *see also engrenage* theory; Eurozone crisis and European integration; liberal intergovernmentalism; neofunctionalism
European Investment Bank (EIB) 52, 55
European Monetary Fund (EMF) 48, 56, 115
European Monetary System 63
European Parliament: and 'Action Programme for the Second Stage' 124; and Basel III/CDR IV 143; and Community method 22; and European Central Bank 101–3; and financial crisis (2007-) 112–13; and financial transactions tax 8, 114, 115; functions and expanding powers of 63, 101; and integration 172; and principal-agent theory 69; and redefined economic governance 2; and reversed qualified majority voting (RQMV) 101; self-confidence and activism of 4, 9; and 'six-pack' of economic reforms 62, 69–70; and supreme emergency debate 18; and TSCG 72; *see also* Community method; Union method
European Semester 9, 66, 67, 68, 70, 71, 170
European Stability Mechanism (ESM): capital and instruments 39; creation 3, 5, 46, 53–4, 113; and European Commission 116, 118; and European integration 169, 170, 178; and OMT Programme 23, 40; as result of path dependence 54–6, 57; and supreme emergency 21, 22, 25; and TSCG 72; *see also* European Financial Stability Facility (EFSF)
European Systemic Risk Board (ESRB) 110
euro-plus countries 175
eurosceptical parties, rise of 177
Eurozone crisis and European integration: abstract and main issues 167–9; liberal intergovernmentalism and national preferences 169, 174–5; neofunctionalism and supranational solutions 169–74, 175–6; popular resistance to EMU redistribution 175–7; summary and conclusion 177–8
Eurozone Summits, and Merkel/Sarkozy letter to van Rompuy 70
Exchange Rate Mechanism (ERM) crises 16
external economic governance *see* G20 and EU external economic governance

Farrell, Henry 105n19
Featherstone, K. 85–6
federalism *see* American federalism; fiscal federalism and Greek debt crisis
Federal Reserve, and sovereign debt 37, 37
financial crisis (2007–): and bank lending 148–50, **149**; and coordination of policy responses 153–4, 158; and 'EMU@10' (European Commission, 2008) 130–2; and European Parliament 112–13; and IMF 112; and popular view of EU 161, 163; and Sarkozy 110; *see also* euro crisis; Eurozone crisis and European integration; supranational entrepreneurship and the Barroso Commission
financial markets: ECB's intervention in 172; and European integration 115, 171–2; and Maastricht governance paradigm 15–16; *see also* market
Financial Stability Board, and EU representation in G20 159
financial supervision 110–11; *see also* Basel Committee on Banking Supervision (BCBS); regulation
financial transactions tax 8, 113–14, 115, 116, 117, 175
Fioretos, O. 54
'Fiscal Compact' treaty *see* Treaty on Stability, Coordination and Governance (TSCG)
'fiscal dominance' issue 32, 36–7, 39
fiscal federalism and Greek debt crisis: abstract and main issues 4–5, 7–8, 77–8; fiscal federalism and risk management 78–81; Greek crisis (characteristics 81–5, 82, 84; first bail-out and moral hazard 85–6; second bailout 86–8); response to crisis and economic governance 88–90
fiscal policies, separation from monetary policies 15, 24
fiscal policy coordination and Community method: abstract and main issues 61–2, 72–3; Community method, delegation and EMU 62–4; 'six-pack' proposals and Van Rompuy Task Force 64–70, 67, 69; Treaty on Stability, Coordination and

185

INDEX

Governance and intergovernmentalism 69–72
fiscal union 8–9, 22, 56, 118, 170, 171, 173; *see also* transfer union
France: banks (diversion of public funds to 1; mutual banks 146; structure of banking and financial systems 146–7, 148); and Basel III/CRD IV 143, 144–6, **144**, 149, 150; *dirigisme* 126; and ECB 100; and EFSF 50, 52, 53, 55; and EMS (European Monetary System) 63; and EU bail-out financing 47; and euro crisis, initial response to 4, 9; financial crisis (2007–) and lending 149–50, **149**; Franco–German alliance 9; and Greek debt crisis 47, 88, 115; and Greek external debt 83, *84*, 86; and Maastricht criteria 7; and reversed qualified majority voting (RQMV) 105n19; and 'six-pack' of economic reforms 67–8, 70; and Union method 22; *see also* Sarkozy, Nicolas
Frankel, Christophe 52, 55

G7, and EU representation 156, 163
G20 and EU external economic governance: abstract and main issues 153–6; collective principal 160–3; multiple agents 156–9; summary and conclusion 163–4; *see also* economic governance and European Commission
Gallagher, E. 63
Geithner, Timothy 139–40
German Debt Management Office (DMO) 52, 55
Germany: and banking union proposals 174; banks (Commerzbank 145; diversion of public funds to 1; *hausbank* 148; Helaba (Hessen-Thüringen LB) 145; Landesbanken 142, 145, 146, 149; structure of banking and financial systems 146–8; *see also* Bundesbank); and Basel III/CRD IV 143, 144–6, **144**, 149, 150; and bilateral loans 48; DMO (German Debt Management Office) 52, 55; dominant role in EU 174–5, 178; and ECB 100, 172; and EFSF 50–1, 52, 53, 55; and elite consensus 10–11; emergency powers in German Basic Law 16–17; and EMF (European Monetary Fund) proposal 48; and EMS (European Monetary System) 63; and ESM (European Stability Mechanism) 22, 54; estimated economic costs of Eurozone exit 36; and EU bail-out financing 47; EU bail-outs and taxpayers 89; and Eurobonds 9; and euro crisis, initial response to 4, 9; and European Commission's stabilization fund proposal 49, 56; financial crisis (2007)

and lending 149, **149**; Franco–German alliance 9; and Greek debt crisis 47, 85–6, 88, 115; and Greek external debt 83, *84*, 86; and intergovernmentalism 70; and Maastricht criteria 7, 9; and Maastricht Treaty 174; Ordo-liberalism 21, 25; and principal-agent theory 73; proposal for EU Budget Commissioner for Greece 39; *Rechtsstaat* (state ruled by law) 17; and revaluation of D-mark (1961) 124; and reversed qualified majority voting (RQMV) 105n19; and 'six-pack' of economic reforms 67–8, 70, 88; social market economy 126; and supreme emergency 18, 19, 25–6; and TARGET2 payment system balances 37; and TSCG 25, 174; and Union method 22; xenophobic stereotypes in press 1–2; *see also* Merkel, Angela
Globalisation Adjustment Fund 112
Glöckler, Gabriel 4, 5
Gocaj, Ledina 5
'golden rule' (structural deficits) 178
Great Recession *see* financial crisis (2007–)
Greek debt crisis: austerity measures 2, 4, 10, 89; bail-outs 47–8, 85–8; characteristics 81–5, *82*, *84*; conditionalities for financial support 11; consolidated BIS bank exposure to 174; crisis contagion and options considered 48–50; and EFSF 45, 46, 57; and ESM 54; estimated economic costs of Eurozone exit 36; and European Commission 47, 81, 84, 85, 86, 113; external debt 83, *84*, 86; government debt and bank-sovereign feedback loop 35; government debt levels 34, *34*; IMF Greek crisis warning exercise 81–2; member states' exposure to 115; proposal for EU Budget Commissioner for Greece 39; xenophobic stereotypes in press 1–2; *see also* fiscal federalism and Greek debt crisis
'grim necessity' quote (*Richard II*, Shakespeare) 13–14
Gros, Daniel 48
Gstöhl, S. 160

Haas, E.B. 89, 108, 109, 110, 176
Haglund, Carl 71
Hallerberg, M. 7, 78, 79, 81
Hallstein, Walter 124, 125, 126, 127, 135n6, 135n7
Hart, H.L.A. 17, 19, 27
hausbank 148
Hawkins, D.G. 155
hedge funds 110, 117
Hegel, G.W.F. 17, 18, 27
Helaba (Hessen-Thüringen LB) 145
Helleiner, E. 150

INDEX

Héritier, Adrienne 105n19
historical institutionalism 30–2, 36, 46, 49, 54, 55, 56–7; *see also* path dependency
Hix, S. 108
Hobbes, Thomas 17, 18, 27
Hodson, Dermot 5, 7, 8, 64, 158
Hoffmann, S. 108
Holmes, Sherlock (Arthur Conan Doyle character's quote) 30
Howarth, David 7, 8
Hungary: budgetary and political problems 10; deficit reduction schedule 174
'hydra factor' 154, 160

IMF *see* International Monetary Fund (IMF)
'incomplete contracts' 158
integration *see* European integration; Eurozone crisis and European integration
intergovernmentalism 57, 61–3, 65, 69–72, 73, 89, 160; liberal intergovernmentalism 169, 174–5
international economic institutions, and EU representation 6
International Monetary Fund (IMF): and CRD IV 142; and EFSF 52; and EU bail-out funding 50; and EU external economic governance 159; and EU representation 156; and EU representation in G20 159; and financial crisis (2007–) 112; and Greek bail-out funding 47, 55, 86; Greek crisis warning exercise 81–2
Ireland: deficit vs public debt ratio 82; and EFSF 52, 53; government's bank bail-out 80; and SGP 35
Issing, Otmar 85
Italy: conditionalities for financial support 11; and ECB 21, 100; and EFSF 52; and Greek debt crisis 115; and Greek external debt 84; and possible eurozone exit 10; and Securities Markets Programme 23; and 'six-pack' of economic reforms 67

Jabko, N. 101, 104n12
Jones, E. 96
Juncker, Jean-Claude, *Towards a Genuine Economic and Monetary Union* (Rompuy, Barroso, Juncker and Draghi) 135n1
Juppé, Alain 35
'just war' theory 17, 19

'keep own house in order' principle 33, 33, 35, 39
Kelemen, D.R. 37–8, 49
Kirkegaard, J. 104n14
Kohl, Helmut 25

Lagarde, Christine 67
Lamfalussy, Alexandre, 2001 Report 16

Landesbanken 142, 145, 146, 149
Larosière, Jacques de 110, 146
LCR (Liquidity Coverage Ratio) 142, 148
legitimacy: and delegation 96, 104n2; and principal-agent theory 97, 101; throughput legitimacy (ECB) 97, 99; *see also* European Central Bank (ECB) and legitimacy
'lender of last resort' function 21
lending: and financial crisis (2007) 148–50, 149; *see also* bilateral loans
Leterme, Yves 48–9
liberal intergovernmentalism 169, 174–5; *see also* intergovernmentalism
liberalism *see* Ordo-liberalism
liquidity provision, and ECB's lender-of-last-resort function 21–2, 23
liquidity rules 140, 141, 142, 147–8
Lisbon Agenda/Strategy 6, 8, 168
Lisbon Treaty 9, 18, 46, 55, 97, 156, 157
'Little Engine' story (Watty Piper), quote from 107
Lloyds–TSB 145

Maastricht criteria: description 32–3; and euro crisis 2, 4; and European elites 10; and European Monetary Fund proposal 48; and financial markets 33–4; France/Germany's divergence from 7; Germany's reaffirming of 9; monetarist-inspired 5
Maastricht Treaty: and Community method 63; and crisis management 31; and crisis resolution failure 3; and differentiated integration 175; and EMU 32, 164; and European Parliament's competencies 101; and fiscal/monetary union 22; German influence on 174; Maastricht governance paradigm and crisis prevention 15–17; 'Maastricht' *status quo* 30; model of exchange-rate policy provisions 21; 'no-bail-out' clause 14, 33, 33, 34, 35, 48; and OMT Programme 40; and supreme emergency 14, 25, 27; *see also* Maastricht criteria; Treaty on the Functioning of the European Union (TFEU)
McCreevy, Charlie 117
Mackenstein, H. 158
McNamara, K. 10
Macroeconomic Imbalances Procedure 38, 81, 111–12
Maggetti, M. 101
Magnette, P. 104n2, 104n17
Majone, G. 101, 176
Marcellino, M. 72
market: market abuse 110; market discipline 33–4, 38, 78–81; market failures 176; *see also* financial markets
Marsh, S. 158

INDEX

Marzinotto, B. 173
Matthijs, M. 89
Mayer, Thomas 48
Merkel, Angela: and Deauville meeting (Oct. 2010) 9; and EFSF 50, 55; and Eurobonds 116; and European Commission's stabilization fund proposal 56; and European Monetary Fund proposal 48; and Greek debt crisis 86; initial dithering response to euro crisis 9, 173; Merkel/Sarkozy letter on Eurozone Summits 70; 'Merkozy' agreement 68; and 'six-pack' of economic reforms 68; and supreme emergency 25, 26; and Union method 4, 61–2; and Van Rompuy Task Force (VRTF) 65; *see also* Germany
'Merkozy' agreement 68
Meunier, Sophie 5
monetary financing prohibition (Article 123 TFEU) 3, 4–5, 14, 23, 24, 30–6, 40–1
monetary policies, separation from fiscal policies 15, 24
Monnet, Jean 45, 108, 118, 125, 126
moral hazard: and European Stability Mechanism 54; and first Greek bail-out 85–6; and supreme emergency 17, 19–20, 22, 24, 27; and TSCG 80
Moravcsik, A. 107, 108, 115, 155, 174
Morelli, M. 173
Multi-Annual Financial Framework (2014–2020) 112
multiple agency 156–9
Musgrave, R. 109
mutual banks 146

neofunctionalism 89, 125, 169–74, 175–6
neoliberalism 8, 32; *see also* Ordo-liberalism
Netherlands: and Greek external debt *84*; and 'six-pack' of economic reforms 67, 69
Net Stable Funding Ratio 142, 148
Nice Treaty 108
Nielson, D. 164n13
'no-bail-out' clause (Maastricht Treaty) 14, 33, *33*, 34, 35, 48
'no-obligation-for transfers' clause (in Article 125 TFEU) 80, 89
normative legal and political theory: justificatory principles 17–19, 27; 'just war' theory 17, 19
northern Europe: and euro crisis 2, 11; and redistribution 177; and Union method 4
Nowotny, Ewald 55

O'Keeffe, Mícheál 4, 5
OMT (Outright Monetary Transactions) Programme 19, 23, 24, 25, 26, 40, 99
Ordo-liberalism 21, 25
Organisation for Economic Co-operation and Development (OECD), and EU representation 156
Osborne, George 148–9
Outright Monetary Transactions (OMT) Programme 19, 23, 24, 25, 26, 40, 99
over-the-counter derivatives 110, 142
'own-house-in-order' principle 33, *33*, 35, 39

Pact for Competitiveness 170
Padoa-Schioppa, T. 100, 104n12, 134, 173
Pagkalos, Theodore 82
Pagliari, S. 150
Papandreou, George 77, 83, 84–5, 86, 88
Partial Protection Certificates 54
path dependency 3, 31, 36, 37–8, 40, 46, 54–7; *see also* historical institutionalism
Peel, Q. 68
'permissive consensus' 168, 177, 178
Peterson, J. 108
Pierson, P. 31–2, 33, 36, 54
Pinder, J. 135n11
Piper, Watty, 'Little Engine' story (quote from) 107
Pisani-Ferry, J. 53
Poland, and European integration 175
Pollack, M. 64, 95, 108, 115, 155
popular opinion: and EMU redistribution 175–7, 178; and external economic governance 154, 160–1, **161**, **162**, 163; *see also* democracy
Portugal: deficit vs public debt ratio 82; and EFSF 53; and Greek external debt *84*
principal-agent theory: and delegation 63–4, 96; and ECB 95, 96, 97, 102–3; and EU representation in G20 154, 155, 157, 158, 160, 163–4; and European Council 69; and European Parliament 69; and European studies 9; and Germany 73; and legitimacy 97, 101; and 'six-pack' 62, 63, 65, 66, 68, 73; and TSCG 72, 73; *see also* agency; collective principal
probit analyses, and EU system of delegation 160–1, **161**, **162**, 163
Prodi, Romano 108, 116
Proissl, W. 55
Project Merlin 149
public opinion *see* popular opinion
Puetter, U. 63, 89, 163

Quaglia, Lucia 7, 8

Rawls, John 17, 27
Rechtsstaat (state ruled by law) 17
redistribution 8, 113–14, 168–9, 175–7, 178
Regling, Klaus 52, 53–4

INDEX

regulation: banking regulation, Europeanization of 11; and Barnier vs Barroso 117; and European Commission entrepreneurship 109–11; and financial markets 15–16; and public opinion 176; *see also* Basel Committee on Banking Supervision (BCBS); capital requirements
Rehn, Olli 53, 56, 88, 111, 112
Renaud-Basso, O. 48, 49, 51, 56
'report of four' 172
responsiveness, vs accountability 95, 98–9
reversed qualified majority voting (RQMV) 70, 71, 79, 101, 178
Richard II, King, 'grim necessity' quote (*Richard II*, Shakespeare) 13–14
risk management, and fiscal federalism 78–81, 89
Robin Hood Tax Coalition 115
Rogoff, Kenneth 104n7
Rommerskirchen, Charlotte 6
Rompuy, Herman van: and EU integration 172; and EU representation in G20 157; and Merkel/Sarkozy letter on Eurozone Summits 70; 'report of four' 172; *Towards a Genuine Economic and Monetary Union* (Rompuy, Barroso, Juncker and Draghi) 135n1; Van Rompuy Task Force (VRTF) 62, 65, 66–7, 68, 69, 112
rule-based approaches, and financial markets 15–16
rule of necessity 19
rule of recognition 17, 18, 19

Sandholtz, W. 107
Santer, Jacques 108
Sarkozy, Nicolas: and Deauville meeting (Oct. 2010) 9; and EFSF 50; and Eurobonds 116; and financial crisis (2007–) 110; and intergovernmentalism 73; Merkel/Sarkozy letter on Eurozone Summits 70; 'Merkozy' agreement 68; and 'six-pack' of economic reforms 68; and Van Rompuy Task Force (VRTF) 65; *see also* France
Scharpf, Fritz 135n11
Schäuble, Wolfgang 36, 48, 56, 67, 115
Schelkle, W. 40
Schmidt, V.A. 95
Schmitt, Carl 16
Schröder, Gerhard 80–1
Securities Markets Programme (SMP) 23, 36, 40, 99, 100
securitization theory 20
Shakespeare, William, *Richard II* ('grim necessity' quote) 13–14
Sherlock Holmes quote 30
Shonfield, A. 135n9
Shore, C. 157
short-selling 110
'silent participations' 145
Single European Act 32
Single Market Act 111
'six-pack' of economic reforms: and Community vs Union method 3–4, 9, 68, 72; and fiscal policy coordination 62; and further integration 172; and national statistical authorities 38; and neofunctionalism 171; overview 64–70, 67, 69; and principal-agent theory 62, 63, 65, 66, 68, 73; and stabilisation 111; unrealistic measures 88
Skocpol, T. 54
Slovakia, budgetary problems 10
Slovenia, budgetary problems 10
Smith, M. 160
SMP (Securities Markets Programme) 23, 36, 40, 99, 100
social market economy 126
Solidarity Fund 112
'sound money and public finances' principle 32
southern Europe: and euro crisis 2, 4, 6, 10, 11; and redistribution 177
sovereign bonds: primary market purchase 14, 23; secondary market purchase 19, 23, 40
sovereign debts: and banks debts 22, 23; bank-sovereign feedback loop 35, 39; and ECB (sovereign bond purchase on primary market 14, 23; sovereign bond purchase on secondary market 19, 23, 40; sovereign debt markets 35, 36, 37); and failure of market discipline 33–4, 38; and Federal Reserve 36, 37; and financial market integration 16; *see also* Economic and Monetary Union (EMU) and sovereign debt crisis; Eurozone crisis and European integration; fiscal federalism and Greek debt crisis; Greek debt crisis
Spaak Report 135n2
Spain: austerity policies, impact of 2, 10; and ECB 21, 100; financial support conditionalities 11
Special Purpose Vehicle (SPV) proposal 49, 50, 51, 56
'spill-over' process 170, 174
stabilisation, European Commission entrepreneurship and financial crisis (2007–) 111–12
Stability and Growth Pact (SGP): and Barroso vs Prodi Commissions 116–17; central surveillance vs national sanctions 80–1; and fiscal discipline 79; and Greek crisis 83, 84; Integrated Economic Policy Guidelines 84; and Maastricht criteria

INDEX

32–4, *33*; penalty system (revised version) 11; and reversed qualified majority voting (RQMV) 101; and 'six-pack' of economic reforms 4, 66, 67, 68, 70; and TSCG 72
'stability begins at home' principle 20
stability culture 17, 18, 25, 26
Stark, Jürgen 23
State intervention 126–7
Stein, J.L. 90n2
'sticky institutions' concept 32, 36
Story, J. 150
Strauss Kahn, Dominique 112
structural adjustment programmes 4
structure, and European Commission entrepreneurship 115–16
subsidiarity 132–3
supervision *see* Basel Committee on Banking Supervision (BCBS); regulation
supranational entrepreneurship and the Barroso Commission: abstract and main issues 107–9; financial crisis (2007–) and Commission entrepreneurship: evaluation (allocation 112–13; redistribution 113–14; regulation 109–11; stabilisation 111–12); financial crisis (2007–) and Commission entrepreneurship: explaining 114 (agency 116–17; structure 115–16; summary and conclusion 117–18); *see also* Barroso, José Manuel
supreme emergency: abstract and main issues 3, 13–14, 26–7; 'grim necessity' quote (*Richard II*, Shakespeare) 13–14; institutional design issues 21–4; vs. intergovernmentalism 63; justificatory principles 17–19; Maastricht governance paradigm 15–16; Maastricht rules and crisis prevention 16–17; moral hazard and contingent commitments 19–21, 23, 24; political strategy for supra-national authority building 24–6; 'supreme emergency exemption' 17, 20–1
Sweden: and Basel III/CRD IV 146, 149; and European integration 175

TARGET2 payment system balances 21, 37
taxpayers: and bank bail-outs 89–90; *see also* Robin Hood Tax Coalition
Temple Lang, J. 63
TEU *see* Treaty on European Union (TEU)
TFEU *see* Treaty on the Functioning of the European Union (TFEU)
throughput legitimacy, and ECB 97, 99
Tierney, M. 164n13
Tinbergen, J. 135n11
Torres, Francisco 6, 62, 101
Towards a Genuine Economic and Monetary Union (Rompuy, Barroso, Juncker and Draghi) 135n1

transfer union 11, 27, 168, 173, 176, 178; *see also* fiscal union
Treaty of Lisbon 9, 18, 46, 55, 97, 156, 157
Treaty of Maastricht *see* Maastricht criteria; Maastricht Treaty
Treaty of Nice 108
Treaty of Rome 124, 126
Treaty on European Union (TEU): Article 10(2) 101; Article 17 156; Article 102 32
Treaty on Stability, Coordination and Governance (TSCG): and delegation 64; and fiscal federalism 79–80; and Germany 25, 174; and intergovernmentalism 62, 69–72; and neofunctionalism 171; non-signing countries 175; overall purpose 38–9; and principal-agent theory 72, 73
Treaty on the Functioning of the European Union (TFEU): Article 120 100; Article 122 113; Article 122(2) 22, 86; Article 123 14, 23, 24, 30–6, 40–1; Article 124 33, 41n3; Article 125 14, 19, 33, 41n4, 80; Article 126(9) 85–6; Article 127 101; Article 136 19, 22, 66, 113; Article 283(2) 104n16; Article 284(3) 104n16; and reversed qualified majority system 71
Trichet, Jean-Claude 36, 53, 100, 102
'troika', and Greek debt crisis 86
TSCG *see* Treaty on Stability, Coordination and Governance (TSCG)
Tsipras, Alexis 88
'two-pack' of legislation 38, 111, 172

Union method 4, 8–9, 22, 61–2, 72, 73; *see also* Community method
United Kingdom: and Basel III/CRD IV 144–6, **144**, 149, 150; and EFSF 50; financial crisis (2007–) and lending 148–9, **149**; government's bank bail-out 80; and Greek external debt 84, 86; Lloyds–TSB 145; Project Merlin 149; and 'six-pack' of economic reforms 67; structure of banking and financial systems 146–7, 148; and TSCG 72, 175
United States: American federalism 80; and Basel III Accord 143; and EFSF 50; Federal Reserve and sovereign debt 37, *37*; and Greek external debt *84*; non-financial company external funding 148

Van Campen Report 124
Van Rompuy Task Force (VRTF) 62, 65, 66–7, 68, 69, 112; *see also* Rompuy, Herman van
venture-capital funds 111
Verwey, Maarten 51
Vilpišauskas, Ramūnas 8

INDEX

Walter, I. 150
Walzer, Michael 19, 27
Warleigh-Lack, A. 63
Weber, Axel 23
Westerwelle, Guido 85
World Bank, and EU representation 156
World Trade Organization, and EU representation in G20 159

xenophobic stereotypes, in German and Greek press 1–2

Yiangou, Jonathan 4, 5, 49

Zahariadis, Nikolaos 4–5, 7–8
Zysman, J. 107